THE GOD OF THE GOSPEL

ROBERT JENSON'S TRINITARIAN THEOLOGY

SCOTT R. SWAIN

IVP Academic

An imprint of InterVarsity Press
Downers Grove, Illinois

InterVarsity Press
P.O. Box 1400, Downers Grove, IL 60515-1426
World Wide Web: www.ivpress.com
Email: email@ivpress.com

InterVarsity Press® is the book-publishing division of InterVarsity Christian Fellowship/USA®, a movement of students and faculty active on campus at hundreds of universities, colleges and schools of nursing in the United States of America, and a member movement of the International Fellowship of Evangelical Students. For information about local and regional activities, write Public Relations Dept., InterVarsity Christian Fellowship/USA, 6400 Schroeder Rd., P.O. Box 7895, Madison, WI 537077895, or visit the IVCF website at <www.intervarsity.org>.

Scripture quotations, unless otherwise noted, are from The Holy Bible, English Standard Version, copyright © 2001 by Crossway Bibles, a division of Good News Publishers. Used by permission. All rights reserved.

Cover design: Cindy Kiple

Images: Resurrection by John Armstrong. Private Collection/The Bridgeman Art Library.

ISBN 978-0-8308-3904-9

Printed in the United States of America ∞

Library of Congress Cataloging-in-Publication Data

Swain, Scott R.
  The God of the gospel : Robert Jenson's Trinitarian theology / Scott R. Swain.
    p. cm.—(Strategic initiatives in evangelical theology)
  Includes bibliographical references and index.
  ISBN 978-0-8308-3904-9 (pbk. : alk. paper)
  1. Trinity. 2. Jenson, Robert W. I. Title.
  BT111.3.S94 2013
  231'.044092—dc23

                                                                      2012051726

P	20	19	18	17	16	15	14	13	12	11	10	9	8	7	6	5	4	3	2	1
Y	30	29	28	27	26	25	24	23	22	21	20	19	18	17	16	15	14	13

The divine being and life and act takes place with ours, and it is only as the divine takes place that ours takes place. To put it in the simplest way, what unites God and us men is that he does not will to be God without us, that he creates us rather to share with us and therefore with our being and life and act his own incomparable being and life and act, that he does not allow his history to be his and ours ours, but causes them to take place as a common history. That is the special truth which the Christian message has to proclaim at its very heart.

Karl Barth, *Church Dogmatics* 4.1:7

CONTENTS

◆

Acknowledgments 7

Abbreviations 9

INTRODUCTION 11

1 The Question Stated 13

2 The State of the Question 32

PART ONE: *Robert Jenson on the Gospel's God* 73

3 The Way of God's Identity According to the Old Testament 77

4 The Way of God's Identity According to the New Testament 96

5 The Triune Identity 121

PART TWO: *Toward a Catholic and Evangelical Account
of the Gospel's God* 143

6 "A Father to You": *God's Fatherly Self-Determination
in the Covenant of Grace* 145

7 Immanuel: *The Son of God's Self-Identification
with Humanity in the Incarnation* 164

8 "Deluged with Love": *The Spirit and the
Consummation of Trinitarian Fellowship* 194

9 Grace and Being: *Bruce McCormack on the Gospel's God* 208

CONCLUSION 229

10 Concluding Reflections on the Question 231

Bibliography 235

Author Index   252

Subject Index   254

Scripture Index   257

ACKNOWLEDGMENTS

◆

This book took much longer to complete than I had originally envisaged. What was to be a light revision of my doctoral dissertation written under the supervision of Kevin Vanhoozer at Trinity Evangelical Divinity School in 2002 has turned out to be a completely new book, only distantly related to its ancestor dissertation. In bringing the present study to publication at last, I have a lot of people to thank.

A number of friends and colleagues read the manuscript, either in part or in its entirety, and offered thoughtful suggestions for improvement. These include Michael Allen, Keith E. Johnson, Matthew Levering, Fred Sanders, Darren Sarisky, Dan Treier and Kevin Vanhoozer. I am especially indebted to George Hunsinger in this regard, who provided numerous helpful comments along with his encouraging commendation.

I am grateful to John Webster for graciously sharing with me the manuscript of his 2007 Kantzer Lectures. John is the supreme contemporary exemplar of dogmatic theology in a (shall we call it?) Reformed and Thomistic key, and an encouragement to many of us who aspire to fulfill the theologian's vocation faithfully and intelligently.

Several persons associated with Reformed Theological Seminary in Orlando, Florida, also deserve recognition. Michael Farrell, our associate librarian, provided assistance in securing books and articles through interlibrary loan. Jonathan Dyer and Alexander Kirk assisted me at different points along the way in preparing the bibliography and proofreading the manuscript. Jennifer Redd produced the indexes with characteristic skill. Here I should also thank Don Sweeting, president of RTS, Orlando, and Ceci Helm, my assistant, who each in different ways promote and protect significant periods of time for research and writing so that I can complete projects like this one.

And then there are the good folks at IVP. Gary Deddo's original interest in a book addressing persons and topics not widely discussed by evangelicals guaranteed that this study would see the light of day. Michael Gibson and Brannon Ellis, my two editors, helped me refine the structure and flow of my argument so that I could make my case as clearly as possible. I am grateful as well to the editorial advisory board of IVP's Strategic Initiatives in Evangelical Theology for their willingness to include this book in that series.

Finally, I want to thank my wife, Leigh, and our four children, Carly, Sophie, Josiah and Micah, for the ways they daily fill my life with joy and encourage me in my calling. Nearly eleven years ago, I dedicated my dissertation to Leigh. I am happy to dedicate this, its offspring, to her now.

"To the King of ages, immortal, invisible, the only God, be honor and glory forever and ever. Amen" (1 Tim 1:17).

ABBREVIATIONS

AO   Robert W. Jenson, *Alpha and Omega: A Study in the Theology of Karl Barth*. New York: Thomas Nelson & Sons, 1963. Reprint, Eugene, OR: Wipf and Stock, 2002.

CD   Karl Barth, *Church Dogmatics*. 14 volumes. Edited by Geoffrey W. Bromily and T. F. Torrance. Edinburgh: T & T Clark, 1936-1969.

GAG   Robert W. Jenson, *God After God: The God of the Past and the God of the Future, Seen in the Work of Karl Barth*. Indianapolis: Bobbs-Merrill, 1969. Reprint, Minneapolis: Fortress, 2010.

ST   Robert W. Jenson, *Systematic Theology*. 2 volumes. New York: Oxford University Press, 1997 and 1999.

TI   Robert W. Jenson, *The Triune Identity: God According to the Gospel*. Philadelphia: Fortress, 1982. Reprint, Eugene, OR: Wipf and Stock, 2002.

UG   Robert W. Jenson, *Unbaptized God: The Basic Flaw in Ecumenical Theology*. Minneapolis: Fortress, 1992.

INTRODUCTION

◆

1

THE QUESTION STATED

◆

INTRODUCTION

God according to the gospel. The phrase epitomizes what must be the
perennial quest of Christian theology: to know the only true God
through Jesus Christ whom he has sent (Jn 17:3; 1:18). The foundation of this quest lies in the reality that God has indeed revealed
himself supremely and reliably through the embassy of the Son's incarnation, atonement, resurrection and enthronement. As Luther
proclaims: "The seals are broken, the stone rolled away from the door
of the tomb, and that greatest of all mysteries brought to light—
that Christ, God's Son became man, that God is Three in One, that
Christ suffered for us, and will reign forever."[1] From the reality
that founds this quest follows a corresponding rule for theological
reflection, eloquently summarized by John of Damascus: Since the
divine benevolence "has revealed to us what it was expedient for us
to know" through his only-begotten Son, "with these things let us be
content and in them let us abide and let us not step over the ancient
bounds or pass beyond the divine tradition" handed down to us "by
the Law and the Prophets and the Apostles and the Evangelists."[2]

---

[1]Martin Luther, *The Bondage of the Will*, trans. J. I. Packer and O. R. Johnston (Grand Rapids:
Revell, 1957), 71.
[2]John of Damascus, *An Exact Exposition of the Orthodox Faith* (New York: Fathers of the Church,
1958), 1.1.

The present study is concerned with one particular dimension of the broad yet bounded place that is the knowledge of the gospel's God, specifically the relationship between God and the evangelical events whereby God becomes our God. Our *quaestio*,[3] to borrow the scholastic idiom, concerns the relationship between God's being and God's self-determination, between the Trinity and election, between God's unfailing character and God's unfolding covenant that reaches its climax in the gospel of Jesus Christ. As this and the next chapter will demonstrate, this question is highly debated in contemporary theology. It is moreover a question that a truly "evangelical"[4] theology cannot ignore.

Theological questions have historical contexts, and this is certainly true of the topic at hand. Though our topic makes indirect appearances here and there in the history of theology, it finds perhaps its clearest and most direct expression in recent debates provoked by the theology of Karl Barth, on many accounts the most significant Protestant theologian of the twentieth century. The historical context for our study is trinitarian theology "after Barth."[5] When it comes to the doctrine of the Trinity, the Basel theologian continues to stimulate diverse, creative and often contradictory proposals about what trinitarian theology should be, about where it is going, and especially

---

[3]Capitalizing on the multivalent possibilities in the term, *quaestio* in the present study connotes a "topic" or "question" of dispute in academic theology and also a "quest" that animates the Christian life. Both senses are held together insofar as the rigors of academic argumentation and debate can serve the spiritual purification of the Christian mind in its pilgrimage toward the eternal kingdom where the *theologia viatorum* is finally exchanged for the *theologia beatorum*.

[4]In this book I use "evangelical" primarily in two senses: (1) to refer to the events announced and explicated in the gospel; and (2) to refer to any form of theology which traces its doctrinal lineage to the confessional documents of the magisterial Reformation. See Friedrich Schleiermacher, *The Christian Faith*, ed. H. R. Mackintosh and J. S. Stewart (Edinburgh: T & T Clark, 1989), § 27. The latter usage enables me to highlight more effectively trends and commitments that have broadly characterized modern Protestant theology than would limiting this term's reference to a specific sociological subset of Anglo-American Protestantism (i.e., "evangelicalism"). This usage also helps us appreciate the fact that competing claims about the gospel's God are also competing claims about what it means to appropriate the theological heritage of the Reformation.

[5]For recent documentation of this lively trajectory in contemporary theology, see Myk Habets and Phillip Tolliday, eds., *Trinitarian Theology After Barth*, Princeton Theological Monograph Series (Eugene, OR: Pickwick, 2011).

about the relationship between God's being Trinity and his being "the electing God"—the God who ordains and constitutes himself the "Friend and Benefactor" of sinners in Jesus Christ.[6] On this latter score especially, Barth's theology poses a question that continues to "give rise to thought" (Heidegger).[7]

While the reception history of Barth's trinitarian theology provides the broad context for the present study, its more immediate focus is Robert W. Jenson's doctrine of God. An American Lutheran theologian of international ecumenical stature, Jenson has devoted nearly fifty years as a professional theologian to delineating a consistently evangelical doctrine of God.[8] In doing so, his theological program provides one of contemporary theology's most sophisticated, comprehensive, and creative responses to many of the questions that Barth poses for a trinitarian dogmatics. Unfortunately, Jenson's theology is only beginning to receive the critical attention it deserves.[9] As David Bentley Hart observes, Jenson's "thought is too little taught

---

[6] *CD* 2.2:26.

[7] Bruce L. McCormack considers Barth's doctrine of election to have brought about "a revolution in the doctrine of God." *Orthodox and Modern: Studies in the Theology of Karl Barth* (Grand Rapids: Baker, 2008), 185. For the debate about how to interpret the significance of this revolution, see the essays collected in Michael T. Dempsey, ed., *Trinity and Election in Contemporary Theology* (Grand Rapids: Eerdmans, 2011).

[8] For Jenson's biography as a theologian, see David S. Yeago, "Catholicity, Nihilism, and the God of the Gospel: Reflections on the Theology of Robert W. Jenson," *Dialog* 31 (1992): 18-22; and Carl E. Braaten, "Robert William Jenson—A Personal Memoir," in *Trinity, Time, and Church: A Response to the Theology of Robert W. Jenson,* ed. Colin E. Gunton (Grand Rapids: Eerdmans, 2000), 1-9; for Jenson's own autobiographical reflections, see his, "A Theological Autobiography, to Date," *Dialog* 46 (2007): 46-54; and also, "God's Time, Our Time: An Interview with Robert W. Jenson," *Christian Century* 123 (2006): 31-35.

[9] Except for several important article-length reviews of Jenson's *Systematic Theology,* responses that have appeared in the journals are largely devoted to individual themes in his theology. The two book-length responses to Jenson's work that have been published do not sufficiently address the issues treated in the present study. The first book, *Trinity, Time, and Church,* edited by Colin Gunton, is an almost entirely sympathetic collection of essays written by Jenson's friends and former students. Though a tribute to Jenson's theological greatness in its own way, it does not critically engage the issues that lie at the heart of this book. The second book, Francesca Aran Murphy's *God Is Not a Story: Realism Revisited* (Oxford: Oxford University Press, 2007), is devoted largely but not exclusively to Jenson's thought. Though it is a work of exceptional dogmatic insight that treats a number of issues addressed in the present book, Murphy identifies Jenson too closely with postliberal projects and consequently fails to consider with full seriousness Jenson's ontological claims (see chapter two, note 177 below).

and too little studied; too few dissertations engage his ideas; not nearly enough attention is paid to his contributions to modern dogmatics; and too little pride is taken in the dignity his work lends to American theology."[10] This is a lamentable situation, not only because a theologian of Jenson's stature remains so largely neglected, but also because of the nature of his proposal. The present study hopes to remedy this situation, at least in part, by rendering a critical exposition of his account of "God according to the gospel."[11] The intention is not merely descriptive, however. Engaging Jenson's doctrine of God provides both stimulus and occasion for outlining my own constructive response to the topic under consideration, the relationship between God's triune being and his triune self-determination to be our God through the gospel.

In order to set the stage for addressing the question before us in this book, the present chapter will seek to accomplish two things: first, to provide the necessary backdrop to the story of trinitarian theology after Barth, and to Jenson's place within that story, by describing the modern roots of the contemporary resurgence of trinitarian theology; second, to introduce the structure and argument of the present study by providing an overview of the chapters that follow.

THE MODERN ROOTS OF THE CONTEMPORARY
TRINITARIAN RESURGENCE

The latter half of the twentieth century and the first decade of the twenty-first have witnessed a resurging interest in the doctrine of the Trinity, a fact now universally recognized and widely documented.[12]

---

[10]David Bentley Hart, "The Lively God of Robert Jenson," *First Things* 156 (October 2005): 28.

[11]This phrase is the subtitle of Jenson's first full monograph devoted to the doctrine of the Trinity, *The Triune Identity: God According to the Gospel* (Philadelphia: Fortress, 1982; Eugene, OR: Wipf and Stock, 2002).

[12]For example, see Ted Peters, *God as Trinity: Relationality and Temporality in Divine Life* (Louisville: Westminster John Knox, 1993); John Thompson, *Modern Trinitarian Perspectives* (New York: Oxford University Press, 1994); Stanley J. Grenz, *Rediscovering the Triune God: The Trinity in Contemporary Theology* (Minneapolis: Fortress, 2004); Bruce D. Marshall, "Trinity," in *The Blackwell Companion to Modern Theology*, ed. Gareth Jones (Malden, MA: Blackwell, 2004), chap. 12; Fred Sanders, "Trinity Talk, Again," *Dialog* 44 (2005): 264-72.

Rather than rehearsing matters that have been treated competently elsewhere, I wish to focus instead on elements of the modern trinitarian resurgence directly related to the question at hand, and to the specific context in which it arises. As we will see more fully in chapter two, although the renewal of trinitarian theology in the work of Karl Barth, and among those doing theology in his wake, represents a novel development in relation to much of modern theology, from another vantage point this renewal also represents the culmination of a consistent trajectory in modern Protestant theology devoted to developing a distinctly evangelical doctrine of God.

Since the time of the Reformation, the doctrine of the Trinity has been a problematic topic, especially for Protestants. The problem did not initially concern the doctrine per se (the virulent anti-trinitarianism of the sixteenth century notwithstanding). Though the early Reformers at times displayed ambiguous postures in relation to traditional trinitarian terminology (e.g., hypostasis, persona, *ousia*) and in relation to the doctrine's place within the broader system of theology (e.g., Melanchthon's 1521 *Loci communes theologici*), these ambiguities never amounted to questioning the substance of the doctrine. Luther located the doctrine of the Trinity among those "sublime articles of majesty" that were "not matters of dispute or contention" between Catholics and Protestants.[13] With Luther, all of the major theologians of the early Reformation era, along with the major confessions and divines of Protestant orthodoxy, roundly affirmed the doctrine of the Trinity as received and confessed by the ancient church. The problem for Protestants, at least initially, did not concern the content of the doctrine. The problem initially concerned what we might call the hermeneutical shape of trinitarian theology: the relationship between Holy Scripture, the ecumenically received form of the doctrine and the constructive task of dogmatics.[14] Whereas me-

---

[13]Martin Luther, "The Schmalkald Articles," in *The Book of Concord: The Confessions of the Evangelical Lutheran Church*, ed. T. G. Tappert (Philadelphia: Muhlenberg, 1959), 291-92.

[14]Though this dimension of the problem was especially acute for Protestants, it was not unknown

dieval theologians had the luxury of pursuing dogmatic reflection on the Trinity on the basis of established ecumenical symbols and the "sentences" of trustworthy ecclesial doctors, the Reformers' commitment to grounding all dogmas in Scripture alone demanded that reflection on the Trinity exhibit a more directly exegetical mode. The point of course is not that the Reformers or their Protestant orthodox heirs sought to engage trinitarian doctrine apart from the church's authoritative pronouncements and teachers, but that their engagement of the tradition had to take place within a transparently exegetical context. The reliability of secondary authorities could not be assumed but rather had to be established. This new hermeneutical setting for trinitarian theology resulted in a complex and often fruitful phase in the development of the doctrine that spanned a period of more than two centuries.[15]

With the rise of Enlightenment thought, the aforementioned hermeneutical problematic became more acute and, as it did, trinitarian theology underwent (oftentimes radical) material transformation.[16] Among many relevant factors contributing to this transformation, three deserve mention here: the rise of new interpretive methods, new attitudes toward classical metaphysics and new agendas for the Protestant university. First, as new approaches to biblical interpretation developed, not only were the biblical bases of the Trinity increasingly brought into question. The very enterprise of what we might call "trinitarian biblical exegesis" was undermined as the locus on the Trinity was segregated to the discipline of dogmatic theology, freeing the discipline of biblical exegesis to devote itself to

to Catholic theologians. See Matthew Levering, *Participatory Biblical Exegesis: A Theology of Biblical Interpretation* (Notre Dame: University of Notre Dame Press, 2008), chap. 2.

[15]For further discussion of the matters treated in this paragraph, see Scott R. Swain, "The Trinity in the Reformers," in *The Oxford Handbook of the Trinity*, ed. Gilles Emery and Matthew Levering (Oxford: Oxford University Press, 2011), 227-39, and the literature cited therein. For the development of trinitarian doctrine in the period of Protestant orthodoxy, see especially Richard A. Muller, *Post-Reformation Reformed Dogmatics*, Volume 4: *The Triunity of God* (Grand Rapids: Baker, 2003).

[16]See now Stephen R. Holmes, *The Quest for the Trinity: The Doctrine of God in Scripture, History and Modernity* (Downers Grove, IL: IVP Academic, 2012).

its "proper" subject matter, that is, the historical development of biblical religion(s).[17] Uprooted from its native scriptural soil, trinitarian doctrine now needed to be rooted in other sources such as history and/or experience, if it was to be rooted at all.[18] Second, the rejection of traditional Christian metaphysics transposed the discourse of both critics and defenders of the Trinity into a new (and increasingly univocal) key, which in turn served to heighten the perceived irrationality of the doctrine.[19] Providing a constructive account of the "essence" of traditional trinitarian teaching under the new metaphysical, epistemological and linguistic conditions of the Enlightenment thus became one of the central tasks of modern trinitarian theology. Third, the restructuring of Protestant universities simultaneously inaugurated a new era of learning and relegated many of the pedagogical sources and religious practices associated with traditional orthodoxy to the status of *terra incognita*.[20] The effects of this relegation were perhaps subtler than other factors contributing to the modern transformation of trinitarian theology. Nevertheless, the significance of

---

[17]The divorce between *sacra doctrina* and *sacra pagina* is formally stated (though certainly not initiated) in Johann P. Gabler's famous 1787 address, "An Oration on the Proper Distinction Between Biblical and Dogmatic Theology and the Specific Objectives of Each," in *The Flowering of Old Testament Theology*, ed. Ben C. Ollenburger, Elmer A. Martens and Gerhard F. Hasel (Winona Lake, IN: Eisenbrauns, 1992), 492-502. See also Nils A. Dahl, "The Neglected Factor in New Testament Theology," *Reflection* 73 (1975): 5-8; and C. Kavin Rowe, "Luke and the Trinity: An Essay in Ecclesial Biblical Theology," *Scottish Journal of Theology* 56 (2003): 1-26.

[18]Samuel M. Powell, *The Trinity in German Thought* (Cambridge: Cambridge University Press, 2001).

[19]William Babcock, "A Changing of the Christian God: The Doctrine of the Trinity in the Seventeenth Century," *Interpretation* 45 (1991): 133-46; and Philip Dixon, *"Nice and Hot Disputes": The Doctrine of the Trinity in the Seventeenth Century* (London: Continuum, 2003). On the implications of this transposition for contemporary philosophy of religion, see David Burrell, "Creator/Creatures Relation: 'The Distinction' vs. 'Onto-Theology,'" *Faith and Philosophy* 25 (2008): 177-89.

[20]Although the social and institutional contexts of Protestant liberalism are often neglected in considerations of modern theology, two recent studies have greatly remedied this situation: Thomas Albert Howard, *Protestant Theology and the Making of the Modern German University* (New York: Oxford University Press, 2006); and Michael C. Legaspi, *The Death of Scripture and the Rise of Biblical Studies* (Oxford: Oxford University Press, 2010). Also of broad relevance to the present point are Michael J. Buckley, *At the Origins of Modern Atheism* (New Haven and London: Yale University Press, 1987); and Antonie Vos, "Scholasticism and Reformation," in *Reformation and Scholasticism*, ed. Willem J. van Asselt and Eef Dekker (Grand Rapids: Baker, 2001), 99-119.

these changes cannot be overestimated. New institutional contexts and aims produced new and sometimes unreliable readers of the classical tradition of trinitarian thought, a fact particularly evident in nineteenth-century histories of dogma and in the constructive trinitarian theologies that emerged under their tutelage.[21]

Protestant responses to this ever deepening problematic were variegated. In his *Conflict of the Faculties,* Immanuel Kant famously concluded that the dogma of the Trinity was inconceivable as a concept and irrelevant to practical religion. He drew similar conclusions regarding the dogmas of Christ's incarnation, resurrection and ascension.[22] Other modern thinkers were not generally so bold. Even when they accepted Kant's critique of classical metaphysics and his basic epistemological framework, many continued to pursue the prize of a consistently evangelical trinitarianism.[23] Friedrich Schleiermacher argued that the traditional dogma could not be established on the basis of biblical exegesis, suggesting that "the Sabellian view" might represent as plausible an exegetical conclusion as "the Athanasian hypothesis."[24] He also regarded the doctrine as saddled with internal contradictions.[25] These criticisms notwithstanding, Schleiermacher did not dispense with the dogma completely because he believed it articulated an essential element of God's saving action as impressed on the Christian self-consciousness, namely, God's active presence with humanity in Jesus Christ and in the church's common Spirit.[26] Far from being merely an appendix to his theology, Schlei-

---

[21]On this point, see especially Lewis Ayres, *Nicaea and Its Legacy: An Approach to Fourth-Century Trinitarian Theology* (Oxford: Oxford University Press, 2004), chap. 16.

[22]Immanuel Kant, *The Conflict of the Faculties,* trans. Mary J. Gregor (New York: Abaris, 1992), 65-73.

[23]Indeed, Schleiermacher perceives in the fact that the doctrine of the Trinity "did not receive any fresh treatment when the Evangelical (Protestant) church was set up," an opportunity for modern evangelical theology to initiate "a transformation [of the doctrine] which will go back to its very beginnings" (*Christian Faith,* 747). Stephen Holmes highlights the importance of this judgment for subsequent Protestant thought. See Holmes, *The Quest for the Trinity,* 186-95.

[24]Schleiermacher, *Christian Faith,* 750; also 741.

[25]Ibid., 742-47.

[26]Ibid., 738, 747-48.

ermacher's discussion of the Trinity therefore functions simultaneously as the capstone of his system and as an attempt to lay the
groundwork for an a posteriori approach to the doctrine that would
flow out of the Christian experience of God's twofold redeeming
presence in Christ and the Spirit.[27] When Albrecht Ritschl later rejected the scholastic approach to God, with its distinction between
God's essential attributes and God's external operations, and reinter-
preted the eternal processions of Son and Spirit in light of their saving missions, he thus brought the approach initiated by Schleiermacher to its natural conclusion: a postmetaphysical doctrine of the
Trinity, chastened by critical exegesis and epistemology, and thoroughly evangelical in impulse.[28]

Widely influential though it was, Schleiermacher's approach to
the Trinity did not prove satisfactory to all. Most notably perhaps,
Georg W. F. Hegel considered Schleiermacher's trinitarianism to
be both theologically and philosophically inadequate.[29] Hegel
sought an objective comprehension of God's being, not merely a
subjective awareness of God's active presence. Only the former, he
believed, would constitute a true knowledge of God. To be sure, for
Hegel as much as for Schleiermacher, the doorway to the classical
resources of trinitarian thought (i.e., scriptural, dogmatic, metaphysical, etc.) was largely a closed one. His concern to revive a robust trinitarian ontology and epistemology was therefore not an
attempt at repristination. Nevertheless, according to Hegel, Christianity contained within itself the path to an objective knowledge

---

[27]Ibid., 747-51.

[28]Albrecht Ritschl, *The Christian Doctrine of Justification and Reconciliation*, 2nd ed., trans. H. R. Mackintosh and A. B. Macaulay (Edinburgh: T & T Clark, 1902), 16-19, 468-72. Ritschl's proj-ect of completing the Reformation by purging Protestantism of its scholastic remainders is dis-cussed in David W. Lotz, "Albrecht Ritschl and the Unfinished Reformation," *Harvard Theologi-cal Review* 73 (1980): 337-72.

[29]My reading of Hegel's trinitarian thought is indebted to Hans Küng, *The Incarnation of God: Hegel's Thought as Prolegomena to a Future Christology* (Edinburgh: T & T Clark, 1987); Peter C. Hodgson, *God in History: Shapes of Freedom* (Nashville: Abingdon, 1989); Cyril O'Regan, *The Heterodox Hegel* (Albany, NY: SUNY Press, 1994); and Powell, *Trinity in German Thought*, chap. 4.

of God in its notion of God's self-revelation in history, with the Trinity standing out as this notion's most "perspicuous symbol."[30] Leaving behind a metaphysics of the self-enclosed divine substance for a metaphysics of the self-revealing divine subject (*Geist*), the doctrine of the Trinity comes to provide in Hegel's thought both the ontological and the epistemological possibility for a true knowledge of God: As the triune God simultaneously reveals and realizes himself in history, human beings are taken up into God's own concrete act of self-understanding, thus rendering to them an objective knowledge of God. Hegel's speculative transgression of Kant's "epistemological strictures" on trinitarian reflection is extended in the later philosophy of Friedrich Schelling. While Schelling's trinitarian thought exhibits a greater familiarity with traditional trinitarianism, as well as a greater emphasis on divine freedom than Hegel's, his modification of Hegel still amounts to a significant "destabilizing" of orthodox trinitarian teaching.[31]

For all the brilliance of these modern theologies of the Trinity, they remain on even the most sympathetic reading distant cousins of the ecumenically received doctrine and, in many cases, rather thin and underdeveloped.[32] A striking exception to this general rule comes in the oft-neglected trinitarian theology of Isaak August Dorner.[33] Working broadly within the Schleiermacherian tradition of inquiry, though drawing also from Hegel and Schelling,[34] Dorner's doctrine of the Trinity represents a significant critique of and development beyond that of his predecessor in the chair of theology at the

---

[30]O'Regan, *Heterodox Hegel,* 64; also 66.
[31]Cyril O'Regan, "The Trinity in Kant, Hegel, and Schelling," in Emery and Levering, *Oxford Handbook of the Trinity* (Oxford: Oxford University Press, 2011), 262-65.
[32]Powell, *Trinity in German Thought,* 142, 146, 165-66.
[33]Isaak August Dorner, *A System of Christian Doctrine,* vol. 1, trans. Alfred Cave (Edinburgh: T & T Clark, 1888), §§ 28-32. On Dorner's trinitarian theology, see Jonathan Norgate, *The Triune God and the Gospel of Salvation* (London: T & T Clark, 2009).
[34]Though he was largely critical of their proposals, Dorner believed that Hegel and Schelling provided important metaphysical foundations for a renewed Protestant trinitarianism insofar as they helped theology "think of God, not as Substance ... but as Movement and as Subject" (*System of Christian Doctrine,* 400).

University of Berlin. While Dorner sought to provide a dogmatic account of God from within the context of faith, and thereby to continue the modern quest for a distinctly evangelical doctrine of God, he nevertheless argued that faith could only serve as the *principium cognoscendi internum* of theology not as its *principium essendi*.[35] Only a robust doctrine of the immanent Trinity could serve the latter function. Dorner's system of doctrine accordingly seeks to demonstrate the way in which God's communication of grace in the incarnation and in the experience of faith find their necessary foundation in the eternal depths of God's triune life.[36]

Other exceptions to the otherwise underdeveloped trinitarianism of modern theology are worth noting. The great Erlangen theologian Johannes von Hofmann sought to ground the experience of faith, as well as a comprehensive vision of history, within a consistently historicized doctrine of the Trinity.[37] Though his revisionist *heilsgeschichtliche* trinitarianism is undoubtedly indebted to Hegel and Schelling, von Hofmann's doctrine is much more eager than theirs to preserve the absolute freedom of God's historical self-determination. In this regard, von Hofmann avoids what Karl Barth would later identify as "the weightiest and most significant of the doubts" that a theologian must have toward Hegel's thought, namely its "failure to recognize that God is free."[38] Working within more traditional frameworks, theologians such as Herman Bavinck continued to articulate sophisticated statements of the orthodox dogma into the early twentieth century.[39]

The preceding discussion is important for understanding the doctrine of the Trinity as developed in the theology of Karl Barth and in the theologies of those he inspires. For all the novelty of

---

[35]Ibid., 169-70.

[36]Ibid., §31.

[37]See Matthew L. Becker, *The Self-Giving God and Salvation History: The Trinitarian Theology of Johannes von Hofmann* (London: T & T Clark, 2004).

[38]Karl Barth, *Protestant Theology in the Nineteenth Century*, trans. Brian Cozens and John Bowden (Grand Rapids: Eerdmans, 2002), 406.

[39]Herman Bavinck, *Reformed Dogmatics*, vol. 2, trans. John Vriend (Grand Rapids: Baker, 2004). See also Marshall, "Trinity," 183-85, 191.

trinitarian theology in and after Barth, this theology does not represent a simple repudiation of modern trinitarian theology but in
many respects fulfills that theology's deepest concerns,[40] including
its commitment to developing the doctrine of the Trinity on the
basis of God's saving action in the gospel, with the assistance of
modern conceptions of subjectivity and personhood, and with
varying degrees of suspicion toward classical doctrinal sources and
formulations. In following Barth's mandate to make the Trinity
"decisive and controlling for the whole of dogmatics,"[41] many prac-
titioners of trinitarian theology after Barth believe they have found
the key to realizing modern theology's quest for a consistently
evangelical doctrine of God.[42] Nevertheless, while these theologians agree on a formal level that the Trinity is the key to a fully
evangelical understanding of God, they disagree quite sharply
about how the Trinity should actually shape that understanding. As
the next chapter will demonstrate, this disagreement partly concerns the extent to which Barth fully grasped the significance of his
trinitarian and christological starting point for the doctrine of God,
and partly concerns the extent to which Barth's trinitarian theology
mandates extending the trajectory of metaphysical revisionism initiated in the modern era.

OVERVIEW

To what extent does an evangelically responsible trinitarian theology
require revising the church's traditional doctrine of God? What must
the church say about the being of "God" if she is to speak "according

---

[40]See McCormack, who makes this point more specifically with respect to Barth's and Alexander
Schweizer's doctrines of election: "Impulses which gave rise to Schweizer's reflections on the
doctrine of election are not simply ignored by Barth but taken up afresh and handled in a different way. What this suggests is that Barth's theology did not constitute a simple repudiation of his
'neo-Protestant' forebear but, rather, a fulfilling of many of his deepest concerns in a new framework" (*Orthodox and Modern*, 42).

[41]*CD* 1.1:303.

[42]Eberhard Jüngel, *God as the Mystery of the World: On the Foundation of the Theology of the Crucified
One in the Dispute Between Theism and Atheism*, trans. Darrell Guder (Edinburgh: T & T Clark,
1983), 41-42.

to the gospel"? These are the questions that modern trinitarian theology raises and that trinitarian theology after Barth seeks to address. In keeping with this quest, the purpose of this book is to consider the relationship between God's being Father, Son and Spirit and God's evangelical self-determination to become our Father, through the Son, in the Spirit.

How shall we proceed? Having stated the question that guides this study, and having identified the roots of that question in modern Protestant theology, we turn in chapter two to consider the state of the question as it has developed in trinitarian theology influenced by Barth. Chapter two traces the development of Barth's trinitarian theology across the *Church Dogmatics*, giving attention along the way to the reception history of his theology among those sympathetic to his basic program. As we will see, Barth's trinitarian theology suggests that a consistently evangelical doctrine of the Trinity must account both for God's eternal self-determination to be our God in the covenant of grace, as well as the realization of that self-determination in the history of the Son's humiliation and exaltation, when confessing the nature and perfection of God's being. As we will also see, trinitarian theology after Barth is characterized by widespread debate about exactly how an evangelical doctrine of the Trinity should accomplish this task. While Barth's theology, and the history of its reception, provides the historical and theological occasion for our question, it is Jenson's answers to this question that primarily concern us in the chapters that follow. Consequently, after tracing the basic contours and influence of Barth's trinitarian thought, chapter two will introduce briefly the theology of Robert Jenson, whose work is the focus of part one of this book.

Part one, composed of three chapters, analyzes Jenson's doctrine of the gospel's God, and thus his own proposal regarding the question under consideration. The chapters are organized according to the hermeneutical logic of Jenson's theology, which moves from the biblical identification of God to the metaphysical implications of

that identification for God's triune identity.[43] Chapter three intro-
duces Jenson's theological interpretation of the Old Testament. Attention is given to the way Jenson reads the biblical naming of God
ante Christum and, in so doing, navigates one of the most critical
challenges facing Christian theology, that is, reading the Old Testament within the context of the canon's coherent presentation of
God's triune identity. As we will see, Jenson's particular solution to
this challenge comes primarily by way of a narrative interpretation of
the exodus, which serves in his theology as both the paradigmatic
identification of God and the anticipatory pattern of God's saving
action in the gospel. Chapter three also considers the way in which
these two realities—God's identity and God's saving action—are
mutually constitutive in Jenson's doctrine of God. Following on this
discussion, chapter four examines Jenson's theological interpretation
of the New Testament. This chapter traces Jenson's arguments about
the way in which Jesus' relation to his Father in the Spirit provides
the dramatic realization of Israel's narrative and thus of God's triune
identity. Jenson's controversial understanding of the Son's preexistence is also introduced, as is his understanding of Jesus' atoning
work and resurrection as events that occur within the life of the triune God. In each instance, the implications of Jenson's narrative
reading for his trinitarian ontology are indicated but not fully developed. Chapter five then analyzes the major implications Jenson
draws from his theological interpretation of Scripture for the being
of the gospel's God, considering both his critique of the church's
traditional doctrine of God as well as his proposed revisionary metaphysics of God's triune identity.

Part two constitutes my constructive response to the question that
animates this study, and also to Jenson's proposal. As stated above, I
am convinced that the questions which Barth's theology raises and
which Jenson's theology addresses are vital, and that they demand

---

[43]See *GAG*, 98-99, 123.

There is the well-documented danger of silencing Reformation in the name of Tradition. Equally destructive, however, is the error of mistaking innovation for Reformation and heralding it as such.

the attention of an evangelical doctrine of God. Moreover, Jenson and many others argue—and I worry—that Barth's proposal suffers from a number of internal ambiguities[44] and therefore that, on its own terms, Barth's proposal ultimately fails to address adequately the questions that it raises. However, as sympathetic as I am to Jenson's concerns and constructive arguments, I am not convinced that the way beyond Barth lies in further metaphysical revision of the church's traditional teaching about God. The way forward, in my judgment, lies in appropriating more deeply certain aspects of traditional dogmatic teaching toward which many contemporary theologians are either ambivalent or openly hostile. These include the analogy of being; the doctrines of divine self-sufficiency, simplicity, immutability and eternity; as well as a rather traditional construal of the relationship between the internal processions and the outward actions of the divine persons. The way to renew the evangelical doctrine of God in the present, I suggest, is through *ressourcement*—retrieving the riches of what the church has confessed about the being and attributes of the triune God on the basis of the Word of God. The doctrine of God may prove more faithful to its evangelical impulse by becoming, in its own way, more catholic.

In this case, as in so many others, the plausibility of such a claim is best defended not simply by providing a genealogical critique of modern Protestant theology, though such critiques are indispensable, or simply by providing a more responsible account of the history of doctrine, though such accounts are indispensable as well. Given theology's status as an exhibitive discipline,[44] the plausibility of this conviction is best defended by "unleashing" these doctrines and allowing them to perform their proper dogmatic work. To that end, I will endeavor to demonstrate the superiority of a more traditional dogmatic response to Barth's queries over those provided by contem-

---

[44] *Theologia non est habitus demonstrativus, sed exhibitivus.* See John Webster, *Word and Church: Essays in Church Dogmatics* (Edinburgh: T & T Clark, 2001), 11.

Ps. 119:104

"Through your precepts I THE GOD OF THE GOSPEL
get understanding, therefore I hate every false way."

porary revisionist approaches like that of Jenson, not by directly engaging those approaches point by point, but by tracing the broad
contours of an alternative account, indicating along the way the pattern of biblical reasoning from which this account emerges and noting criticisms of other approaches where relevant.[45]

I suggest that a constructive treatment of the topic at hand may
proceed profitably by considering three dimensions of God's evangelical self-determination: (1) the relationship between God's being
and his self-determination to become our Father; (2) the relationship between God's being and his self-determination to become one
of us in the incarnation of the Son; (3) the relationship between
God's being and his self-determination to perfect us in the fellowship of the Holy Spirit. These dimensions are appropriate benchmarks for critical analysis and constructive description because they
reflect the Bible's own intrinsically trinitarian presentation of the
gospel, a presentation that both announces the events of the Son's
sending, incarnation, atonement and exaltation (Mk 12:1-12; Rom
1:1-4; 1 Cor 15:1-4) and proclaims in those events the realization of
God's covenant promise to be our God and Father and to dwell
among us by his Spirit (Lev 26:12; Is 40:9; Jn 20:17; 2 Cor 1:20;
6:16-18). These three dimensions of God's evangelical self-determination may serve as appropriate benchmarks for our discussion not
only because they reflect the biblical witness to God's identity but
also because they are capacious enough to house debates concerning
most of the issues that have emerged in trinitarian theology after
Barth, preeminently, the nature of God's electing self-determination,

---

[45]See John Webster's comments on the proper ordering of dogmatic description to polemical engagement: "Critical-polemical considerations are subordinate to positive dogmatic description,
and must not be allowed to distort the matter of doctrine. . . . Indeed, often critical engagement
is most effectively and charitably undertaken by better portrayal of the material content of dogmatics, especially when it has an eye to the placement of particular doctrines in the entire dogmatic corpus, and to the need to retain proportion, coherence and order. Good dogmatics un-
leashes doctrines and lets them run, so to speak, lets them explicate themselves with a bit of help
from conceptual analysis and systematic organization." "The Eternal Begetting of the Son," in
God Without Measure: Essays in Christian Doctrine (London: T & T Clark, forthcoming).

of God's incarnate history, and (as Jenson requires us to address) of the eschatological perfecting of fellowship between God and his people in the Spirit.

Part two includes four chapters. Chapter six addresses the first of the above-mentioned dimensions of God's evangelical self-determination, namely, the relationship between God's being and his self-determination to be our Father in the covenant of grace. In this chapter, I argue that the traditional notion of a "relative attribute" enables us to affirm that the biblical description of God as "our Father" truly belongs to God's identity, and not merely to the way we identify him, without requiring us to historicize the being of God. Furthermore, it is precisely the unchanging self-sufficiency of God's being that explains the sort of historical economy witnessed in the gospel: an economy of divine self-giving for the sake of creaturely blessing and progress toward filial glory. Appeal is then made to the doctrine of divine simplicity to show that such an understanding of God's fatherly identity, far from introducing an unwarranted gap between God's identity *in se* as the Father of the Son and God's identity *pro nobis* as the Father of his elect children, actually accounts better for the utter reliability of God's self-revelation in the gospel than does Jenson's proposal insofar as it enables us to perceive in God's fatherly will *ad extra* the free and contingent extension of his natural and necessary fatherly will *ad intra*.

Chapter seven then addresses the second dimension of God's evangelical self-determination: the relationship between God's being and his self-identification with us in the incarnation of the Son of God. Building on the discussion of the previous chapter, it argues that God's gracious assumption of human nature in the incarnation requires a more robust understanding of the Son's prevenience to the evangelical economy than Jenson's theology affords. Such an understanding may be found, I suggest, in the doctrine of the *pactum salutis* and, more deeply, in the doctrine of the Son's eternal generation from the Father. This chapter also responds to Jenson's view that a tradi-

tional understanding of the so-called incommunicable attributes inhibits any meaningful assertion of the incarnation of the Word. The
response involves engaging with the so-called Hellenization thesis
and explicating an evangelically appropriate understanding of God's
infinite perfection. The latter task is aided by a radical conception of
divine transcendence and by the analogy of being. This chapter also
posits a Thomistic conception of the distinction/relationship between the Son's eternal procession and temporal mission as the best
way of accounting for the reality of God's presence with us as one of
us in the Word made flesh.

In chapter eight, we turn to the third dimension of God's evangelical self-determination and consider the relationship between
God's being and his consummation of fellowship with us in the
Spirit. This chapter draws on concepts discussed in the preceding
two chapters, along the way addressing certain defects in Jenson's
pneumatology. Because many of the issues relevant to this dimension
of our topic are treated in previous chapters, this chapter is at once
briefer and more focused—concerned almost exclusively with the
relationship between the Spirit's eternal procession and temporal
mission. I argue that the Spirit eternally proceeds in the perfect, mutual love of the Father and the Son, and that his procession extends
into the economy as a "deluge" of divine love (Jonathan Edwards),
equipping and empowering the *totus Christus*, both head and body,
with all that is requisite to our inclusion as redeemed creatures within
the perfect, mutual love of the Father and the Son.

Chapter nine circles back to the broader discussion of trinitarian
theology after Barth introduced in chapter two in order to engage
Bruce L. McCormack's trinitarian thought. Although McCormack's
constructive dogmatic thesis is still in its provisional stages of articulation, it merits our attention for a number of reasons. Not only does
it engage many of the issues treated throughout the present study in
a clear and compelling manner, providing one of the most controversial answers to our question available today, it engages this question

from a perspective significantly different from that of Jenson. Whereas Jenson provides a distinctly Lutheran and eschatologically oriented example of what I describe in chapter two as "evangelical historicism," McCormack provides a distinctly Reformed and protologically oriented example of evangelical historicism. Accordingly, the goal of chapter nine is to provide a summary analysis of McCormack's argument about what an evangelical doctrine of God after Barth should look like, as well as a critique. Although I am highly influenced by McCormack's reading of Barth, and although I am sympathetic to many of his theological concerns, I argue that his proposal ultimately remains unsatisfactory insofar as it fails to account for the proper evangelical relationship between "the eternally rich God" (Martin Rinckart) and the economy of salvation. Chapter ten, the concluding chapter, provides a brief summary of the argument of this book.

2

THE STATE OF
THE QUESTION

◆

INTRODUCTION

In the previous chapter, we identified the modern roots of the question which animates this study. In the present chapter, we turn to "the Barthian shoot" in which this question has flowered.[1] Our approach will be to survey the main lines of Barth's doctrine of the triune God, looking in rough sequence at sections of the *Church Dogmatics* where the doctrine is addressed. Within the context of our survey, we will also consider the main lines of debate surrounding Barth's significance for contemporary trinitarian dogmatics, focusing specifically on dimensions of that debate which touch on the topic at hand: the relationship between God's triune being and his covenantal self-determination. As we will discover, trinitarian theology after Barth demands that a consistently evangelical doctrine of God wrestle with the implications of divine election and divine incarnation for the being of God.

Among Protestant theologians working in the wake of Barth's trinitarian program, none have offered a more dogmatically rigorous or comprehensive response to the demands imposed by Barth

---

[1]See Stanley Grenz, *Rediscovering the Triune God: The Trinity in Contemporary Theology* (Minneapolis: Fortress, 2004), 72, who follows Ted Peters in this description.

on the evangelical doctrine of God than Robert Jenson. Jenson's theology self-consciously seeks to meet these demands, even as it seeks to transcend what it perceives to be the limitations of Barth's own thought, especially in the areas of pneumatology and eschatology. Along with our summary of Barth's trinitarian theology and its reception, therefore, the present chapter will also introduce the trinitarian theology of Robert Jenson in order to lay the foundation for a fuller engagement with his thought in the chapters that follow.

THE TRINITY IN *CHURCH DOGMATICS* 1.1

In the theology of Karl Barth, the "mediating theology" (*Vermittlungstheologie*)[2] that dominated so much nineteenth century Protestant thought simultaneously came to an abrupt end and found a new beginning.[3] In its place, and over the course of several decades, Barth sought to construct a dogmatics that did not require pretheological apologetic defense and that was not anxious to demonstrate its continuity with general conceptions of human reason, history or religious experience. The starting point of Barth's theology was the sheer singularity of God's self-revelation in Jesus Christ as attested in Holy Scripture, a starting point that required no foundations and that entered the sphere of dogmatic reasoning as *novum*, not as the summation of previously comprehended realities.[4] Though his earlier

---

[2]For a recent introduction to this movement, see Matthias Gockel, "Mediating Theology in Germany," in *The Blackwell Companion to Nineteenth-Century Theology*, ed. David A. Fergusson (Oxford: Blackwell, 2010), 301-18.

[3]Contrary to earlier "neo-orthodox" readings of Barth which tended to interpret Barth as making a complete break with Protestant liberalism, more recent scholarship suggests that in Barth we have the sublation (*Aufhebung*) of many of modern Protestant theology's aims and concerns. See chiefly in this regard, Bruce L. McCormack, *Karl Barth's Critically Realistic Dialectical Theology: Its Genesis and Development 1909-1936* (Oxford: Clarendon, 1997). Also instructive is Ryan Glomsrud, "Karl Barth and Modern Protestantism: The Radical Impulse," in *Always Reformed: Essays in Honor of W. Robert Godfrey*, ed. R. Scott Clark and Joel E. Kim (Escondido, CA: Westminster Seminary California, 2012), chap. 5.

[4]A complete discussion of the *Realdialektik* of revelation in Barth cannot be pursued here. For an instructive introduction, see Bruce L. McCormack, "'The Limits of the Knowledge of God': Theses on the Theological Epistemology of Karl Barth," in *Orthodox and Modern: Studies in the Theology of Karl Barth* (Grand Rapids: Baker, 2008), chap. 6.

attempts to displace/replace the modern liberal theological agenda were not without success, it was only in the *Church Dogmatics* that Barth's positive alternative to modern Protestant theology began to emerge in its mature form. It is also in the *Church Dogmatics* that the doctrine of the Trinity assumed its commanding position within this alternative tradition of theological inquiry.[5]

We find Barth's first extensive treatment of the doctrine of the Trinity in the first part-volume of the *Church Dogmatics,* within the context of his discussion of God in his revelation. As John Webster observes, Barth's preoccupation with the concept of revelation in this section is not primarily epistemological in nature. His concern is primarily theological, even metaphysical. In other words, Barth takes up the question of *revelation* because he is fundamentally concerned with addressing the question, "Who is God?"[6] According to Barth, it is only in light of God's distinctive identity as Father, Son and Holy Spirit that we may think properly about the nature of revelation and the nature of God.[7]

Given its defining significance, Barth argues that the doctrine of the Trinity must be located "at the head of all dogmatics."[8] In taking this approach, Barth is self-conscious of his departure not only from "Modernist Protestantism," which stumbled at the utter mystery of God's self-revelation as Trinity,[9] but also of his departure from the theologies of the Reformation and Protestant orthodoxy, which rightly revered the mystery of the Trinity but (in Barth's estimation) failed to perceive the significance of this mystery for theological

---

[5]It should be noted that Barth's placement of the doctrine of the Trinity in a position of prominence in *Church Dogmatics* is in keeping with a move already made but less developed in his earlier dogmatic texts. See *The Göttingen Dogmatics: Instruction in the Christian Religion,* trans. Geoffrey W. Bromiley (Grand Rapids: Eerdmans, 1991), §5; and *Die Christliche Dogmatik in Entwurf,* ed. Gerhard Sauter (Zürich: Theologischer Verlag Zürich, 1982), §§10-13.
[6]John Webster, *Barth's Ethics of Reconciliation* (Cambridge: Cambridge University Press, 1995), chap. 1.
[7]*CD* 1.1:300-301.
[8]Ibid., 300.
[9]Ibid., 303-4.

method and for the doctrine of God.[10] Taking leave of his forebears at this point, Barth argues that the Trinity must be programmatic in our conception of God's being and work. Given the sheer singularity of God's self-revelation as Trinity, this revelation can provide the *only* foundation for theological reflection on God. This conviction holds both a negative and a positive methodological implication. Negatively, theological reflection on God may never attempt to "illustrate" that which God reveals about himself on the basis of or in comparison with any other analogue or object. Because "God is not in a class" (*Deus non est in genere*),[11] our understanding of the Trinity of persons in God cannot be modeled after other "trinities" within creation, the so-called vestiges of the Trinity (*vestigium Trinitatis*),[12] nor can our understanding of God's being and perfection be interpreted on the basis of some "master concept" that purports to comprehend the being and perfection of both God and his creatures.[13] Positively, the singularity of God's self-revelation as Trinity requires that theological reflection on God only take the form of an "interpretation" of that revelation as it is mediated through the canonical witness of the prophets and apostles.[14] As revelation constitutes God's self-interpretation to the church through the medium of Holy Scripture, so the doctrine of the Trinity constitutes the church's interpretation of God's revelation on the basis of that scriptural medium.[15] By closing the hermeneutical circle that traces the movement of revelation from the triune God, through its mediation in Holy Scripture, to its conceptual elaboration

---

[10]Ibid., 300-301, 303. For a penetrating critique of Barth's judgment in this regard, see Willem van Asselt, "The Fundamental Meaning of Theology: Archetypal and Ectypal Theology in Seventeenth-Century Reformed Thought," *Westminster Theological Journal* 64 (2002): 319-35.

[11]See *CD* 2.1:310-11.

[12]*CD* 1.1:333-47.

[13]*CD* 2.1:311-12. In Barth's judgment, both Protestant and Catholic dogmatics failed to observe this methodological rule with consistency, a failure that bore severe consequences in their doctrines of God (*CD* 2.1, 261, 287-88). This methodological rule also explains Barth's rejection of the *analogia entis*.

[14]*CD* 1.1:333-47.

[15]Ibid., 308-11. For an incisive commentary on this dimension of Barth's theological method, see Eberhard Jüngel, *God's Being Is in Becoming: The Trinitarian Being of God in the Theology of Karl Barth*, trans. John Webster (Edinburgh: T & T Clark, 2001).

in church dogmatics, Barth believes he has identified the only possible path to a knowledge of the gospel's God—a path that Barth would follow with rigorous consistency throughout his career.[16]

As many of his interpreters have pointed out, Barth's understanding of "God in his revelation" at this point is not a complete departure from modern trinitarianism. Following a consistent theme of modern theology, Barth considers the triune being, and thus the triune revelation, primarily under the category of divine "subject" and not under the category of divine "substance." For Barth, rightly interpreting the divine identity demands that we first consider God as a "who" and not as a "what." This emphasis on the divine subjectivity explains Barth's strict identification of the subject of revelation with the content of revelation.[17] Given his thoroughly personal nature, the God who reveals himself cannot ultimately be distinguished from the God who is himself revealed. This strict identification of the subject and content of revelation in turn accounts for the sheer singularity of God's self-revelation. As Pannenberg notes, it is Barth's "linking of the thought of God's self-revelation with that of its uniqueness" that enabled him to rule out "all ideas of a second source of the knowledge of God."[18] Barth's emphasis on the divine subjectivity also explains his focus on the eventful nature of revelation. Barth credits Hegel for teaching modern theology the lesson that the God who reveals himself by himself reveals himself as an "event that comes and goes, like a passing thunder-shower (Luther), like the angel at the pool of Bethesda." This God is "the Living God" with a "real history" whose truth must be encountered in the singular movement of that history or nowhere at all.[19]

[16]*CD* 2.1:262-63; see also *CD* 1.1:380.
[17]Wolfhart Pannenberg, *Systematic Theology*, trans. Geoffrey W. Bromiley (Grand Rapids: Eerdmans, 1991), 1:219-23. See also Bruce L. McCormack, "The Doctrine of the Trinity After Barth: An Attempt to Reconstruct Barth's Doctrine in the Light of His Later Christology," in Myk Habets and Phillip Tolliday, eds., *Trinitarian Theology After Barth*, Princeton Theological Monograph Series (Eugene, OR: Pickwick, 2011), 90-92.
[18]Pannenberg, *Systematic Theology*, 1:223.
[19]Karl Barth, *Protestant Theology in the Nineteenth Century*, trans. Brian Cozens and John Bowden

For all Barth's indebtedness to modern conceptions of divine subjectivity, when it comes to his material description of the Trinity his doctrine continues to exhibit a fairly traditional "Western" shape.[20] According to Barth the doctrine of the Trinity is the fulfillment of monotheism: "The name of the Father, Son and Spirit means that God is the one God in threefold repetition."[21] The doctrine speaks "not of three divine I's, but thrice of the one divine I."[22] In keeping with this understanding, Barth defines the controverted concept of "person" as a subsisting mode of being within the one God, distinguished by its particular relations to the other persons.[23] Barth also

---

(Grand Rapids: Eerdmans, 2002), 402. Speaking elsewhere on the eventfulness of God's self-revelation, Barth summarizes the matter: "What is concerned is always the birth, death and resurrection of Jesus Christ, always his justification of faith , always his lordship in the Church, always his coming again, and therefore himself as our hope. We can only abandon revelation, and with it God's Word, if we are to dispense with it. With it we stand, no, we move necessarily in the circle of its event or, in biblical terms, in the circle of the life of the people of Israel. And in this very event God is who he is. God is he who in this event is subject, predicate and object; the revealer, the act of revelation, the revealed; Father, Son, and Holy Spirit. God is the Lord active in this event. We say 'active' in this event, and therefore for our salvation and for his glory, but in any case active. Seeking and finding God in his revelation, we cannot escape the action of God for a God who is not active. This is not only because we ourselves cannot, but because there is no surpassing or bypassing at all of the divine action, because a transcendence of his action is nonsense. We are dealing with the being of God: but with regard to the being of God, the word 'event' or 'act' is *final*, and cannot be surpassed or compromised. To its very deepest depths God's Godhead consists in the fact that it is an event—not any event, not events in general, but the event of his action, in which we have a share in God's revelation. . . . *Actus purus* is not sufficient as a description of God. To it there must be added at least '*et singularis*'" (*CD* 2.1:262-64).

[20]Barth's trinitarian theology exhibits a "Western" character (1) in the material affirmations that it makes related to the nature of divine persons, the *filioque,* etc. and also (2) in the sources from which it draws (e.g., Augustine, Anselm, Thomas Aquinas, Protestant orthodoxy, modern Catholic dogmatics). I do not identify Barth's trinitarian theology as "Western" in contrast to "Eastern" *if* the latter label intends to distinguish a different starting point (the three persons vs. their consubstantial nature) or to identify a social model of the Trinity. Recent scholarship has severely criticized this widely popular construct of distinguishing Western and Eastern trinitarian types. For a helpful introduction to this line of criticism, see Sarah Coakley, ed., *Re-Thinking Gregory of Nyssa* (Oxford: Blackwell, 2003). It is, moreover, a construct that strikes me as unprofitable for interpreting Barth's trinitarian thought.

[21]*CD* 1.1:350.

[22]Ibid., 351.

[23]Ibid., 366. For a sympathetic critique of Barth's understanding of trinitarian persons as "modes of being," see Alan J. Torrance, *Persons in Communion: An Essay on Trinitarian Description and Human Participation, With Special Reference to Volume One of Karl Barth's "Church Dogmatics"* (Edinburgh: T & T Clark, 1996). More severe criticism may be found in Jürgen Moltmann, *The Trinity and the Kingdom: The Doctrine of God,* trans. Margaret Kohl (Minneapolis: Fortress, 1993), 139-44.

affirms the Father's eternal generation of the Son, as well as Spirit's eternal procession from the Father and the Son (the *filioque*).[24] In a rather elegant discussion of the relationship between the *opera Trinitatis ad intra* and the *opera Trinitatis ad extra*, Barth treats the manner in which the distinct modes of "being in becoming"[25] by which the three persons subsist in the one God serve to ground the distinctive appropriations by which the three persons exhibit themselves in the inseparable external works of God.[26] While Barth is keen to emphasize throughout his discussion that the singular event of divine self-revelation provides our only epistemological access to the Trinity,[27] he is equally keen to deny that divine self-revelation provides the ontological basis of the Trinity, "as though God were the triune God only in his revelation and only for the sake of his revelation."[28] To say otherwise, Barth fears, would compromise the free and gracious nature of revelation and reconciliation. It would also cut off the divine movement of grace from its ontological basis in God's antecedently rich triune life, leaving us to interpret this movement solely according to immanent, this-worldly criteria and thus outside the sphere of faith.[29] In this, as in nearly all of the aforementioned instances, Barth's characteristically "modern" doctrine of the Trinity bears closer resemblance to that of Dorner than it does to that of Hegel. A debated point among Barth interpreters concerns whether and to what extent Barth's version of the doctrine of the Trinity as expounded in *Church Dogmatics* 1.1 can sustain later developments in his theology, most notably his revised doctrine of election and his historicized doctrine of Jesus Christ.

---

[24]Barth *CD* 1.1:414-47, 466-89.

[25]See ibid., 427.

[26]Ibid., 394-98.

[27]Ibid., 479-83; also 371.

[28]Ibid., 312.

[29]Ibid., 420-22. This particular line of argument is thoroughly developed by Paul Molnar, *Divine Freedom and the Doctrine of the Immanent Trinity: In Dialogue with Karl Barth and Contemporary Theology* (London: T & T Clark, 2002).

THE TRINITY IN *CHURCH DOGMATICS* 2.1

In *Church Dogmatics* 2.1 Barth turns his attention more directly to the being and perfection of the God identified as triune in the first part-volume of his dogmatics.[30] According to Barth, the task of expounding the statement "God is" represents both "the hardest" and "the most extensive" task of Christian dogmatics, the way in which dogmatics expounds this statement being definitive for the way it expounds "the subject of all other statements."[31] Barth lays the foundation for pursuing this task by considering two erroneous approaches that have plagued Protestant dogmatics, both of which are traceable to Philipp Melanchthon. The first approach refuses the task of conceptual reflection on God's being and instead focuses exclusively upon the *beneficia Christi*. This approach, followed by many modern theologians,[32] is traceable to Melanchthon's 1521 *Loci communes*, wherein he argued that the divine mystery is more worthy of adoration than of investigation. The second approach does not refuse the task of conceptual reflection on God's being. However, Barth considers this error the worse of the two because it fails to consider God's being in light of the only peculiar basis on which it might be known—God's act in his revelation. In other words, this approach failed to remember "that a Church dogmatics derives from a doctrine of the Trinity."[33] In so doing, it allowed its conception of the divine being to be determined by pagan philosophy and thereby unwittingly "paved the way for the later Enlightenment with all that that involved."[34] Barth traces this approach to Melanchthon's "disastrous" example in later editions of his *Loci communes*, and identifies

---

[30]An illuminating commentary on §§28-31 of *Church Dogmatics* 2.1 may be found in Robert B. Price, *Letters of the Divine Word: The Perfections of God in Karl Barth's Church Dogmatics* (London: T & T Clark, 2011).

[31]*CD* 2.1:257-58.

[32]In the immediate context, Barth identifies Hermann Cremer's *Die christliche Lehre von den Eigenschaften Gottes* as falling prey to this approach (*CD* 2.1:260).

[33]Ibid., 259-61.

[34]Ibid., 266; also 288.

Protestant orthodoxy as one of its major culprits.[35]

If these two fatal routes are to be avoided, reflection on God's being must follow the path laid out by God in the singular movement of his self-revelation. Following this path leads Barth to offer the following gloss on the statement "God is": "God is who he is in the act of his revelation. God seeks and creates fellowship between himself and us, and therefore he loves us. But he is this loving God without us as Father, Son and Holy Spirit, in the freedom of the Lord, who has his life from himself."[36] More tersely, "God is the one who loves in freedom." It is immediately evident that these descriptions seek to guard against both of the aforementioned errors. God's being is known in his loving movement toward us in Christ and nowhere else.[37] Indeed, Barth insists that God "does not will to *be himself* in any other way than in *this relationship*."[38] Generic, nontrinitarian concepts of divine being are thus ruled out. And yet, according to Barth, if we are to understand the character of this divine movement correctly, we must understand God's movement toward us in the gospel as the free "overflow" of his triune being.[39] God loves us and in doing so he *is* the one he is; but his love for us is not the beginning of his love. God's love for us is the overflow of his free and eternal love as Father, Son and Holy Spirit. God loves us by granting

[35]Ibid., 259-60, 261, 263-67, etc. For an insightful interrogation of Barth's reading of Reformed orthodoxy on this point, specifically focusing on Barth's reading of Amandus Polanus, see Rinse H. Reeling Brouwer, "The Conversation Between Karl Barth and Amandus Polanus on the Question of the Reality of Human Speaking of the Simplicity and the Multiplicity in God," in *The Reality of Faith in Theology: Studies on Karl Barth, Princeton-Kampen Consultation 2005*, ed. Bruce L. McCormack and Gerrit Neven (Bern: Peter Lang, 2007), 51-110.

[36]*CD* 2.1:257. This statement summarizes Barth's understanding of the divine being and serves "as shorthand for the whole of his doctrine of the perfections" (Price, *Letters of the Divine Word*, 11).

[37]*CD* 2.1:261: "What God is as God, the divine individuality and characteristics, the *essentia* or 'essence' of God, is something which we shall encounter either at the place where God deals with us as Lord and Saviour, or not at all."

[38]Ibid., 274, italics mine.

[39]As Edwin Christian van Driel notes, "overflow" is one of Barth's favorite terms to describe the relationship between God's triune life *ad intra* and his triune life *ad extra*. Van Driel, *Incarnation Anyway: Arguments for Supralapsarian Christology* (Oxford: Oxford University Press, 2008), 92-94. See also Barth, *CD* 2.2:175: "His being and activity *ad extra* is merely an overflowing of his inward activity and being, of the inward vitality which he has in himself."

us a fellowship in the life of love that he is "without us" in the freedom of the Trinity.[40] Concepts of divine being that would speak of
God's loving movement toward us without acknowledging the inner-
trinitarian depth from which that movement springs are thus ruled
out as well. In sum, then, God is the one who loves in freedom both
ad intra—as Father, Son and Spirit, and *ad extra*—in the gospel of
his Son wherein he "seeks and creates fellowship between himself
and us." And God's being as the one who loves in freedom *ad extra*
corresponds to God's being as the one who loves in freedom *ad intra*.

This twofold depth of God's triune being indicates "the reality of
God."[41] The doctrine of the divine perfections that unfolds in the
remainder of volume 2.1 is a commentary on this twofold depth, a
tracing out of what it means to speak of the Trinity as the one who
determines to be who and what he is *only* in relation to us and as
the one whose determination in this regard springs forth from the
fullness of who and what God is *wholly* without us as Father, Son
and Spirit.

Although a survey of Barth's presentation of the divine perfections lies beyond the scope of the present study,[42] it is important to
note one further feature of Barth's trinitarian ontology before proceeding to discuss his doctrine of election, specifically, his understanding of the being of God as "the being of a person." To identify
God as the one who loves in freedom is to identify God as "hypostatic being,"[43] as one who exists in "the freedom of a knowing and
willing I."[44] That God exists in this manner means that he is "self-
moved," that his being is his "own, conscious, willed and executed
decision."[45] Indeed, according to Barth, only the triune God truly

[40]*CD* 2.1:273.
[41]Barth prefers to speak of trinitarian ontology under the description of "the reality of God" because he believes this description "holds together being and act, instead of tearing them apart like
the idea of 'essence'" (*CD* 2.1:262).
[42]See Price, *Letters of the Divine Word*.
[43]The terminology is Robert Jenson's, but it aptly characterizes Barth's ontology at this point.
[44]*CD* 2.1:267.
[45]Ibid., 271.

exists "in the strict and proper sense" as an event of absolute self-determination.[46] The fact that God exists in this decision includes the fact that "his life, that is, his life in himself, which is originally and properly the one and only life, leans towards this unity with our life." The determination by which God *is* God as *our* God "is therefore the divine, the θεόν, the essence of God in the revelation of his name."[47]

What does it mean to say that God consciously wills and executes the decision to be God? Certain answers to this question can be ruled out immediately. The point for Barth is not merely that God wills his existence in reference to the creature, that his being is a decision only in the sense that he determines to give himself to us in the covenant of grace. Already in his trinitarian ontology Barth affirms a point that becomes emphatic in his doctrine of election: God's existence is a freely willed existence—both *ad intra* as Trinity and *ad extra* in the covenant of grace.[48] "God's freedom constitutes the essential positive quality, not only of his action towards what is outside himself, but also of his own inner being."[49] God's being is voluntive being through and through.[50] Nevertheless, having established this point, we are very far from answering the question regarding what any of this means. Should we say that God *necessarily* wills his existence as the triune God who loves in freedom and that he *contingently* wills to be this God for us in Jesus Christ? Does God's decision refer to his free choice either to will or to nil a specific state of affairs? And, if so, does this free choice apply as equally to God's being and existence as it does to his decision to seek and create fel-

---

[46]Ibid.

[47]Ibid., 274-75.

[48]See *CD* 2.2:79: "God is the living God . . . inwardly as well as outwardly, a quality expressed and attested in concrete decision." And later in the same paragraph: "God is not *in abstracto* Father, Son and Holy Ghost, the triune God. He is so with a definite purpose and reference."

[49]*CD* 2.1:303, 550. See also Barth's qualified endorsement of the notion that God's freedom is a matter of his "self-realization" as Trinity (*CD* 2.1:305-6).

[50]See Eberhard Jüngel: "Decision does not belong to the being of God as something supplementary to this being; rather, as event, God's being is his own decision" (*God's Being Is in Becoming*, 81).

lowship with human beings? Does divine freedom indicate God's capacity to be what he is and to do what he does in sovereign self-affirmation, apart from external or internal constraint? Or does divine freedom indicate God's capacity for projecting and realizing his being and ours, a capacity that is wholly indeterminate apart from the act of projection and realization itself? Furthermore, how do God's being, power, knowledge and will relate to possibility and actuality? Are both divine and creaturely possibilities and actualities consequences of divine willing? Or is it only the case that creaturely actualities are a consequence of divine willing, their possibility being a consequence of divine power (the so-called *potentia absoluta*)? These questions are difficult to answer, not least because one can find proof-texts for almost all of the aforementioned senses of divine willing in the sprawling discourse of the *Church Dogmatics*![51]

A potentially promising path for addressing these questions lies in examining the ways in which Barth critically appropriates the sophisticated apparatus of conceptual distinctions pertaining to the *voluntas Dei* that are available in the theological tradition.[52] Though rarely explored by those engaged in contemporary Barth debates,[53] this path provides a broad range of categories within which we might classify the many different things that Barth has to say about God's decision to be God. However, this path does not wholly resolve the

---

[51]Witness George Hunsinger, "Election and the Trinity: Twenty-Five Theses on the Theology of Karl Barth," *Modern Theology* 24 (2008): 179-98; and Bruce L. McCormack, "Election and the Trinity: Theses in Response to George Hunsinger," *Scottish Journal of Theology* 63 (2010): 203-224.

[52]In *CD* 2.1 alone, Barth critically engages the following traditional distinctions related to the *voluntas Dei*: *voluntas naturalis* and *necessaria*, *voluntas libera*, *voluntas beneplaciti* and *occulta*, *voluntas signi* and *revelata*, *voluntas absoluta*, *voluntas conditionalis*, *voluntas antecedens*, *voluntas consequens*, *voluntas efficiens*, *voluntas permittens*, *voluntas efficax*, *voluntas inefficax*; closely related here is the distinction between *potentia absoluta* and *potentia ordinata*. See *CD* 2.1:519-97.

[53]A notable exception is Dolf te Velde, *Paths Beyond Tracing Out: The Connection of Method and Content in the Doctrine of God, Examined in Reformed Orthodoxy, Karl Barth, and the Utrecht School* (Delft, The Netherlands: Eburon, 2010). This volume not only provides an extensive comparison between Barth and Reformed scholasticism on the doctrine of God. It also demonstrates keen sensitivity to the distinctive ways in which Barth employs traditional scholastic distinctions in his doctrine of God.

aforementioned questions, as Barth's stance toward traditional distinctions pertaining to the divine will is rarely one of simple adoption or simple rejection but is more often one of critical appropriation in service of his own distinctive theological program.[54] Consequently, interpreters are left with the challenge of applying various concepts of freedom and decision (both classical and modern) to the various dimensions of what Barth has to say about the divine willing, and to debate which applications make the most sense of Barth's theology, either taken as a whole or viewed from the perspective of its diachronic development. At the end of the day, interpreters are also left with the question of whether or not Barth's doctrine of divine freedom is comprehensible *on its own terms*.

THE TRINITY IN *CHURCH DOGMATICS* 2.2

In the second part-volume of *Church Dogmatics* volume 2, we come to Barth's most creative and controversial *theologoumenon* in his doctrine of election. In treating this doctrine, Barth is once again self-conscious of his departure from the tradition; but in this instance his departure is more substantial in comparison to earlier modifications

---

[54]To note just one significant example: Barth uses the distinction between God's *voluntas naturalis* and *necessaria* (i.e., God's "natural and necessary will") and God's *voluntas libera* (i.e., God's "free will") to distinguish between God's will concerning himself and God's will concerning "everything else," immediately adding the qualification that God's *voluntas necessaria* concerning himself is also "free" and that his *voluntas libera* concerning everything else is in some sense "necessary" (*CD* 2.1: 591). Read in its immediate context, this distinction and its accompanying qualification are fully in keeping with traditional Reformed ways of speaking of the *voluntas Dei* (see also *CD* 2.1:518-19). However, this reading is complicated when examined within the larger context of *Church Dogmatics* 2.1, for earlier in the volume Barth insists that we understand God's status as *ens necessarium* (i.e., "necessary being") to be "the effect of his freedom." He goes on to say: "If we seek to establish the intrinsic impossibility that God could not be, or could be other than he is, i.e., if we seek the necessity of his being, or of his being in this particular way, on any other basis than that of *this empirical decision*, we have to consider whether we are not concerned with a God who in his need to be is not God but the postulated apotheosis of our creaturely existence" (*CD* 2.1:307, italics mine). In other words, it is only following from the "empirical fact" of God's existence, which itself follows from God's actual decision to exist, that we may conclude that God necessarily exists (*CD* 2.1, 307). In contrast to the reading of Barth's distinction between God's necessary will and his free will provided above, this passage suggests that *God* necessarily exists in the same way that *anything* that actually exists necessarily exists: as a consequence of God's free decision (i.e., by a "necessity of the consequence"). Understood in this manner, Barth's use of traditional terminology seems quite distant from traditional Reformed ways of speaking of the *voluntas Dei*.

of the tradition that he has undertaken.[55] Much of the controversy that engages us in the present study is about how to interpret the significance of Barth's innovation at this point.

Building on two premises developed earlier in volume two—that God alone reveals God, and that God reveals himself as the one who loves in freedom—Barth turns to the doctrine of election, the doctrine which concerns God's free and irrevocable relationship to that which is not God, God's determination to be the one who loves in freedom *also* for us.[56] According to Barth, the decree of election is God's *primal decision*. Election is God's first and fundamental decree, the *opus internum ad extra* that determines the shape of all other divine decrees and all other divine actions which flow from it.[57] Election is the beginning of the ways and works of the God who himself has no beginning.[58] According to Barth, the decree of election is also God's *concrete decision*. As a *decretum concretum*,[59] election assigns a definitive shape to the way in which God relates to all things *ad extra*. Specifically, election is God's good pleasure to relate to creation definitively in and as Jesus Christ, who is both the subject and the object of election, the electing God and the elect human being.[60] "The name Jesus Christ," Barth tells us, is "the basis of the doctrine of election."[61] Perhaps most significantly, as God's primal, concrete

---

[55]Compare Barth's discussion of the mostly cosmetic differences between his doctrine of the divine perfections and that of the dogmatic tradition (*CD* 2.1:344-50) with his discussion of the "innovation" that his doctrine of election brings in relation to the dogmatic tradition (*CD* 2.2:77-93).

[56]*CD* 2.2:3-6.

[57]Ibid., 8-9.

[58]Ibid., 94, 102-3.

[59]Karl Barth, *Die Kirchliche Dogmatik* 2.2 (Zürich: Theologischer Verlag Zürich, 1980), 172-73. Cornelis van der Kooi points out that the English version of *Church Dogmatics* here mistranslates *decretum concretum* as *decretum absolutum*. See *As in a Mirror: John Calvin and Karl Barth on Knowing God: A Diptych* (Grand Rapids: Eerdmans, 2005), 371n113.

[60]*CD* 2.2:3-8, 94-145.

[61]Ibid., 60. Barth explains: "If we would know who God is, and what is the meaning and purpose of his election, and in what respect he is the electing God, then we must look away from all others, and excluding all side-glances or secondary thoughts, we must look only upon and to the name of Jesus Christ, and the existence and history of the people of God enclosed in him. We must look only upon the divine mystery of this name and this history, of this Head and this body" (*CD* 2.2:54). See also *CD* 4.1:16-18.

decision in Jesus Christ, the doctrine of election belongs to the doc-trine of God. The doctrine of election is not only a determination about matters that are "'downstream' from the eternal moment of election"—including creation, anthropology, evil and christology—but also a determination about matters that are "'upstream' from the moment of election," specifically the being and identity of God.[62] The doctrine concerns God's free and irreversible *self*-determination to be God only in relation to us as our God.[63] "The election of grace in the beginning of all things is God's self-giving in his eternal purpose."[64] Consequently, the failure to appreciate the doctrine of election is not simply a failure to appreciate God's plan for creation and history, it is a failure to appreciate God's being and existence. God is not the living and triune God *in abstracto*; he is the living and triune God in this "definite purpose and reference."[65]

To say that Jesus Christ is the *subject* of election is to say that he is *the electing God*. The identification of Jesus Christ as the electing God serves as a kind christological shorthand for a doctrine with trinitar-ian and covenantal depth.[66] That Jesus Christ is the electing God means (1) that Jesus' Father eternally wills also to be our Father by giving up his Son Jesus to death on a cross; (2) that the Son of God eternally wills also to unite himself with the man Jesus in order to fulfill his Father's commission and to effect the covenant of grace; (3)

---

[62]Edwin Christian van Driel, "Karl Barth on the Eternal Existence of Jesus Christ," *Scottish Journal of Theology* 60 (2007): 45-46.

[63]*CD* 2.2:5-11, 76-77. As Bruce McCormack notes, the implications of Barth's doctrine of election *for creatures* (i.e., its implied universalism) has drawn the most attention from "those who have been weaned on Reformed understandings of predestination." However, it is the implications of Barth's doctrine of election *for God* that is of primary interest for Barth and of greatest theologi-cal significance (*Orthodox and Modern*, 185).

[64]*CD* 2.2:161.

[65]Ibid., 79. Elsewhere, Barth puts the matter this way: "In no depth of the Godhead shall we en-counter any other but him. There is no such thing as Godhead in itself. Godhead is always the Godhead of the Father, the Son and the Holy Spirit. But the Father is the Father of Jesus Christ and the Holy Spirit is the Spirit of the Father and the Spirit of Jesus Christ" (*CD* 2.2:115).

[66]Paul Nimmo, "Election and Evangelical Thinking: Challenges to our Way of Conceiving the Doctrine of God," in *New Perspectives for Evangelical Theology: Engaging with God, Scripture, and the World*, ed. Tom Greggs (New York: Routledge, 2010), 37.

that the Spirit eternally wills that the unbroken unity of the eternal Father and the eternal Son should also come to include the union of God with sinful human beings in Jesus Christ, the mediator of the covenant of grace.[67] So described, Barth's doctrine of election closely resembles the Reformed doctrine of the *pactum salutis,* the eternal pact between the Father and the Son concerning the salvation of elect sinners.[68] Like the *pactum salutis,* Barth's doctrine of election is the eternal movement within the *opera Trinitatis ad intra* that grounds the temporal saving movement of God in the *opera Trinitatis ad extra.* The difference between Barth's doctrine of election and the *pactum salutis* lies in his particular modulation of double predestination. Whereas God assigns to all human beings the decree of salvation in and through Jesus Christ, God assigns to himself the decree of reprobation in and through Jesus Christ. In this decree, "There is a sure and certain salvation for man, and a sure and certain risk for God."[69] When the triune God commits himself to fallen human beings in Jesus Christ, he ordains "the surrender of . . . his own impassibility" and the assumption of "reprobation, perdition and death."[70] For God, election "means severe self-commitment."[71] In "his overflowing glory God is sacrificial love: love which seeks not her own but the things of others."[72] In Jesus Christ, the triune God thus determines his being as a being for covenant fellowship with sinful human beings.

Accordingly, to say that Jesus Christ is the *object* of election is to say that he is *the elect human being* in and through whom all other human beings are exalted to fellowship with God. Jesus Christ is the elect human being whose particular existence is the free creaturely deter-

---

[67]*CD* 2.2:101-2.
[68]Similarly, Paul Dafydd Jones, *The Humanity of Christ: Christology in Karl Barth's Church Dogmatics* (London: T & T Clark, 2008), 81. Cf. Barth's criticisms of the *pactum salutis* in *CD* 4.1:65-66.
[69]*CD* 2.2:162.
[70]Ibid., 163.
[71]Ibid., 164.
[72]Ibid., 173; also 121.

mination that corresponds to God's free self-determination in election. *As* this one and *through* this one—through his free obedience
unto death and through his exaltation as the royal man—the determination of all human beings to live in correspondence to God's
self-determination is realized.[73] The man Jesus is "himself the plan
and decree of God, himself the divine decision with respect to all
creation and its history whose content is already determined."[74]
Whereas God in Christ assigns to himself "reprobation, perdition
and death," God in Christ assigns to all human beings "glory, goodness and blessedness."[75] In Jesus Christ, the triune God thus determines sinful human beings for covenant fellowship with himself.[76]

Because Jesus Christ is the electing God and the elect human
being, neither the subject nor the object of election remains hidden
to us. Both the identity of God and the identity of elect human beings are *wholly revealed* in the gospel.[77] In making this point, Barth
seeks to correct his own Reformed heritage which, in his judgment,
left both the identity of the electing God and the identity of elect
human beings *hidden* within an "absolute decree" (*decretum
absolutum*)—a decree in which God "is neither conditioned" (as in
the Remonstrant doctrine of "conditional election," where the presence or absence of human faith conditions God's election) "nor self-
conditioned" (as in Barth's doctrine, where God's eternal determination to unite himself with the man Jesus conditions God's election).[78]
Jesus' identity as the electing God and the elect human being also
explains why the doctrine of election is "the sum of the gospel."[79] The
doctrine of election in Jesus Christ not only makes "our knowledge

---

[73]Ibid., 116-18, 177-80.
[74]Ibid., 104.
[75]Ibid., 174.
[76]Insofar as the creature's determination in election is a determination toward free correspondence
with God's free self-determination, Barth's doctrine of election lays the foundation for his theological ethics. See Paul Nimmo, *Being in Action: The Theological Shape of Barth's Ethical Vision*
(London: T & T Clark, 2007).
[77]*CD* 2.2:13, 48, 76, 111, 134.
[78]Ibid., 134. See also McCormack, *Orthodox and Modern*, 188-89.
[79]See *CD* 2.2:25-34.

of salvation . . . certain," but, more importantly, it also makes our knowledge of God certain, because it "is the description of the decision in which God is God."[80] According to Barth, "There is no height or depth in which God can be God in any other way."[81] "In no depth of the Godhead shall we encounter any other but him. There is no such thing as Godhead in itself. Godhead is always the Godhead of the Father, the Son and the Holy Spirit. But the Father is the Father of Jesus Christ and the Holy Spirit is the Spirit of the Father and the Spirit of Jesus Christ."[82] In his doctrine of election, Barth thus realizes his quest for an "unequivocal Emmanuel."[83]

While many consider Barth's innovative doctrine of election to be his "greatest contribution" to Christian theology,[84] its implications for the doctrine of God remain a matter of considerable and complex controversy.[85] The controversy not only concerns scores of interpretive judgments about hundreds of passages within Barth's published writings. It also concerns the nature and extent of Barth's ongoing theological development across the years of writing the

---

[80]*AO*, 144-45.

[81]*CD* 2.2:77.

[82]Ibid., 115.

[83]See *CD* 1.2:170.

[84]McCormack, *Orthodox and Modern*, 183. See also Gary Badcock, who says Barth's doctrine of election is "perhaps" his "most original and profound contribution to Christian theology." *Light of Truth and Fire of Love: A Theology of the Holy Spirit* (Grand Rapids: Eerdmans, 1997), 173.

[85]The contemporary debate surrounding the doctrine of election was sparked by Bruce L. McCormack, "Grace and Being: The Role of God's Gracious Election in Karl Barth's Theological Ontology," in *The Cambridge Companion to Karl Barth*, ed., John Webster (Cambridge: Cambridge University Press, 2000), 92-110; republished in McCormack, *Orthodox and Modern*, chap. 7. See also McCormack, "Election and the Trinity"; Molnar, *Divine Freedom;* Kevin Hector, "God's Triunity and Self-Determination: A Conversation with Karl Barth, Bruce McCormack, and Paul Molnar," *International Journal of Systematic Theology* 7 (2005): 246-61; Kevin Hector, "Immutability, Necessity, and Triunity: Towards a Resolution of the Trinity and Election Controversy," *Scottish Journal of Theology* 65 (2012): 64-81; Matthias Gockel, *Barth and Schleiermacher on the Doctrine of Election: A Systematic-Theological Comparison* (Oxford: Oxford University Press, 2007); van Driel, *Incarnation Anyway;* Adam Eitel, "The Resurrection of Jesus Christ: Karl Barth and the Historicization of God's Being," *International Journal of Systematic Theology* 10 (2008): 36-53; George Hunsinger, "Election and the Trinity"; Aaron T. Smith, "God's Self-Specification: His Being Is His Electing," *Scottish Journal of Theology* 62 (2009): 1-25; Justin Stratis, "Speculating about Divinity? God's Immanent Life and Actualistic Ontology," *International Journal of Systematic Theology* 12 (2010): 20-32; as well as the essays in Michael T. Dempsey, ed., *Trinity and Election in Contemporary Theology,* (Grand Rapids: Eerdmans, 2011).

Church Dogmatics: Does *CD* 2.2 mark a significant point of evolution in Barth's thought, or does the *Church Dogmatics* as a whole exhibit Barth's more or less mature perspective on the doctrine of God? The controversy concerns, furthermore, the relative interpretive importance that should be attached to the major historical contexts within which Barth theologized, the "great tradition" of Christian theology on the one hand and modern Protestant thought on the other. To put the matter crudely: Do the concerns of Augustine, Thomas, and Calvin or those of Schleiermacher, Hegel, and Schelling more directly animate Barth's theologizing? Nevertheless, for all its complexity, the controversy is at its heart a matter of *dogmatic coherence*: Does Barth's identification of Jesus as the electing God cohere with other material claims that he makes regarding God's identity, not only in *Church Dogmatics* 2.2 but also elsewhere in the *Church Dogmatics*? The issue concerns the relation between election and Trinity, between God's being and God's self-determination toward fellowship with us in the covenant of grace. Specifically, does the *theologoumenon*, "Jesus Christ is the electing God," require us to affirm that God's being and identity "is a function of the divine election,"[86] or is this *theologoumenon* consistent with the affirmation that God's being and identity constitutes "the essential presupposition and ground"[87] of election? Is God who he is eternally in himself because of who he is for us in Jesus Christ, or is God who he is for us in Jesus Christ because of who he is eternally in himself? Because the former viewpoint argues that Barth's identification of Jesus as the electing God does not cohere with other material claims that he makes about God's identity in the *Church Dogmatics*, we will call it the "inconsistency thesis." Because the latter viewpoint argues that the identification of Jesus as the electing God

---

[86]McCormack, *Orthodox and Modern*, 266.

[87]George Hunsinger, "Election and the Trinity," 179. Hunsinger later states: "The autonomy of God's eternal self-relationship is a necessary condition for the fulfillment of the covenant, since God's people and all things are to be taken up into it" (189).

does cohere with other material claims that Barth makes in the *Church Dogmatics,* we will call it the "consistency thesis."[88]

The consistency thesis appeals to passages scattered widely throughout the *Church Dogmatics* and also to passages contained specifically within volume 2.2 which affirm that God's triune identity is not determined by the election of grace but that God's triune identity is wholly complete apart from and prevenient to the election of grace.[89] Thus, for example, at the beginning of § 33, "The Election of Jesus Christ," Barth states that election constitutes God's free determination concerning all things "except . . . for God himself."[90] A few pages later, Barth affirms that while Jesus Christ—the subject and object of election—"was at the beginning of all things," he was "not at the beginning of God, for God has indeed no beginning."[91] According to passages such as these, election functions as the hinge *between* God and all things. And election forever determines God's *relationship* to all things. But election does not function to determine God's being *as God.* It functions to determine God's being *as our God.*

The consistency thesis also appeals to the architectonic structure of Barth's theology as a whole to support its claim that his doctrine of election does not demand a revision of his doctrine of God. Far from requiring that Barth rescind earlier statements about God's replete and independent being, Barth's doctrine of election fits quite nicely within his broader account of the relationship between God's triune being *ad intra* and God's triune economy *ad extra.* This broader account teaches (1) that God's wholly realized triune identity is the natural and necessary object of his eternal self-affirmation, (2) that

---

[88]I believe that these labels are preferable to the labels of "traditionalist" vs. "revisionist" (cf. Hunsinger, "Election and the Trinity," 179; and McCormack, "Election and the Trinity," 204-205) in that they sidestep the historiographical issue concerning which interpretation enjoys historical precedence, and also the issue concerning which interpretation is more faithful to Barth, and instead focus on the dogmatic issue of whether Barth's *theologoumenon* coheres with the rest of his doctrine of God or whether it requires modification of that doctrine.

[89]See especially Hunsinger, "Election and the Trinity."

[90]*CD* 2.2:94.

[91]Ibid., 102.

God's movement toward us in Jesus Christ is the free and contingent object of his eternal self-determination, a self-determination which guides and governs the realization of all God's works *ad extra*, and (3) that the former object of God's self-affirmation constitutes the ontological ground and goal of the latter object of God's self-determination which is its "repetition" and "confirmation":[92] the election of grace flows from God's perfect triune life and runs to God's perfect triune life.[93] This broader account of the relationship between God's being *in se* and God's economy *pro nobis* accordingly prohibits us from interpreting Barth's claim that Jesus is the electing God "absolutely or without qualification."[94] Instead it requires us to interpret it as a statement which summarizes the primal event of "God in God's movement towards humanity."[95] Such an interpretation, it is argued, preserves the "inseparable unity, abiding distinction, and irreversible asymmetry" of the relationship between God's triune being and God's triune self-determination.[96]

Proponents of the consistency thesis worry about the implications of its alternative. If God's eternal self-affirmation as God is a function of God's eternal self-determination to be our God, then is not God's freedom compromised and is not "God's triune being" made dependent on "his relationship to the world"?[97] And would not such a situation in turn hazard the very values which Barth's doctrine of election seeks to preserve? If God's being is dependent on his relationship to the world, then election is robbed of its status as a *gracious* election.[98] Moreover, if God's being is dependent on his relationship to the world, then our knowledge of God is robbed of its

---

[92]*CD* 4.2:346.

[93]Edwin Christian van Driel, "Karl Barth on the Eternal Existence," 52-53, 58-59; van Driel, *Incarnation Anyway*, 93-98; George Hunsinger, "Election and the Trinity," 189, 193. See also *CD* 2.2:155-56; *CD* 4.2:344-47.

[94]Hunsinger, "Election and the Trinity," 183.

[95]Van Driel, "Karl Barth on the Eternal Existence," 59.

[96]Hunsinger, "Election and the Trinity," 194.

[97]Ibid.,190.

[98]Van Driel, "Karl Barth on the Eternal Existence," 55; Molnar, *Divine Freedom*, 63, 71-72, 312.

status as a truly *objective* knowledge of God, abandoning us to a doctrine of the Trinity that is "nothing more than a description of our relations among ourselves," an idol "of our own invention."[99]

For their part, proponents of the inconsistency thesis wonder whether their counterparts have fully considered "the meaning and ontological implications" of Barth's assertion that Jesus Christ is the electing God.[100] These interpreters do not deny the presence, nor do they dispute the interpretation, of passages in the *Church Dogmatics* which portray God as naturally and necessarily complete antecedent to his eternal act of election. What they deny is the consistency of such passages with Barth's fundamental methodological commitment to interpreting God's *being* solely and exclusively on the basis of God's *self-revelation* in Jesus Christ,[101] and more specifically the consistency of such passages with Barth's mature doctrine of election and his later Christology.[102] These interpreters wonder whether the consistency thesis can really account for what is perhaps the cardinal point of Barth's doctrine of election, namely, its claim that the identity of the electing God and the identity of the elect humanity are *wholly revealed* in Jesus Christ, that there is "no height or depth in which God can be God in any other way."[103]

According to the inconsistency thesis, Barth's early understanding of God's triune being is not yet adequately controlled by God's evangelical self-determination in Jesus Christ. Barth's early doctrine of the Trinity remains a "highly formal"[104] doctrine, a doctrine that is

---

[99]Molnar, *Divine Freedom*, 64; see also 120-24, 167-81.

[100]McCormack, *Orthodox and Modern*, 264.

[101]Bruce L. McCormack, "Why Should Theology be Christocentric? Christology and Metaphysics in Paul Tillich and Karl Barth," *Wesleyan Theological Journal* 45 (2010): 64.

[102]Bruce L. McCormack, "God *Is* His Decision: The Jüngel-Gollwitzer 'Debate' Revisited," in *Theology as Conversation: The Significance of Dialogue in Historical and Contemporary Theology: A Festschrift for Daniel L. Migliore*, ed. Bruce L. McCormack and Kimlyn J. Bender (Grand Rapids: Eerdmans, 2009), 57, 62, 64.

[103]*CD* 2.2:77.

[104]Bruce L. McCormack, "Karl Barth's Version of an 'Analogy of Being': A Dialectical No and Yes to Roman Catholicism," in *The Analogy of Being: Invention of the Antichrist or the Wisdom of God?* ed. Thomas Joseph White (Grand Rapids: Eerdmans, 2011), 112.

derived "from the formal *logic* of revelation" (i.e., the proposition
"God reveals himself as Lord") rather than "from the *history* of Jesus
Christ."[105] Along the same lines, proponents of the inconsistency
thesis argue that "Barth's early vision of God's self-sufficient Lordship sits awkwardly with the later contention . . . that God wills
eternally to be 'with us.'"[106] The triune Lord of *Church Dogmatics* 1.1
is "free *from* us." But the triune Lord of *Church Dogmatics* 2.2 is "free
for us." These interpreters furthermore contend that the distinction
(a "metaphysical gap"[107] on this reading) between God's will *ad intra*,
whereby God naturally and necessarily *affirms* his triune identity, and
God's will *ad extra*, whereby God freely and contingently *determines*
himself for covenant relationship with humanity through Jesus
Christ, does not seem to account for Barth's claim that God is "absolutely" his "own, conscious, willed and executed *decision*,"[108] the singular and wholly realized decision *only* to be God *as* our God in Jesus
Christ.[109] As one commentator summarizes the point: "the action of
God in electing to be God for humanity in Jesus Christ is *not* the act
of an already existing agent"—that is, a wholly and antecedently realized Trinity. "Rather it is an act in the course of which God determines the very being of God."[110]

While those committed to the inconsistency thesis hold different
views about its implications for the relationship between divine election and divine triunity in particular,[111] there is nevertheless a considerable amount of agreement regarding its implications for the
relationship between God's evangelical self-determination and God's
being. According to this perspective, because God's being is deter-

---

[105]McCormack, "Election and the Trinity," 215.

[106]Jones, *Humanity of Christ*, 64-65; McCormack, "God *Is* His Decision," 63.

[107]See McCormack, "Election and the Trinity," 208-210, 212-14, 219 n 37, 222.

[108]*CD* 2.1:271.

[109]McCormack, "Election and the Trinity," 217-18.

[110]Paul Nimmo, *Being in Action*, 8.

[111]Bruce McCormack believes that election is logically prior to Trinity (*Orthodox and Modern*, 266).
Kevin Hector believes that Trinity is logically prior to election ("God's Triunity and Self-determination," 246-61). Paul Dafydd Jones believes that Trinity and election are "coincident" and
"coordinate" (*Humanity of Christ*, 81).

mined by God's decision, his being must be understood "as *plastic* in nature, as susceptible of a 'determination.'"[112] In contrast to creatures whose natures are never wholly self-determined, "God is the subject who determines his own nature.... He himself determines what sort of being he is."[113] What is "natural" or "necessary" in God's being therefore is not antecedent to God's decision to be our God but is shaped by that decision and the historical movement that flows there from. On this interpretation, God's essential triune identity "exists nowhere—neither in eternity nor in time—in abstraction from the concrete material 'determination' which makes it what it is." God's essential triune identity is "actualized in the history of Jesus Christ."[114]

In summary of this viewpoint: Because God is his decision to be our God in Jesus Christ—because Jesus Christ is the electing God, God's triune being is eternally and unalterably shaped according to the sovereign, historical movement which extends from God's primal decree *ad intra* and which issues in the humiliation and exaltation of Jesus Christ *ad extra*.[115] And because God's being is wholly determined by this movement, the gospel is able to announce a salvation that is wholly secure and the identity of a God that is wholly revealed.

THE TRINITY IN *CHURCH DOGMATICS* 4.1

Mention of the humiliation and exaltation of the Son of God *ad extra* brings us to the last volume in our survey of the *Church Dogmatics* and its reception: volume 4, *The Doctrine of Reconciliation*. Here Barth expounds the manner in which the triune Lord realizes the election of grace in the history of Christ's reconciling movement. For Barth, expounding this movement in its fullness requires that it

---

[112]Bruce L. McCormack, "Let's Speak Plainly: A Response to Paul Molnar," *Theology Today* 67 (2010): 59.

[113]*GAG*, 127.

[114]McCormack, *Orthodox and Modern*, 239.

[115]Jones, *Humanity of Christ*, 93-94.

be viewed from three "perspectives."[116] The first perspective concerns the downward movement of reconciliation—"The Way of the Son of God into the Far Country"—in which God effects atonement for sin. This movement is the subject matter of *Church Dogmatics* 4.1. The second perspective concerns the upward movement of reconciliation—"The Homecoming of the Son of Man"—in which humanity is restored to fellowship with God. This movement is the subject matter of *Church Dogmatics* 4.2. The third perspective does not concern an additional movement, for the twofold reconciling movement of God in Christ constitutes an "intrinsically perfect and unsurpassable action."[117] The third perspective therefore concerns the manner in which the complete and perfect act of reconciliation "declares itself";[118] it concerns the "revelation" that "takes place in and with reconciliation."[119] This declaration, summarized under the description, "Jesus Christ, the True Witness," is the subject matter of *Church Dogmatics* 4.3.1.

As the preceding summary suggests, we find in volume four of the *Church Dogmatics* Barth's most consistent application of the lesson he attributes to Hegel, specifically, the lesson that the gospel's God reveals himself as an "event that comes and goes," as a "living God" with a "real history" whose being is to be found in the particular movement of that history and nowhere else.[120] Abiding by this rule, Barth "re-translates" all of the topics of traditional catholic and Reformed Christology (including the person and work of Christ, the two states of Christ, and the union and communion of Christ's two natures) "into the sphere of a history."[121] According to Barth, it is only by "re-translating" the entire doctrine of reconciliation into historical categories that the status of Jesus Christ as "the *living* Jesus

---

[116]These three perspectives are initially summarized in *CD* 4.1:128-54.
[117]*CD* 4.3.1:7.
[118]Ibid., 10.
[119]Ibid., 8.
[120]Barth, *Protestant Theology*, 402.
[121]*CD* 4.2:106.

Christ" can be preserved.[122] In volume four of the *Church Dogmatics,* we thus find Barth's "historicized Christology."[123]

In terms of theological ontology, and therefore of the subject matter of the present study, Barth concerns himself in *The Doctrine of Reconciliation* with the following questions: "How can a being be interpreted as an act, or an act as a being? How can God, or man, or both in their unity in Jesus Christ, be understood as a history?"[124] Because our present concern is the being *of God* in light of his evangelical self-determination, we shall focus on Barth's discussion in *Church Dogmatics* 4.1 of the divine movement of self-humiliation in the events of the Son of God's incarnation and atonement, leaving aside Barth's discussion of the human movement of exaltation which accompanies that event, as well as his discussion of the way in which this double movement attests itself as "the light of life."

The condescending movement of God in the incarnation constitutes "the indispensable basis and substance" of the entire doctrine of reconciliation.[125] In this movement, we are concerned with the God who "shows himself to be the great and true God in the fact that he can and will let his grace bear this cost, that is he *capable, and willing and ready* for this condescension, this act of extravagance, this far journey."[126] In other words, we are concerned with what the gospel reveals about the being and nature of "the true God." According to Barth, the New Testament reveals that God in his necessary being and essence is *obedient:* "What distinguishes the man Jesus as the Son of God is that which apparently stands in the greatest possible contradiction to the being of God: the fact that in relation to God—and therefore to the world as well—this man wills only to be obedient—obedient to the will of the Father, which is to be done on earth

---

[122]Ibid., 110, italics mine.
[123]On which, see McCormack, *Orthodox and Modern,* chap. 8.
[124]*CD* 4.2:108.
[125]*CD* 4.1:159.
[126]Ibid., italics mine.

for the redemption of man as it is done in heaven."[127] The obedience of Jesus is not simply an adjunct of the human nature and vocation that the Son of God assumes in the incarnation in order to realize the perpetually unrealized obedience of Adam and Israel.[128] The obedience of Jesus is the revelation and enactment of the inner reality of his identity as the Son of God. The relationship between the Father and Jesus, where there is one who commands and another who obeys, is "a matter of the mystery of the inner being of God as the being of the Son in relation to the Father."[129]

Consequently, accounting for the deity of Christ in light of the gospel demands that Barth consider both the inner and outer moments "of the mystery of the deity of Christ," that is, his eternal relationship to the Father *ad intra* and his incarnation, humiliation and death *ad extra*.[130] Barth first discusses the second moment of the Son's deity, as revealed on his way into the far country in the incarnation. In discussing this topic, Barth seeks to preserve the orthodox and ecumenical consensus that in the incarnation of the Son of God "the divine being does not suffer any change, any diminution, any transformation into something else, any admixture with something else, let alone any cessation."[131] His reasoning is that any diminution of or change in the divine being as a consequence of the incarnation "would at once throw doubt upon the atonement made by him."[132] This same line of reasoning drives Barth to reject modern kenotic christologies.[133]

Nevertheless, though he rejects modern kenotic theories of the incarnation, Barth credits these theories with identifying an ambiguity which lies at the heart of the church's confession that the Word

---

Ibid., 164.
[128]Although it *is* that. See ibid., 166-76.
[129]Ibid., 177.
[130]Ibid., 179.
[131]Ibid., 179.
[132]Ibid., 180.
[133]See ibid., 180-83.

became flesh. The ambiguity is indicated in the church's (in)ability to answer sufficiently the question *Quo iure Deus homo?* By what right or inner law of the divine being did God become a man?[134] Barth refuses to interpret the ontological *ratio* of the incarnation and crucifixion as an inscrutable paradox or (worse in his judgment) as evidence of a rift or contradiction in the inner being of God.[135] According to Barth, "A God who found himself in this contradiction can obviously only be the image of our own unreconciled humanity projected into deity."[136] No, Barth insists that our understanding of the event of the incarnation, and of its inner divine necessity, be controlled by the Pauline doctrine "that God is 'not a God of confusion, but of peace'" (1 Cor 14:33).[137] In the incarnation, God does assume a creaturely form of existence, a form that is not his own form, a form that exists in a state of alienation from and contradiction against God.[138] But in condescending to assume this creaturely form, God does not contradict his deity. God expresses and enacts his true deity in humbly condescending to assume the form of a servant, the form that bears the weight of God-forsakenness on the cross. God's humility is therefore the revelation not the veiling of God's true deity.[139] Barth explains:

> It corresponds to and is grounded in his divine nature that in free grace he should be faithful to the unfaithful creature who has not deserved it and who would inevitably perish without it, that in relation to it he should establish that communion between his own form and cause and that of the creature, that he should make his own its being in contradiction and under the consequences of that contradiction, that he should maintain his covenant in relation to sinful man (not surrendering his deity, for how could that help? but giving up

---

[134]Ibid., 184.
[135]Ibid., 184-86.
[136]Ibid., 186.
[137]Ibid.
[138]Ibid.,185, 191-92.
[139]Ibid., 185-92.

and sacrificing himself), and in that way supremely asserting himself and his deity. . . . God does not have to dishonour himself when he goes into the far country, and conceals his glory. For he is truly honoured in this concealment. This concealment, and therefore his condescension as such, is the image and reflection in which we see him as he is. His glory is the freedom of the love which he exercises and reveals in all this. In this respect it differs from the unfree and loveless glory of all the gods imagined by man. Everything depends on our seeing it, and in it the true and majestic nature of God: not trying to construct it arbitrarily; but deducing it from its revelation in the divine nature of Jesus Christ. From this we learn that the *forma Dei* consists in the grace in which God himself assumes and makes his own the *forma servi*.[140]

Barth summarizes the law that must consequently govern our thinking about the incarnation and our answer to the question, *Quo iure Deus homo?* "By doing this God proves to us that he can do it, that to do it is within his nature. And he shows himself to be more great and rich and sovereign than we had ever imagined."[141]

Thinking through what it means for the humble, incarnate God to be "more great and rich and sovereign than we had ever imagined" leads Barth from the second and outer moment of the Son's deity to the first and inner moment of the Son's deity, to the truth about the Son of God within the *opera Trinitatis ad intra* that accounts for and grounds his divine humiliation in the *opera Trinitatis ad extra*. According to Barth, if the divine humiliation of the Son of God in the incarnation is not to be understood as the retraction or the contradiction of his deity, then we must acknowledge that obedience belongs to the Son of God in the deepest, inner reality of his being.

This is an acknowledgement, however, that both subordinationism and modalism fail to make. Whereas subordinationism takes the obedience of the Son of God as evidence of his ontological inferior-

---

[140]Ibid., 187-88.
[141]Ibid., 186.

ity to the Father, modalism takes the obedience of the Son of God as "only . . . a kind of forecourt of the divine being," a temporal surface that that does not in fact "bring us into touch with God himself."[142] The error of both subordinationist and modalist understandings of God's triune being is that "they try to evade the cross of Jesus Christ."[143] If we are to avoid both errors and to follow through with a theological ontology that corresponds to the cross, then we must acknowledge that within the singular and incomparable being of the gospel's God there is "an above and a below, a *prius* and a *posterius,* a superiority and a subordination" and that "far from preventing this possibility, his divine unity consists in the fact that in himself he is both one who is obeyed and another who obeys."[144] God's unity is not so solitary that it does not admit the distinction between "one who rules and commands in majesty" and "one who obeys in humility." Neither is God's dignity so human that it does not admit alongside the glory of the one who is first and superior an equal glory of the one who is second and subordinate.[145] Barth applies this cruciform conception of the *opera Trinitatis ad intra* as follows:

> In his mode of being as the Son he fulfils the divine subordination, just as the Father in his mode of being fulfils the divine superiority. In humility as the Son who complies, he is the same as is the Father in majesty as the Father who disposes. He is the same in consequence (and obedience) as the Son as is the Father in origin. He is the same as the Son, that is, as the self-posited God (the eternally begotten of the Father as the dogma has it) as is the Father as the self-positing God (the Father who eternally begets).[146]

This, according to Barth, is the mystery of God's trinitarian being *ad intra* that constitutes the inner necessity and law of God's trinitarian

---

[142]Ibid., 196.
[143]Ibid., 199.
[144]Ibid., 200-201.
[145]Ibid., 202-3.
[146]Ibid., 209.

movement toward humanity *ad extra*. Because the history of the Father commanding and of the Son obeying occurs within God's triune life, the history of the Father commanding and of the Son obeying occurs within the economy of salvation. Because commanding and obeying, superiority and subordination, is the structure of God's inner life, the incarnation is not the occasion for surrendering or sacrificing the Son's deity but for expressing and enacting it. Because God is this sort of God, "the way of the Son of God into the far country" is the supreme and reliable revelation of the glory of God in the highest.[147]

In my judgment, Barth's historicized christology, and the trinitarian ontology that accompanies it, exhibits at this point in his theological development what he elsewhere calls "a bit of Hegeling."[148] Barth did not expect his Hegeling/historicizing interpretation of God to elicit praise for its orthodoxy "from any quarter."[149] However, his historicizing did elicit emulation. Indeed, in many cases, those who followed Barth's historicizing lead have engaged in *more than* a bit of Hegeling (sometimes to Barth's own consternation),[150] and this without apology. Thus Hans Küng encourages Christian theology to recognize "just how right Hegel was when, inspired by genuinely Christian motives, he attempted, as one who at once completed and overcame the Greek metaphysical concept of God, to take seriously the great themes of God's suffering, of dialectic in God and of God's involvement in becoming."[151] Similarly, Eberhard Jüngel credits Hegel with correcting the classical doctrine of God in light of the cross, destroying "the axiom of absoluteness, the axiom of apathy, and the axiom of immutability, all of which are unsuitable axioms for

---

[147]See Barth, *Dogmatics in Outline* (New York: Harper and Row, 1959), chap. 5.

[148]See McCormack, *Orthodox and Modern*, 271.

[149]*CD* 4.2:106. But cf. George Hunsinger, "Karl Barth's Christology: Its Basic Chalcedonian Character," in *Disruptive Grace: Studies in the Theology of Karl Barth* (Grand Rapids: Eerdmans, 2000), chap. 6.

[150]See, for example, Barth's response to Jürgen Moltmann's theology in Karl Barth, "To Prof. Jürgen Moltmann, Bonn," in *Letters 1961-1968*, trans. Geoffrey W. Bromiley (Grand Rapids: Eerdmans, 1981), 174-76.

[151]Hans Küng, *The Incarnation of God: Hegel's Thought as Prolegomena to a Future Christology* (Edinburgh: T & T Clark, 1987), 457.

the Christian concept of God," and encourages theology not to "be embarrassed to express that debt."[152] The story of trinitarian theology "after Barth" is therefore not only the story of debates about how to interpret Barth's claim that Jesus is the electing God. It is also the story of debates about whether and to what extent Barth's historicizing agenda, and its concomitant metaphysical revisionism, requires affirmation and extension.[153]

ROBERT JENSON'S TRINITARIAN THEOLOGY AS A SPECIES OF POST-BARTHIAN EVANGELICAL HISTORICISM

As the preceding discussion demonstrates, addressing the identity of the gospel's God "after Barth" requires addressing God's identity as both the electing and the incarnate God, as the God who wills to be who and what he is in the fellowship he establishes with us in the Word made flesh. Few have perceived this point with greater clarity, or pursued it with greater boldness, than Robert Jenson, whose theology is the major focus of this book. It is time therefore to provide a brief orientation to his thought, and thus to matters that will occupy us at greater length in the chapters that follow.

Jenson's quest for a theological ontology appropriate to the gospel's God belongs to the historicizing family of approaches to the doctrine of God that have emerged in the wake of Barth's theology. Like Barth, these theological kin reject the largely antimetaphysical stance of the earlier Ritschlian dogmatics and seek instead to offer constructive accounts of God's being.[154] Moreover, like Barth, these

[152]Eberhard Jüngel, *God as the Mystery of the World: On the Foundation of the Theology of the Crucified One in the Dispute Between Theism and Atheism*, trans. Darrell Guder (Edinburgh: T & T Clark, 1983), 373.

[153]Stanley J. Grenz describes the particular "Barthian shoot" that extends his trinitarian historicizing under the heading, "The Trinity as the Fullness of History," in *Rediscovering the Triune God,* chap. 3.

[154]See, for example, Albert Ritschl, "Theology and Metaphysics," in *Three Essays*, trans. Philip Hefner (Minneapolis: Fortress, 1972 [1881]), 151-217. For a response, see Pannenberg's now classic essay, "The Appropriation of the Philosophical Concept of God as a Dogmatic Problem of Early Christian Theology," in *Basic Questions in Theology: Collected Essays*, vol. 2, trans. George H. Kehm (Philadelphia: Westminster, 1971), esp. 119-22.

theologians share the conviction that the doctrine of the Trinity is the key to a truly Christian theological ontology. These thinkers have moved beyond Barth, however, by offering more radical critiques of classical metaphysics and by developing more fully historicized accounts of the divine nature. For these "evangelical historicists,"[155] the metaphysical center of gravity for the Christian doctrine of God lies in the unfolding historical relationship between the *man* Jesus and his Father in the Spirit,[156] a relationship often viewed from the perspective of its eschatological consummation rather than from its protological initiation,[157] and often interpreted according to a radical application of the Lutheran doctrine of the communication of attributes. According to the latter perspective, the divine attributes of the Son of God are communicated directly to the human nature and history of Jesus (the so-called *genus majestaticum*), while the human attributes and experiences of Jesus—sometimes including his death[158]—are communicated directly to his divine nature (the so-called *genus tapeinoticum*).[159] Jenson worked out the basic elements of his own distinctive theological ontology in his early engagements with Barth's theology within this particular stream of Barth appro-

---

[155]I owe this label to a personal conversation with Michael Allen.

[156]To cite but one example: Jürgen Moltmann describes his doctrine of God as "an attempt to start with the special Christian tradition of the history of Jesus the Son, and from that to develop a historical doctrine of the Trinity." *The Trinity and the Kingdom: The Doctrine of God*, trans. Margaret Kohl (Minneapolis: Fortress, 1993), 19. See also Jürgen Moltmann, *The Way of Jesus Christ: Christology in Messianic Dimensions*, trans. Margaret Kohl (Minneapolis: Fortress, 1993), 69.

[157]Foundationally in this regard, see Wolfhart Pannenberg, *Jesus—God and Man*, 2nd ed., trans. Lewis L. Wilkins and Duane A. Priebe (Philadelphia: Westminster, 1968); see also Jüngel, *God as the Mystery*, 331-68. A helpful introduction to this stream of Lutheran theology is provided in LeRon Shults, "The Futurity of God in Lutheran Theology," *Dialog* 42 (2003): 39-49.

[158]Jürgen Moltmann, *The Crucified God: The Cross of Christ as the Foundation and Criticism of Christian Theology*, trans. R. A. Wilson and John Bowden (Minneapolis: Fortress, 1993), esp. chap. 6.

[159]According to confessional Lutheran teaching on the "communication of attributes," the divine attributes of Christ are communicated *directly* to his human nature and not merely *indirectly* via the divine person's assumption of that nature. This doctrine undergirds Lutheran sacramental theology regarding the real presence of Christ's body and blood in the Lord's Supper. While confessional Lutheran theology accepts the *genus majestaticum*—the communication of divine properties directly to Jesus' human nature, it rejects the *genus tapeinoticum*—the communication of human properties directly to Jesus' divine nature. The affirmation of the latter doctrine has been made possible under the influence of Hegel. On which, see Jüngel, *God as the Mystery*, chap. 3, §7.

priation.[160] These elements remain a central feature of his project to this day.

Following Barth, Jenson argues that the divine being must be understood as a self-determining sort of being. In contrast to creatures whose natures are never wholly self-determined, "God is the subject who determines his own nature. . . . He himself determines what sort of being he is."[161] Jenson's appropriation of Barth on this point, however, is not without qualification. He finds in Barth's doctrine of divine self-determination a troubling ambiguity. Jenson worries that by locating God's self-determination in his "primal decision"—the decision God makes "before the foundation of the world" (Eph 1:4), Barth threatens to turn the electing God into a Platonic form and the evangelical events into his temporal shadow, thus undermining the connection between God's being and the evangelical events, and also between the eternal person-constituting relations of the Trinity and the actual history of the man Jesus with his Father in the Spirit.[162] Jenson wonders, in turn, whether Barth's overemphasis on protology is the consequence of a pneumatological deficit in his theology, a deficit that keeps Barth from appreciating the full significance of the eschatological nature of the gospel and of the gospel's God.[163] Jenson's proposed corrective is to relocate God's gracious self-determination from Barth's *primal* history to *our* history: "In *our* history God makes his *eternal* decision."[164]

---

[160]See Jenson, *AO* and *GAG*. On the significance of Lutheran christology for his own theological program, see Jenson, "Thanks to Yeago," *Dialog* 31 (1992): 23. On Jenson's debt to and disappointment with Pannenberg's eschatological orientation, see Jenson's review of the second volume of Pannenberg's *Systematic Theology* in Jenson, "Parting Ways?" *First Things* 53 (May 1995): 60-62. For Jenson's more recent reflections on theology's eschatological orientation, see Jenson, "Second Thoughts about Theologies of Hope," *Evangelical Quarterly* 72 (2000): 335-46.

[161]*GAG*, 127.

[162]*AO*, esp. 155, 161-63; *GAG*, 151-55. A judgment regarding the legitimacy of Jenson's critique of Barth lies beyond the scope of the present study. For Barth's attempt to address the kind of worry expressed by Jenson, see *CD* 2.2:184-94.

[163]Robert W. Jenson, "Karl Barth," in *The Modern Theologians*, 2nd ed., ed. David F. Ford (Cambridge, MA: Blackwell, 1997), 33-34; and more fully Robert W. Jenson, "You Wonder Where the Spirit Went," *Pro Ecclesia* 2 (1993): 296-304.

[164]Jenson, *AO*, 163.

Consequently, according to Jenson, the doctrine of the Trinity must be an "interpretation of God under rigorous obedience to this rule: God is in himself precisely what he is in the history between Jesus, and the one he called 'Father,' and us in their mutual Spirit."[165] Only when interpreted in light of this rule can Barth's precious insight into the nature of the gospel's God as the self-determining historical God be preserved.

In Jenson's theology, the doctrine of the Trinity thus synthesizes, among other things, the concepts of divine relatedness and divine temporality.[166] With respect to divine temporality, the doctrine of the Trinity enables him to say that God is something that *happens*, "like a kiss or a train wreck."[167] God's being is not one that remains forever unchanging and therefore immune to the events of history (and therefore also to us). His being is an event that happens in history and as history because it is an event that happens in Jesus by virtue of God's free self-determination. With respect to divine relatedness, trinitarian doctrine enables Jenson to see in Jesus' death and resurrection the *interpersonal* event which constitutes God's own life: "God is what happens *between* Jesus and his Father in their Spirit."[168]

ROBERT JENSON'S TRINITARIAN THEOLOGY AS A THEOLOGICAL INTERPRETATION OF HOLY SCRIPTURE

For Jenson, theologizing "God according to the gospel" requires not only a sophisticated theological ontology but also a sophisticated theological hermeneutic,[169] the latter being dictated by the former. Because God's being is constituted in the particular events of the gospel, theological reason can know God's being only by giving in-

---

[165]Jenson, "Karl Barth," 31.
[166]Jenson, *GAG*, 119.
[167]Jenson, *ST* 1:214.
[168]Ibid., 221, italics mine.
[169]On which, see Darren Sarisky, "What is Theological Interpretation? The Example of Robert W. Jenson," *International Journal of Systematic Theology* 12 (2010): 201-16.

terpretive attention to the biblical rendering of the events in which his being is constituted.[170]

Jenson argues that the doctrine of the Trinity's primary function in Christian theology is to identify *who* God is, that is, to distinguish the personal identity of the Christian God from that of other putative gods.[171] The doctrine of the Trinity fulfills this function in primarily two ways: first, by identifying God's proper name, "the name of the Father and of the Son and of the Holy Spirit" (Mt 28:19); and second, by identifying God's distinctive personal actions, preeminently according to Jenson: "God is whoever raised Jesus from the dead."[172] Jenson's point in emphasizing *who* the Trinity identifies God to be is certainly not meant to deny that the Trinity has something to say about *what* God is like, that is, concerning the divine being and nature. The point is that we may only address the question regarding God's being and nature by following after the particular, self-determined path of God's personal identity. Only by attending to who he is may we understand what he is like.[173]

Such an approach requires that we take the particular way that Scripture identifies God with utter seriousness. Because narrative is the overarching genre by which Scripture identifies God, Jenson argues that God has a *narrative identity*.[174] For Jenson, this means not only that God's personal identity is one which unfolds according to a temporal structure and which is determined by temporal, interpersonal relations. It also means that "the Lord's self-identity . . . is established not from the beginning but from the end." As Jenson explains: "The biblical God is not eternally himself in that he persistently instantiates a beginning in which he already is all he ever will be; he is eternally himself in that he unrestrictedly anticipates an end in

---

[170]Compare this with Eberhard Jüngel's discussion of "the hermeneutical problem of theology" in *God's Being Is in Becoming*, 9-11.

[171]Here, again, Jenson follows Barth's lead. See *CD* 1.1:301 and *ST* 1:60.

[172]*ST* 1:63. See also *GAG*, 98; *TI*, xii-xiii; and chap. 1; *ST* 1:42-46.

[173]*GAG*, 98-99, 123.

[174]*ST* 1:57-58.

which he will be all he ever could be. It holds also—or, rather, primarily—with God: a story is constituted by the outcome of the narrated events."[175] In Jenson's theology, "narrative identity" thus becomes the operative concept for developing the Pannenbergian notion of the "ontological priority of the future."[176]

Given his understanding of God's narrative identity, Jenson's constructive theological work consists largely in a theological interpretation of biblical narrative, an attempt to follow Scripture's narrative portrayal of who God is in order to understand what God is like.

Jenson's attention to the distinctive literary form of evangelical discourse in no way signals a declension from substantive theological assertion to mere "talk about talk."[177] Jenson's theological ontology and theological hermeneutic are intrinsically related. Scripture's particular way of recounting the economy of salvation (narrative) is inseparable from the particular sort of God the gospel announces (the Trinity) because the God identified *by* the events rendered in biblical narrative is identified *with* those events.[178] The events of creation, exodus, incarnation, crucifixion, resurrection, and enthronement are not merely "clues" to an otherwise timeless and unchanging Trinity.[179] These "blatantly temporal events"[180] constitute God as Trinity. For this reason, God's identity is not "paraphrasable" apart from the

---

[175]Ibid., 66.

[176]Besides *Jesus—God and Man,* Pannenberg's early reflections on this topic may be seen in his essay, "The God of Hope," in *Basic Questions in Theology,* 2:234-49.

[177]Contra Francesca Aran Murphy, *God Is Not a Story: Realism Revisited* (Oxford: Oxford University Press, 2007), 18. Murphy's reading of Jenson depends upon classifying him with the Yale School and certain Wittgensteinian versions of Thomism. To be sure, there are some analogies between Jenson and his Anglo-American counterparts—supremely, all of them have taken the so-called "linguistic turn" and are thus attentive not only to *what* is said about God but also to *how* it is said. However, as we have argued already, it is (primarily) German systematic theology after Barth, not Anglo-American Barthianism and Thomism, that provides the most immediate context for and the closest analogy to Jenson's theological program. Indeed, if conceptual dependence is traceable to anyone when it comes to Jenson's early interest in the category of narrative, it is Fuchs and not Frei who is responsible. See Robert W. Jenson, *The Knowledge of Things Hoped For* (Oxford: Oxford University Press, 1969), 196-233.

[178]*ST* 1:59.

[179]Ibid.

[180]Ibid., 49.

particular literary mode of narrative. Narrative *represents* God *as* the sort of God whose *being* takes its concrete form *in* a temporally ordered dramatic plot.[181]

In order to appreciate Jenson's theological hermeneutic we must briefly mention one further aspect of his approach: his "ruled reading" of Holy Scripture.[182] According to Jenson, reading Scripture with the rule of faith does not involve imposing an external hermeneutical principle on the text.[183] There is "a logical fit" between the Ecumenical Creeds and "the evangelical history narrated in the gospel."[184] Because both creed and canon attest to "the true ontology of historical being,"[185] creeds function as "hermeneutical principles for the reading of Scripture" even as Scripture "displays" the doctrine of the creeds.[186] Within this understanding of the relationship between canon and creed, Jenson finds specifically dogmatic backing for his dramatic conception of God. In particular, he finds in the second article of the Nicene-Constantinopolitan Creed, one of the church's most widely accepted, enduring, and therefore normative summaries of the faith, warrant for some of the most daring moves of his theology.

For Jenson, it is the grammar of the second article, specifically its subject and predicates, which captures most faithfully the logic of the Christian doctrine of God. According to the second article of the creed, the Son who appears in the evangelical events is *homoousios* with the Father. The personal subject of the gospel story is "*God* with us."[187] Furthermore, according to the creed, this divine

---

[181]Compare with Martha Nussbaum's comments regarding the intrinsic relationship between certain visions of being and certain literary forms. *Love's Knowledge: Essays on Philosophy and Literature* (Oxford: Oxford University Press, 1990), 5. See also Jüngel, *God as the Mystery*, 299-314.

[182]For Jenson's most recent discussion of this topic, see Robert W. Jenson, *Canon and Creed* (Louisville: Westminster John Knox, 2010).

[183]Robert W. Jenson, "The Bible and the Trinity," *Pro Ecclesia* 11 (2002): 330, 338-39.

[184]*TI*, 50. For Jenson's understanding of the formation and development of creeds, see *TI*, 48-50.

[185]Robert W. Jenson, "Identity, Jesus, and Exegesis," in *Seeking the Identity of Jesus: A Pilgrimage*, ed. Beverly Roberts Gaventa and Richard B. Hays (Grand Rapids: Eerdmans, 2008), 50.

[186]Jenson, "Bible and the Trinity," 339.

[187]*TI*, 86-87.

Son is the personal protagonist of utterly creaturely, utterly temporal events. The creed predicates of the Son that he "was incarnate by
the Holy Ghost of the Virgin Mary, and was made man; and was
crucified under Pontius Pilate; he suffered and was buried."[188] From
womb to tomb, Jesus is "God *with us*."[189] Rightly understood, this
subject and these predicates constitute the theological grammar of
Nicene dogma. Consequently, according to Jenson, Scripture is
never properly read unless we perceive that *this one* who endured
these events is "one of the holy Trinity."[190] Cyril of Alexandria (one
of Jenson's theological heroes) expresses this grammar with clarity:
"He who endured the precious cross for our sake and experienced
death was not an ordinary man to be regarded as separate and distinct from the Word of God the Father. On the contrary, the Lord
of glory suffered in the flesh, according to the Scriptures."[191] *Unus
ex Trinitate passus est.*[192]

Jenson's trinitarian theology in its entirety is a sustained and ener-
getic attempt to draw out the full ontological implications of what
we might call the gospel's "Nicene-narrative grammar," to say what
must be true of God if indeed the story of *Jesus* is the story of *God
with us*. According to Jenson, saying this in the context of the late
modern West requires that he take up Jeremiah's prophetic mantle of
"tearing down" and "building up" (Jer 1:10 NLT) in relation to received

[188]The Nicene-Constantinopolitan Creed in Philip Schaff, ed., *The Creeds of Christendom* (repr. Grand Rapids: Baker, 1996), 2:59.

[189]See Robert W. Jenson, "For Us . . . He Was Made Man," in *Nicene Christianity: The Future for a New Ecumenism*, ed. Christopher R. Seitz (Grand Rapids: Brazos, 2001), 83-84.

[190]See the Second Council of Constantinople, Tenth Anathema: "If anyone does not confess that our Lord Jesus Christ who was crucified in the flesh is true God and Lord of glory and one of the holy Trinity, let him be anathema," in *Christology of the Later Fathers*, ed. Edward R. Hardy (Louisville: Westminster John Knox, 1954), 381.

[191]Cyril of Alexandria, "An Explanation of the Twelve Chapters," in Norman Russell, *Cyril of Alexandria* (London: Routledge, 2000), 189.

[192]For a discussion of this post-Chalcedonian formula, which represents a Nicene-Cyrilline inter-pretation of Chalcedonian Christology, see Basil Studer, *Trinity and Incarnation: The Faith of the Early Church*, trans. Matthias Westerhoff (Collegeville, MN: Liturgical Press, 1993), 222-29; also John Meyendorff, *Christ in Eastern Christian Thought* (Crestwood, NY: St. Vladimir's Seminary Press, 1987), 77-78.

ecclesiastical teaching about God. In other words, speaking truly of the gospel's God requires a trinitarian metaphysics that is at once *deconstructive* and *reconstructive*.[193]

In Jenson's judgment, the history of trinitarian doctrine is the all too depressing account of theology's evasion of the fact that Jesus' story is God's story. To be sure, this history has its high points, the Nicene Creed standing near the pinnacle in this regard. Nevertheless, the history of theology has bequeathed to the church what is in many respects an "unbaptized God,"[194] a conception of God still soiled by pagan notions such as divine immutability, impassibility and timelessness, notions designed "to protect deity from contamination by temporality's slings and arrows, above all from women's wombs or the tombs women tended."[195] Jenson's prescription for remedying this situation is clear: theology must purge itself of this all too Greek view of God. Fulfilling the church's baptismal office therefore requires a deconstructive metaphysics. Nevertheless, because baptism signifies not only a dying but also a rising again, theology's task is never simply deconstructive. A trinitarian theology derived from the gospel must also have a reconstructive moment. Having cast off its pagan legacy, theology must awaken to the full significance of Jesus' name of "Immanuel." Jenson's theology seeks to serve just such an awakening. The result is a fully historicized account of God's trinitarian being. As we have seen, "God is what happens between Jesus and his Father in their Spirit."[196]

CONCLUSION

In this chapter we have considered the historical and theological context that gives rise to the question of this study: What is the re-

---

[193]See Yeago's comments: "All of Jenson's theological work is ordered around a central polemical axis: the conflict between 'the gospel about Jesus' and the assumptions of what Jenson . . . tends to call 'normal religion.'" David S. Yeago, "Catholicity, Nihilism, and the God of the Gospel: Reflections on the Theology of Robert W. Jenson," *Dialog* 31 (1992): 18.

[194]See *UG*.

[195]Jenson, "For Us," 84.

[196]*ST* 1:221.

lationship between God being Father, Son and Spirit and the evangelical events whereby God realizes his determination to become our Father, through the Son, in the Spirit? As we have seen, Barth's trinitarian theology and the debate which it has provoked require that evangelical theology give its attention to the implications of divine election and divine incarnation for its understanding of God's trinitarian being. In this chapter, we have also introduced one of contemporary theology's most sophisticated and comprehensive responses to the demands of Barth's theology, that of Robert Jenson. Having set forth the historical and theological context of our question, and having introduced Jenson's particular answer to this question, we are therefore in a position to consider more fully Jenson's hermeneutical and theological proposal regarding the being of the gospel's God. To this proposal we now turn.

PART ONE

◆

ROBERT JENSON ON THE
GOSPEL'S GOD

Trinitarian theology after Barth poses a question for us: What is the relationship between God being Father, Son and Spirit and God electing to become our Father, through the Son, in the Spirit? Robert Jenson provides one of contemporary theology's most sophisticated, if not yet fully explored, answers to this question. According to Jenson, the relationship between God's triune being and God's triune self-determination is a relationship of strict identity: The triune God is identified *by and with* the evangelical events whereby he becomes our God.

That the triune God is identified by and with the events of the evangelical story line is the governing conviction of Jenson's theological program.[1] As we have seen already, this conviction is rooted in a Nicene-narrative reading of the Bible and refracted through a Lutheran understanding of the communication of idioms. Under the guidance of this catholic and evangelical rule of faith, Jenson reads the story of the man Jesus as the story of *unus ex Trinitate*. As we have also seen, Jenson regards the constitution of God's identity by and with the history of Jesus as a contingent fact, a matter of God's free self-determination. God has chosen the pathway of Jesus' death and resurrection as the pathway of his triune being. He

---

[1] In Jenson's own words: "The whole argument of this work [i.e., *Systematic Theology*] depends on this" conviction (*ST* 1:59).

has resolved to be God only as our God.

Because the biblical story is the story of the triune God's free identification by and with the story of his people, the triune identity is structured according to the plot of this particular story, which is dramatic in shape. This means, first, that God's identity is constituted temporally: Because Jesus' identity is constituted within the context of Israel's temporal, conflicted story of election, blessing, apostasy and redemption, God's identity must be so constituted as well. This means, second, that God's identity is constituted from the end of the story, not from the beginning: Because the identity of God's sinful people is settled only at death—at the conclusion of their existence, the identity of the God of Jesus Christ must be so as well, for he is the God of *this* people.[2] To be sure, the triune identity can be known before the story ends. But this is not because God's identity is forever unchanging. It is because God by the Spirit *anticipates* the final determination of his identity. Because God possesses the final outcome of his being by anticipating it, he can reveal himself, through his promises, in dramatically appropriate ways before the great dénouement of his being.[3]

According to Jenson, there are finally only two alternatives when it comes to thinking about "God" in relationship to "the gospel."[4] On the one hand, there is the timeless God of the past, whose identity is eternally self-same and unchanging and therefore who can only redeem creation by turning back the clock to creation's timeless beginning. For this God, redemption can only mean *Endzeit gleich Urzeit*.[5] On the other hand, there is the timely God of the future, who constitutes his identity at the end and is therefore able to transcend the past (via resurrection) and bring about a better future for his creation through inclusion within the triune life. Jenson insists that it is only

[2]*ST* 1:65.
[3]*ST* 1:67-68.
[4]*TI*, 4; *ST* 1:67.
[5]See Jenson, "Creator and Creature," *International Journal of Systematic Theology* 4 (2002), 220.

the latter sort of God who truly "fits" the Bible's dramatic plot. It is only the latter sort of God who can save humanity from its basic metaphysical predicament, the meaninglessness of time, and bring humanity, in and with time, into metaphysical perfection: the infinitely glorious harmony of God's triune life with us.

The task for part one of the present study is to explore more deeply the meaning and logic of the claims summarized in the preceding paragraphs. For reasons that will become transparent below, the nature of Jenson's claims about the identity of God calls for a peculiar method for analyzing those claims. Because his doctrine of God exhibits a "narrative identity"—that is, an identity constituted by and with historical events—it cannot be distilled by attending to a list of divine "attributes" or "perfections." Jenson's systematic theology provides no such list.[6] The logic of Jenson's doctrine of God is most easily grasped by tracing the way he reads the Bible's narrative rendition of God's triune name as it unfolds in the Old and New Testaments (the focus of chapters three and four respectively), and by considering the ontological judgments he draws from that narrative rendition (the focus of chapter five).

---

[6] *ST* 1:223.

THE WAY OF GOD'S
IDENTITY ACCORDING
TO THE OLD TESTAMENT

◆

DE DIVINIS NOMINIBUS

The Christian doctrine of God is that species of biblical reasoning devoted to the prayerful contemplation and explication of the divine names revealed in Holy Scripture.[1] Christian teaching about God is dependent on the biblical revelation of the divine names for reasons close at hand. Due to "the weakness of human intelligence," that which may be known of God through creation is known only "by a few, and that after a long time, and with the admixture of many errors."[2] Moreover, due to the darkening effects of sin on human understanding, "scarcely one man in a hundred is a true spectator" of the glory of God that shines forth in creation.[3] The doctrine's dependence on "what the sacred scriptures have divinely revealed"[4] is not

---

[1] For a recent and insightful discussion of the present topic, see Janet Martin Soskice, "Naming God: A Study in Faith and Reason," in *Reason and the Reasons of Faith*, ed. Paul J. Griffiths and Reinhard Hütter (London: T & T Clark, 2005), 241-54.

[2] Thomas Aquinas, *Summa theologiae*, trans. Fathers of the English Dominican Province (New York: Benzinger Bros., 1948), 1.1.5 ad 1 and 1.1.1, respectively.

[3] John Calvin, *Institutes of the Christian Religion*, trans. Ford Lewis Battles (Philadelphia: Westminster, 1960), 1.5.8 (61).

[4] Dionysius, *The Divine Names*, in *Pseudo-Dionysius: The Complete Works*, trans. Colm Luibheid (New York: Paulist, 1984), 1.1.

cause for despair, however. For the divine naming in Holy Scripture reflects the divine largesse from which it flows,[5] exhibiting to theological reason a "surplus of description."[6] The biblical writers praise God by "many names."[7] God is identified as "Lord," "Almighty," "one," "good," "eternal," and supremely in his tripersonal identity as "Father," "Son," and "Holy Spirit." God is the one who created heaven and earth, who entered into covenant with Abraham, Isaac, and Jacob, who rescued Israel from Egypt and caused them to possess the land of Canaan as an inheritance. He is the one who delivered over Jesus because of our transgressions and raised him up because of our justification, who poured out his Spirit on all flesh, and who promises to make all things new. Because the biblical naming of God is so very "great," the Christian doctrine of God is afforded with resources that are truly "unsearchable" (see Ps 145:3).

As it seeks to fathom the wealth of resources available to it, the Christian doctrine of God must be cognizant of several challenges intrinsic to the task of explicating the divine names.[8] Not only are there issues of scope (to what extent has Christian teaching about God faithfully borne witness to the fullness of biblical revelation?) and meaning (does calling God "good" mean the same thing as calling the creature "good"?), but there is also the issue of fidelity in conceptual paraphrase—that is, which words count as faithful repetitions of the biblical witness and which words count as betrayals of that witness? Are, for example, divine immutability and impassibility faithful renditions of the biblical claim that with God "there is no variation or shadow due to change" (Jas 1:17)? Or do these predications distort the biblical presentation of divine constancy?

---

[5]Dionysius, *Divine Names* 1.2.
[6]Denys Turner, "On Denying the Right God: Aquinas on Atheism and Idolatry," *Modern Theology* 20 (2004): 148.
[7]Dionysius, *Divine Names* 1.6.
[8]For a fuller discussion of the issues raised in the present paragraph, see Stephen Holmes, "The Attributes of God," in *The Oxford Handbook of Systematic Theology*, ed. John Webster, Kathryn Tanner and Iain Torrance (New York: Oxford University Press, 2009), 54-71.

Then there is the more complex issue of interpreting the logical status of the various biblical descriptions of God: Does naming God "creator of heaven and earth" or "the one who brought Israel out of Egypt" carry the same significance for God's identity as naming him "holy" or "just"? Is Yhwh's relation to Israel of the same sort as the Father's relation to the Son? If not, what is the difference between these kinds of naming and these kinds of relations?[9] As these questions suggest, the doctrine of God is a proposal not only regarding which descriptions are "necessary and appropriate" to faithful speech about God, but also regarding how various descriptions of God "work."[10] To the extent that it must consider how these various descriptions work, the Christian doctrine of God engages in "ontological reflection," reflecting on who God is, what sort of one he is, and how he is the one he is—all on the basis of "what the sacred scriptures have divinely revealed."[11]

Jenson's theology creatively and critically retrieves this tradition of expounding the doctrine of God by explicating the divine names revealed in Holy Scripture. Over the course of the next three chapters, we will consider Jenson's interpretation of the divine names with a careful eye toward the hermeneutical and theological moves that he makes in navigating the various challenges outlined above. This approach will enable us to appreciate better Jenson's dogmatic proposal. It will also prepare us for part two of the present study, where I will register my chief criticisms of Jenson's proposal and offer a constructive response to the question under consideration.

The remainder of the present chapter will consider the way Jenson reads the Old Testament naming of God. According to Jenson, the New Testament's way of naming God as triune must be under-

---

[9]Book five of Augustine's *The Trinity* wrestles with such questions in a way that becomes foundational for the later history of the doctrine of God.

[10]Stephen Holmes, "Divine Attributes," in *Mapping Modern Theology: A Thematic and Historical Introduction,* ed. Kelly M. Kapic and Bruce L. McCormack (Grand Rapids: Baker Academic, 2012), 48.

[11]*GAG,* 123; *ST* 1:63.

stood as a *new* way of naming the God *already* identified in the Old Testament as the God of the exodus, because the gospel fulfills the scriptures of Israel.[12] As Irenaeus argued in the second century, the God of Israel and the God of Jesus Christ are "one and the same."[13] For this reason, trinitarian theology can never be merely a matter of New Testament exegesis. Trinitarian theology is an exercise in ecclesial exegesis of a two-testament Bible, a point the church must always acknowledge if it is to avoid the "perennial temptation" toward Marcionism.[14]

In discussing his interpretation of the Old Testament witness to the divine identity, we will first discuss what Jenson regards as the Bible's primary grammar of naming God—its predication of "proper names" and "narrative descriptions." We will then discuss how Jenson's understanding of this grammar informs his interpretation of other biblical patterns of divine naming, including his understanding of the YHWH-Israel relation as an internal relation, and his understanding of God's self-identity as a matter of "dramatic coherence." Finally, we will discuss Jenson's understanding of the Isaianic servant's vital role in the dénouement of covenant history and of God's identity.

THE GRAMMAR OF GOD:
PROPER NAME AND NARRATIVE DESCRIPTION

Jenson's claim regarding the relationship between the triune identity and the evangelical events is in large part determined by his theological interpretation of the exodus. For Jenson, the exodus provides not only the Bible's fundamental image of salvation, but also its fundamental grammar for naming God.

In biblical theology, the definition of salvation is "exodus." This claim may be an oversimplification, but only by a pinch. As Gordon McConville observes, the exodus "is the supreme example of Yah-

---

[12]*TI*, 8; *ST* 1:63.
[13]Irenaeus, *Against Heresies*, Ante-Nicene Fathers 1: Apostolic Fathers, Justin Martyr, and Irenaeus (repr. Grand Rapids: Eerdmans, 1996), 3.10.5.
[14]*ST* 1:42-43.

weh's saving activity on behalf of his chosen people, and as such it becomes the paradigm for all acts of salvation."[15] Thus understood, *exodus* refers not only to the second book of the Pentateuch but also to a narrative pattern of events that begins with Israel's redemption from Egypt, continues through the wilderness wanderings, and ends in the Promised Land.[16] Variations on this pattern recur throughout both testaments in narrative, prophecy and praise. Canonically, the fulfillment of the exodus occurs in Jesus Christ, whose Passover sacrifice and exodus from the grave inaugurated the great eschatological deliverance of God's people.[17]

The exodus is not only concerned with Israel's rescue from peril to inherit a blessing, however. The exodus is also concerned quite centrally with the identity of Israel's God. Indeed, we may read the entire book of Exodus as rendering in narrative form the answer to Pharaoh's question: "Who is YHWH . . . ?" (Ex 5:2, my translation).[18] According to the book of Exodus, YHWH is the one "who brought you out of the land of Egypt, out of the house of slavery" (Ex 20:2), thereby revealing his unique and unrivalled power in relation to the gods of Egypt (Ex 15:11). He is also the one who, faced with Israel's primal sin at Sinai, manifests the fullness of his sovereign goodness (Ex 33:19) in exhibiting "steadfast love and faithfulness" toward his people (Ex 34:6), pardoning Israel's transgression, and taking them as his own possession (Ex 34:9) in order that he might dwell in their midst (Ex 29:46). The narrative stretching from Leviticus through Kings constitutes an extended portrayal of YHWH's covenant faithfulness. Thus Solomon summarizes the story in his prayer of dedication for the temple: "Blessed be the LORD who has given rest to his people

---

[15]J. Gordon McConville, "Exodus," in *New International Dictionary of Old Testament Theology and Exegesis*, ed. Willem A. VanGemeren (Grand Rapids: Zondervan, 1997), 4:601.
[16]See R. E. Watts, "Exodus," in *New Dictionary of Biblical Theology*, ed. T. Desmond Alexander and Brian S. Rosner (Downers Grove, IL: IVP Academic 2000), 478-87, esp. 479; Walter Brueggemann, *Theology of the Old Testament: Testimony, Dispute, Advocacy* (Minneapolis: Fortress, 1997), 211-12; also Jenson, *TI*, 7.
[17]See Watts, "Exodus."
[18]See *ST* 1:44.

Israel, according to all that he promised. Not one word has failed of all his good promise, which he spoke by Moses his servant" (1 Kings 8:56). And so, the answer to Pharaoh's question—the meaning of "the name"—is rendered by the narrative.[19]

The identification of God by proper name (i.e., YHWH) and narrated action (i.e., the deliverance of Israel from Egypt) thus represents what is perhaps the Old Testament's most characteristic grammar for naming God.[20] Taking this characteristic grammar as a *reliable* revelation of God's identity entails a number of materially significant decisions for the Christian doctrine of God, preeminently in Jenson's case: the identification of God both *by and with* the saving events of history. According to Jenson, if God is identified only *by* the events that name him and not *with* those events, then the doctrine of God's connection to biblical revelation is severed. On such a scheme, the Bible's narrative descriptions become mere clues to a God who actually remains unknown and unrevealed. On such a scheme, such clues can only serve as an occasion for projecting our own idolatrous conceptions about God.[21]

Jenson's concern to guard the reliability of biblical revelation is to be commended. Discounting the phenomenal form of biblical revelation has sometimes occasioned imaginative approaches to constructive theology proper in the modern era.[22] This point notwithstanding, it is not entirely clear why Jenson's two alternatives must be the only ones: either identify God by and with the events of history or undercut any access to a revealed God. (The main stream of Christian theo-

---

[19]*ST* 1:43-44; so Christopher R. Seitz, *Figured Out: Typology and Providence in Christian Scripture* (Louisville: Westminster John Knox, 2001), 135-36.

[20]See *TI*, chap. 1; *ST* 1, chap. 3. See Walter Brueggemann, *Theology of the Old Testament*, 122-26, also chap. 4. While Jenson acknowledges that "a proper name is proper just insofar as it is used independently of aptness to the one named," he argues that the proper names of God in Scripture, especially the name of Father, Son and Spirit, function not simply to identify God (i.e., to pick him out as a distinct individual among others) but also to reveal something about his identity (i.e., to summarize his distinctive personal character and being). See Jenson, *TI*, 18.

[21]Jenson, *ST* 1:59-60, 63.

[22]For a textbook example, see Sallie McFague, *Models of God: Theology for an Ecological, Nuclear Age* (Minneapolis: Fortress, 1987).

logical reflection on God, for example, has affirmed that the events of the exodus and the evangel are both *true and revelatory* descriptions of God without affirming that they are ingredient to the *being* of God, that historical events truly constitute a *relation* between God and his creatures even though they do not constitute God *as God*. The question of whether the tradition has been consistent and right to do so will occupy our attention in part two.) What is clear is that Jenson's commitment to one horn of the dilemma that he proposes represents perhaps the fundamental interpretive judgment that he makes in his doctrine of God, determining the logical status of the various biblical names for God in a historicist direction.[23]

Before unpacking the significance of this interpretive judgment, we should pause to mention two of its most notable consequences. First, by treating the exodus as the fundamental identification of God, Jenson picks up the biblical naming of God "midstream." Rather than beginning where the canonical rendering of God begins, with God as the creator of the world and its history (Gen 1:1), or perhaps antecedently with the eternal procession of the Word (Jn 1:1), Jenson begins with the revelation of God within history.[24] This decision in turn raises a couple of questions that must be kept in mind as we proceed to analyze and engage Jenson's doctrine of God. One question concerns the Bible's most fundamental distinction—the distinction between created and uncreated being: Does allowing the exodus to function as the primary grammar for identifying God threaten to leave the Creator-creature distinction underdeveloped when discussing God's mighty acts of salvation?[25] It is one thing to affirm that

---

[23]According to Jenson, "Israel's theology can all be derived from the identification of God by the Exodus" (*TI,* 34).

[24]The point, of course, is *not* that Jenson fails to recognize that creation is the canon's first description of God (see *ST* 2:3-5). The point concerns whether Jenson fails to account for the material significance of this description's primacy. For hermeneutical reflections on and defense of an approach like that of Jenson, see Neil B. MacDonald, *Metaphysics and the God of Israel: Systematic Theology of the Old and New Testaments* (Grand Rapids: Baker, 2006), chap. 7.

[25]That Jenson affirms the Creator-creature distinction is undisputed (see *ST* 1:99, 110, etc.). The question concerns whether this distinction can be accounted for sufficiently within the gamut of historical categories.

God acts in history and quite another to affirm that God acts in history *as* the one who is that history's origin and end. The question may be put in a slightly different way: Does allowing the exodus to function as the primary grammar for identifying God run the risk of accommodating God's first act *ad extra*, that is, the act of creation, to God's historical acts of salvation?[26] The point is not to question the necessity of relating creation, salvation and consummation within the organic execution of God's single decree. Nor is it to insist on a specific order of teaching in the exposition of the divine names. (Here too the dictum applies: *methodus est arbitraria*.) The question concerns whether "history" is capacious enough a category for explicating the identities and agencies of both God and God's creatures.

Second, because of its primacy for Jenson, the exodus grammar (including its extension in the events of the gospel) becomes the nearly *exclusive* grammar for naming God in his theology. In expounding the name of the triune YHWH, Jenson focuses almost entirely on the Bible's *historical* predicates—above all, God's raising of Israel from Egypt and Jesus from the dead. Furthermore, when he brings in *other* predicates and concepts to explicate the identity of God (e.g., eternity, infinity), he consistently historicizes them, translating them into historical categories. The question to keep in mind is this: Is this nearly exclusive focus on historical predicates advisable? Can other biblical ways of naming God be ignored without significant distortion to the doctrine of God (see the discussion above about the issue of scope)?[27] As Michael Horton observes, the Bible not only

[26] The concern is not merely hypothetical. See *ST* 2:14.

[27] It is not entirely clear how Jenson would respond to this line of questioning. On the one hand, he affirms that systematic theology is measured "by its success or failure as a hermeneutical principle for Scripture *taken as a whole*" (*ST* 1:33, emphasis mine). On the other hand, he seems to deny the possibility of rendering a coherent doctrine of God on the basis of the biblical witness in its entirety, suggesting instead that only a "dramatic" conception of God's identity can account for the Bible's "mutually conflicted" descriptions of God (*ST* 1:64; see also 33). Although the tradition has from time to time been guilty of spiritualizing certain biblical descriptions of God in the name of preserving a coherent portrait of God, the countenancing of "mutually conflicted" descriptions of God in Scripture seems to give up in principle on the hermeneutical task that is the Christian doctrine of God.

names God by "strong verbs," identifying God by his mighty historical acts. It also names God by "adverbs," which identify how God acts
(e.g., impartially, mercifully), as well as by "adjectives" (e.g., just, loving, merciful, almighty, everlasting), and "nouns" (e.g., father, king,
warrior, judge). The latter two categories especially move beyond
identifying God by the ways he has acted in *particular* situations to
the ways God characteristically (predictably?) acts in *every* situation
(see Jon 4:1-2).[28] Exclusive focus on historical description thus runs
the risk of reductionism. It may also run the risk of projecting modern
historicist understandings of personal identity onto the biblical material. We will return to these matters in due course.

"ISRAEL IS MY SON": THE YHWH-ISRAEL RELATION IN HISTORICIST TRINITARIAN PERSPECTIVE

According to Jenson, when the exodus story is read from the standpoint of its fulfillment in the gospel, we discover in its *dramatis
personae* a distinctly trinitarian pattern: "Israel is my son, my firstborn" (Ex 4:22 NASB).[29] Indeed, the whole sequence of exodus
events—from the disinheriting of Pharaoh in the final plague to the
granting of an inheritance to Israel in the Promised Land—may be
seen as the embattled outworking of a father-son relationship between YHWH and Israel.[30] Moreover, Jenson argues, because the pat-

---

[28]Michael Horton, *Lord and Servant: A Covenant Christology* (Louisville: Westminster John Knox, 2005), 22-23; with Brueggemann, *Theology of the Old Testament*, chaps. 4-6.

[29]Jenson explains his approach to reading the Old Testament as follows: "My exegetical ventures have of course not been altogether neutral. I have been supposing from the start that a serious doctrine of the Trinity and an accompanying Christology are true. Yet if these doctrines were external hermeneutical principles otherwise obtained and then imposed on Scripture, they themselves could not be authoritative. It is therefore important to see that Trinity and Chalcedonian Christology in fact *show* themselves in Scripture.... Or one might put it so: it is important to see that there is indeed a hermeneutical circle between Scripture and the doctrines of Nicaea, Constantinople and Chalcedon. The doctrines are hermeneutical principles for the reading of Scripture, and Scripture displays the doctrines" (Robert W. Jenson, "The Bible and the Trinity," *Pro Ecclesia* 11 [2002]: 338-39). For further discussion of his approach to biblical interpretation, see *ST* 1:76; 2:282-84. See also Barth's similar way of interpreting the Old Testament witness in terms of the Father-Son relation in *CD* 4.1:169-76.

[30]See Dennis J. McCarthy, "Notes on the Love of God in Deuteronomy and the Father-Son Relationship Between Yahweh and Israel," *Catholic Biblical Quarterly* 27 (1965): 144-47.

tern of this relationship is so integral to the warp and woof of the
Old Testament, it recurs under the guise of various other figures,
including the Shekinah cloud, the Word and the Servant.[31] While
the figures may change, the pattern of relationship embodied in these
various figures remains constant.[32]

As we have already suggested, Jenson's understanding of this relational pattern is determined by his historicizing interpretation of the
exodus grammar: God is not only identified *by* his paternal relation to
Israel; God is identified *with* his paternal relation to Israel. Jenson explains: "The primary trinitarian sense of 'the Son' may be so stated: he is
another by and with whom God is identified, so that what he does to
and for this other he does to and for himself—in a way to which the
relation between human parent and child is a created analogy—and so
that he is related to himself as the one who is related to this other in this
way."[33] Yнwн's relationship to his son Israel is a relationship *internal* to
his identity and therefore *constitutive* of his identity.

In order to feel the full force of this claim, we must consider the
nature of an "internal relation." An internal relation is one that follows the following logic: for the proposition "A is related to B," if A
were no longer related to B, then A would no longer be A, because the
two terms of the relationship are mutually constitutive ontologically.[34]
Thus, without his *son* Israel, Yнwн is not a *father*. Without his *servant*
Israel, Yнwн is not a *lord*. What is so striking about this relationship,
of course, is that the second term of this father-son relationship is in
this case a *creature*: "It is precisely as flesh that the people of Israel
have their Son-relation to God."[35] God constitutes himself *as* God by
constituting himself the God of *this* creaturely people.

---

[31]*ST* 1:76-81.
[32]Jenson, "Bible and the Trinity," 332.
[33]*ST* 1:75-76.
[34]Jenson states: "The relation to the Son is an internal relation to the Father, a relation necessary to
his being as God the Father. *To be God is to be related.*" "The Triune God," in *Christian Dogmatics,*
ed. Carl E. Braaten and Robert W. Jenson (Philadelphia: Fortress, 1984), 127.
[35]*ST* 1:78.

Jenson's claim thus constitutes a rejection of the traditional understanding of God's fatherly relation to his creatures as a "mixed relation," that is, a relation that is "internal" (ontologically constitutive) for one member of the relationship but "external" (not ontologically constitutive) for the other. His reason for rejecting the traditional understanding is one that we have already seen: "Since God's *identity* is told by his story with creatures . . . those others cannot be merely extrinsic to him."[36] Reject the internal nature of God's relation to his people and one rejects the reliable nature of God's revelation to his people.

If giving primacy to the exodus grammar is the fundamental interpretive judgment of Jenson's doctrine of God, classifying God's fatherly relation to his covenant people as an internal relation is the fundamental ontological judgment of Jenson's doctrine of God. As in the case of his fundamental interpretive judgment, Jenson's fundamental ontological judgment raises its own set of questions: If God's fatherly identity is constituted by and with his relationship to his creaturely son Israel, then is not God's identity as father dependent on Israel's existence? To affirm as much would seem to deny the freedom of God's decisions to create the world and to enter into covenant with Israel. Or else, it would seem to suggest that God's status as father is not intrinsic to his identity, regardless of his decisions to create and to elect.

These are significant questions indeed, to which we will return in due course. For now, we should recall that, for Jenson, the fact that God's fatherhood is constituted in relation to his creaturely covenant partner is a consequence of his free and sovereign decision.[37] God has bound himself to Israel, not due to external compulsion, but rather as an expression of his lordly freedom. Therefore, God only *is* father in relation to Israel his son. But he is so *freely*, as a consequence of his sovereign self-determination. Moreover, Jenson insists,

---

[36]Ibid., 75, italics in the original.
[37]Ibid., 47, 53, 75.

God would have been father to a son had he never chosen the path of creation and covenant. He adds, however, that we can know nothing at all about what such a divine father-son relation would have been like.[38] The Father of Israel is in fact the only God who can be known, for he is in fact the only God who exists.

YHWH'S SELF-IDENTITY IN DRAMATIC COHERENCE

Having discussed the hermeneutical and ontological judgments fundamental to Jenson's explication of the triune name, we are now in a position to appreciate a concept central to his historicized doctrine of God, the concept of dramatic coherence. The logic of this Jensonian concept emerges quite naturally from the previous analysis.

If Yhwh's identity as father is indeed constituted by and with his relationship to Israel, then Yhwh's identity must be a "blatantly temporal" identity.[39] This is so because the relationship by which God's identity is constituted is a *temporal* relationship, one that unfolds over the course of historical events. More specifically, Yhwh's identity is constituted by a particular set of historical events with a particular shape, namely, that of the exodus.

The exodus story, as we have seen, is a story of "contested victory."[40] Unlike many ancient myths, the exodus story is not the mere repetition of eternally self-same principles that happen "at no time and at all times."[41] Rather, the exodus is a story of God's fidelity to specific promises in the face of concrete conflict and opposition. And therefore it is also a story whereby God's personal identity (defined in

---

[38]Ibid., 65, 141; *TI*, 139, 141. Jenson no longer considers meaningful the counterfactual statement, "God would presumably have been the same triune God that he is" had he not created the world, covenanted with Israel, or commissioned Jesus to be his Son (see Robert W. Jenson, "Once More the *Logos Asarkos*," *International Journal of Systematic Theology* 13 [2011]: 131). However, because Jenson has not unpacked the significance of this retraction, and because such counterfactual statements are ubiquitous in his dogmatic œuvre, my custom throughout the present study will be include such statements where they fit within Jenson's system and to engage them accordingly, while noting the retraction.
[39]*ST* 1:49.
[40]Ibid., 48.
[41]Ibid.

terms of constancy vis-à-vis specific promises) is actually *determined* by whether or not he actually overcomes Pharaoh and rescues Israel. God is Israel's father *only insofar as* he trounces her oppressor and makes good on his promises. Because he does so, and only because he does so, he is who he is.[42] This means that the conflicts and resolutions inherent to any good drama are inherent to the triune identity. God *is* the God of Israel only *as* he suffers and overcomes the twists and turns of Israel's history. He transcends history—as all gods must according to Jenson—and thus establishes his identity as God. But he transcends history not by existing in a changeless, timeless manner, but by virtue of his self-constancy through time.[43]

Because YHWH's identity is established on the basis of his personal constancy through time, his identity—what makes him this God and not another—is "constituted in *dramatic coherence*."[44] Jenson explains: "The classic definition of this sort of coherence is provided by Aristotle, who noticed that a good story is one in which events occur 'unexpectedly but on account of each other,' so that before each decisive event we cannot predict it, but afterwards see it was just what had to happen." According to Jenson, "God is one with himself just by the dramatic coherence of his eventful actuality."[45]

Furthermore, just as the coherence of a good story is determined by the climax and resolution of its plot and not at its beginning, so the dramatic coherence of YHWH's identity is determined by the *outcome* of the biblical events and not at the beginning. The Lord's self-identity "is established not from the beginning but from the end, not at birth, but at death, not in *persistence* but in *anticipation*."[46] Jenson's claim is not merely that we can only *know* the whole truth about YHWH's identity at the conclusion of the story. Jenson's claim is that YHWH's identity is *constituted* only at the conclusion of the

---

[42]*TI*, 39-40.
[43]Ibid.
[44]*ST* 1:64.
[45]Ibid.
[46]Ibid., 66.

story. To be sure, this does not mean that God is nonexistent before the story of his relationship with Israel reaches its fulfillment. Rather, it means that, before the story's conclusion, God exists *in anticipation of* the fulfillment of his father-son relationship with Israel: "God *anticipates* his future and so possesses it."[47]

How, then, can God be known to Israel *before* his identity is settled, before the story ends? We have already indicated the answer: God's being-in-anticipation can be known to Israel before the end of Israel's history under the mode of *promise*: "I will be who I will be."[48] Jenson states that YHWH "is understood to have been antecedently identifiable by a promised future that then *turned out* to be the Exodus, and so by the event precisely in its temporal contingency."[49] Through his promises, then, YHWH's identity is rendered in "dramatically appropriate"[50] ways before the story ends. And thus Israel can place its hope in *this* particular God and not another in anticipation of the story's end.[51]

We will discuss the more fully ontological implications of this "dramatic" conception of the triune identity in chapter five. Before doing so, we must explore more closely the nature of the conflict that drives the Old Testament story line, as well as the figure in whom that story line's resolution is promised. Only then can we appreciate the way in which the evangelical events constitute the great denouement of the biblical drama and of God's triune being.

THE SOURCE OF DRAMATIC DISSONANCE AND THE PROMISE OF DRAMATIC RESOLUTION

David Bentley Hart, one of Jenson's most notable critics, worries that Jenson's theology poses insuperable difficulties, specifically in its identification of the being of God with the drama of history. Such an

---

[47]*ST* 2:121.
[48]*ST* 1:67-68.
[49]Ibid., 49.
[50]*GAG*, 163-64.
[51]*ST* 1:68-71.

identification, according to Hart, means that "every painful death of a child, every casual act of brutality, all war, famine, pestilence, disease, murder . . . all are moments in the identity of God, resonances within the event of his being, aspects of the occurrence of his essence."[52] While such a god "may evoke fear and awe," Hart insists it cannot evoke "genuine desire." He therefore concludes: "If, speculatively, Jenson's theology seems to fail Anselm's test, morally it seems to fail the test of Ivan Karamazov."[53] While I do not wish to evaluate the legitimacy of Hart's assessment at this point, it does highlight an issue that historicist conceptions of God like that of Jenson must address, namely, the relationship between God's being and the atrocities of sin and suffering. It is one thing to say that God is identical with the events of the exodus and Easter. It is another thing to say that God is identical with the events of Hitler's Auschwitz or Pol Pot's killing fields. Jenson's theology does address this issue, and, as one might expect, it does so from within the narrative logic of Israel's story. Whether or not Jenson's theology acquits itself of Hart's charges may be left finally for the reader to judge.

According to Jenson, *sin* is the great crisis of the biblical narrative: The story of "God with us" that the Old Testament narrates is a story of Israel's "betrayal of the 'with us.'"[54] This betrayal alone explains why the story of God with his people is a story of suffering and death. Death is not "natural"[55] or intrinsic to the created order; it cannot be "harmonized" with the being of God or with his purposes for Israel in a Hegelian scheme of thesis, antithesis and synthesis.[56] Nor is death a given in the relationship between God and his people;

---

[52]David Bentley Hart, *The Beauty of the Infinite: The Aesthetics of Christian Truth* (Grand Rapids: Eerdmans, 2003), 165.

[53]Ibid.

[54]*ST* 1:72.

[55]Ibid.

[56]Jenson states: "The Hegelian or Tillichian ideas that creation and fall are more or less the same thing cannot stand." "The Church's Responsibility for the World," *The Two Cities of God: The Church's Responsibility for the Earthly City*, ed. Carl E. Braaten and Robert W. Jenson (Grand Rapids: Eerdmans, 1997), 3.

it is a threat to that relationship. Consequently, Jenson asserts: "From first to last of biblical faith, God is death's *opponent*."[57]

Nevertheless, according to Jenson, death is Israel's *reality*, a reality which puts YHWH's relationship with Israel—and therefore the identities of both YHWH and Israel—in jeopardy. The Old Testament story line thus concludes with the question that must be asked, given the reality of death: "Son of a human—what do you think? Can these bones live? These bones that are the whole of my people? Can the death of my people be reversed?"[58] According to Jenson, the Old Testament does not itself provide a resolution to this dramatic crisis. That the death of God's people can be reversed and therefore that YHWH will be a father to his son Israel is fully and finally announced in the good news that God has raised Jesus *the* Son from the dead.

Before we can appreciate the way in which the gospel resolves the dissonance of sin and death, however, we must trace one further pattern in the relationship of YHWH and Israel. This pattern at once brings us to the climax of the Old Testament story line and to the event that finally constitutes the triune identity. The pattern in question concerns yet another of the Old Testament titles under which YHWH's father-son relation to Israel recurs: Servant. The Servant figures significantly in the great denouement of Israel's drama with God as the one through whom YHWH establishes "eschatological peace."[59] The Servant does so by playing a role which is at once corporate and individual; the Servant is at once Israel and an individual within Israel.[60] Jenson expounds the relationship between the Ser-

---

[57] *ST* 1:66.

[58] Ibid., 12. Jenson argues that sin and death do not surprise YHWH, such that the evangelical resolution to Israel's plight must be understood as "a mission of emergency repair" (*ST* 1:48). Quite to the contrary, the supralapsarian Jenson confesses "Christ crucified" to be "the wisdom of God" —that is, God's eternal and deepest plan for creation. Moreover, this eternal plan is unintelligible apart from sin. Jenson's point is only that the roles of sin and death in that divine plan must be acknowledged for what they are: "what God does not want" (*ST* 2:133), even while we see that sin and death "belong to God's intent precisely—but *only*—as they do appear in Christ's victory over them" (*ST* 1:73).

[59] *ST* 1:80.

[60] Ibid., 81.

vant as an individual *within* the community and the Servant *as* the community using the Augustinian concept of the *totus Christus* (the "whole Christ"). Though the phrase does not appear in Holy Scripture, the concept does.[61] This concept indicates the Messiah's *corporate* reality consisting of a "head" and "members." As such, the Messiah may be considered either as an individual or as a communal whole (e.g., 1 Cor 12:12-27; Eph 5:23; Col 1:18; 2:19). But the Servant not only plays the role of Israel within Israel. He also appears in the biblical drama as one of the three *dramatis dei personae* that constitute God's triune life. According to Jenson, it is precisely in this role—as one who fulfills the role of Israel within Israel, and as one who does so as a character in God's triune life—that the Servant enables the resolution of the Old Testament narrative.

How so? The crisis of the biblical drama reaches its climax and resolution as the individual Servant fulfills his unique role by means of a twofold representation. First, the Servant represents YHWH to the community, thus acting on YHWH's behalf in the face of death. Second, the Servant simultaneously represents the community to YHWH.[62] Jenson explains: "How is God . . . as a participant within her story, to face Israel's death with Israel? . . . Within the confrontation of the *totus puer domini* with death, there is one to die and there is his community to be died for. Just so, there is among the *dramatis dei personae* one to die and one before whom the death is enacted."[63] The implications of this event are noteworthy. Because the Servant dies on Israel's behalf as her corporate representative, the Servant secures Israel's eschatological "inclusion in the divine life."[64] This, Jenson argues, is the goal of Israel's election as son: "You shall call me, my Father, and not turn away from following me" (Jer 3:19 NASB). Because of his unique identity, however, the Servant is able to secure

---

[61]See, for example, N. T. Wright's discussion of this concept of the Messiah in *The Climax of the Covenant: Christ and the Law in Pauline Theology* (Minneapolis: Fortress, 1993), chap. 3.

[62]*ST* 1:83.

[63]Ibid., 82.

[64]Ibid., 83.

Israel's inclusion in the divine life without eliding of the Creator-creature distinction (a distinction which Jenson regard as "the first axiom" of Christian theology).[65] Jenson explains:

> Were there only a singular creature who in his own person was "one of the Trinity," in his instance, the difference between God and creature would simply be abolished; but, in that the one person is the one he is only as identified with a community whose members are *not*, in their singular persons, identities of God, the one Israelite's membership in God in fact sustains the difference between God and creature. Were there to be only a homogenous plurality of persons to be taken into the triune life, again, the difference between God and creature would vanish in religious murk; but, in that the community subsists only in that the one is within it, this one is, just so, a unique individual whose reality as "one of the Trinity" does not release a proliferation of divine hypostases.[66]

Jenson's trinitarian historicism thus takes a specifically Servant form. God participates in Israel's plight as the Servant who undergoes a sin-bearing death and as the Lord who accepts that death as an offering for sin. Israel participates in the divine life by participating in the Servant, the one who dies on Israel's behalf as a member *of* Israel and who is yet distinct *from* Israel as "one of the Trinity" and therefore as the one who opens filial space *for* Israel in the triune life.[67] Or so, Jenson insists, Israel was taught to hope.

CONCLUSION

Although the preceding analysis certainly does not address all of Hart's concerns, it does perhaps at least clarify the nature of Jenson's claim. Whatever "dramatic coherence" the gospel may provide in relation to the conflicted story of God's internal, historical relation to his people, that coherence is not one which mitigates the evils of sin, suf-

---

[65]*ST* 2:37; see also Jenson, "Jesus in the Trinity," *Pro Ecclesia* 8 (1999): 311.
[66]*ST* 1:83.
[67]Ibid., 82-85; *ST* 2:98.

fering, and death, either by naturalizing the reality of evil or by explaining its existence in light of some higher "rationality." According to Jenson, Yʜwʜ dramatically responds to sin, suffering and death by *overcoming* sin, suffering and death. Furthermore, whatever identification Jenson wishes to posit between God and history, it is not a simple, direct identification.[68] God's identification with history is his identification with the specific nation of Israel within history and, within Israel, with the specific Israelite Servant sung about in Isaiah. It is the song of this Servant, and this song alone, that promises to harmonize the story of God with his people in Jenson's theology.

Of course, Jenson argues that we have not heard this song in its full resonance unless we have heard its crescendo in the gospel of Jesus Christ. The God who raised Israel from Egypt and who promised to exalt his suffering Servant is also the God who raised Jesus from the dead. Jenson's interpretation of the identification of God by the resurrection of Jesus will be our focus in the next chapter.

---

[68]Hart acknowledges as much, but he does not believe that Jenson's "small but drastic amendment" to Hegel actually works (Hart, *Beauty of the Infinite,* 163).

4

THE WAY OF GOD'S
IDENTITY ACCORDING TO
THE NEW TESTAMENT

♦

INTRODUCTION

Robert Jenson's theology addresses the central question of this study—what is the relationship between God and the evangelical events in which God becomes our God?—with the claim that the triune God is *identified by and with* these historial events. As we have seen, explicating the meaning of this claim requires that we trace Jenson's theological interpretation of God's "narrative identity" as it is rendered in the Old and New Testaments. According to this narrative identity, "God is whoever raised Jesus from the dead, having before raised Israel from Egypt."[1] Having traced the way Jenson reads the Old Testament naming of God as the one who "raised Israel from Egypt," we turn in the present chapter to a consideration of the way he reads the New Testament naming of God as the one who "raised Jesus from the dead," and to some of the integral hermeneutical and theological moves that belong to this reading.

For Jenson, the New Testament announcement that God raised Jesus from the dead represents the necessary but not yet narrated

---

[1]*ST* 1:63.

conclusion to the Old Testament story of God and his people. Because the Old Testament does not itself proclaim the actual fulfillment of Isaiah's Servant pattern, it ends as "a story in search of a conclusion."[2] With the appearance of the man Jesus, however, the coherence of Israel's plight with its messianic solution becomes intelligible.[3] Read from the viewpoint of its conclusion in the story of Mary's child, the Old Testament story line is illuminated as "a pattern pointing to what had to happen"[4] (and thus as "a plotted sequence of christological prophecy-events"[5]), even as the fulfillment of the Old Testament story line remains traceable only "from the viewpoint of faith that a resurrection has indeed occurred."[6] This hermeneutical situation should not surprise us, according to Jenson, because it is only the conclusion of a story which provides that story's narrative coherence.[7]

In Jenson's historicized trinitarian theology, the story of the man Jesus not only renders the scriptural plot line dramatically coherent, but renders God's triune identity dramatically coherent as well. In order to appreciate the way it does so, we will first consider the way Jenson unpacks his fundamental ontological judgment (i.e., the characterization of God's fatherly relation to his creaturely people as a relation "internal" to his identity) vis-à-vis the story of Jesus. As we will see, Jenson employs Wolfhart Pannenberg's concept of reciprocal self-distinction to describe the constitutive significance of the man Jesus for God's identity, a concept that in Jenson's theology entails a creative reinterpretation of Jesus' divine filial preexistence. We will then consider the way Jenson explicates the events of Jesus' cross and resurrection as events internal to God's triune life. This analysis

---

[2] N. T. Wright, *The New Testament and the People of God* (Minneapolis: Fortress, 1992), 217; see *ST* 1:84.

[3] *ST* 2:275.

[4] *ST* 1:81.

[5] *ST* 2:283.

[6] *ST* 1:84.

[7] See, for example, *ST* 2:275; for further discussion of Jenson's understanding of the relationship between prophecy and its fulfillment, see *ST* 2:282-84 (note Jenson's appreciation of de Lubac).

will prepare us for chapter five, which further elucidates and summarizes the revisions to the Christian doctrine of God required by
Jenson's theological interpretation of Scripture.

JESUS IN THE TRINITY

Talk of the person in whom both the story of Scripture and the identity of God find dramatic coherence leads us to the topic of christology. Jenson's christology may be stated succinctly: Jesus is the one
who, in eschatologically filling and fulfilling Israel's son-relation to
YHWH in the Spirit, decisively defines the triune identity and thereby
accomplishes human salvation in fulfillment of Israel's Scriptures.[8]
As we have seen, to put things this way is not to adopt the Marcion-
ite position that God's identity is not truly or appropriately por-
trayed in the story of Israel. Rather, it is to insist that God's identity
is only finally and eternally established in what happens between the
God of Israel and the Israelite Jesus.

To explain Jesus' role in this regard, Jenson strikes a Pannenbergian note, appealing to the latter's concept of "reciprocal self-
distinction"[9] to describe Jesus' constitutive significance for the divine
life.[10] According to Pannenberg, the identities of the Father and
Jesus are mutually constituted in the history of their unfolding relationship as narrated in the New Testament. The triune identity is
constituted by Jesus' utter obedience to the Father's lordship, by the
Father's entrusting of the kingdom to Jesus, and by the Father's re-
ceiving of the kingdom back from Jesus in the eschaton.[11] In other
words, the events that unfold between the Father and Jesus do not

---

[8]*ST* 1:77, 138; see also *ST* 2:98-99. Again, compare with Barth *CD* 4.1:170: "For all its originality
and uniqueness what took place in Christ is not an accident, not a historical *novum*, not the ar-
bitrary action of a *Deus ex machina*, but that it was and is the fulfillment—the superabundant
fulfillment—of the will revealed in the Old Testament of the God who even there was the One
who manifested himself in this one man Jesus of Nazareth—the gracious God who as such is able
and willing and ready to condescend to the lowly and to undertake their case at his own cost."

[9]See Wolfhart Pannenberg, *Systematic Theology*, trans. Geoffrey W. Bromiley (Grand Rapids: Eerdmans, 1991), 1:308-19.

[10]For Jenson's appeal to Pannenberg at this point, see *ST* 1:108-10.

[11]Pannenberg, *Systematic Theology*, 1:310.

merely *reveal* who and what God is (epistemology). They *determine* who and what God is (ontology).[12] Pannenberg explains:

> The rule or kingdom of the Father is not so external to his deity that he might be God without his kingdom. The world as the object of his lordship might not be necessary to his deity, since its existence owes its origin to his creative freedom, but the existence of the world is not compatible with his deity apart from his lordship over it. Hence lordship goes hand in hand with the deity of God. It has its place already in the intratrinitarian life of God, in the reciprocity of the relation between the Son, who freely subjects himself to the lordship of the Father, and the Father, who hands over his lordship to the Son.[13]

Though Pannenberg's notion of triune reciprocal self-distinction may be developed in a number of different ways,[14] Jenson's radical appropriation of this concept is unambiguous. According to Jenson, God *is* as God *does* in the relationship of reciprocal self-distinction that obtains between the Father and Jesus in the Holy Spirit. Jenson explains the significance of the historical-relational structure of the triune life in a manner that is as strikingly clear as it is amusing:

> What if Jesus were in fact a sort of male Shirley Maclain [*sic*]? And *he* were risen to be the Son? Then that is the kind of God there would be: Almighty Boopsie in heaven. What if Jesus were in fact a liberal politician? And *he* were risen to be the Son? Then standard Protestantism would be *true*. What if Jesus were in fact an unconditionally accepting therapist? One can only set one's nightmares in order.[15]

Who the man Jesus actually is and what the man Jesus actually does in relation to YHWH his Father quite literally constitutes God as who

---

[12]Wolfhart Pannenberg, "Eternity, Time, and the Trinitarian God," in *Trinity, Time, and Church: A Response to the Theology of Robert W. Jenson*, ed. Colin E. Gunton (Grand Rapids: Eerdmans, 2000), 66.

[13]Pannenberg, *Systematic Theology*, 1:313.

[14]See Pannenberg "Eternity, Time, and the Trinitarian God." For Jenson's disappointment with Pannenberg's construal of this notion, see his review of Pannenberg's *Systematic Theology*, vol. 2, in *First Things* 53 (1995): 60-62.

[15]Jenson, "Jesus in the Trinity," 318.

and what God is. If someone else had filled the eschatological-dramatic role of "Son" in relation to God, then God would be different. As a matter of fact, however, "the identity of the eternal Son is the human person Jesus."[16]

REINTERPRETING JESUS' DIVINE FILIAL PREEXISTENCE

The previous chapter suggested that construing God's relation to his people as an internal relation raises certain questions about the freedom of God's relation to his people and also about whether or not God's identity is intrinsically trinitarian. Jenson's christological claim once again puts such questions before us. How can the man Jesus, who enters center stage rather late in the biblical drama, simply *be* the second person of the Godhead without denying the Trinity's prevenience to the gospel, Israel or even creation? In christological terms, how does Jenson's christology avoid the charges of adoptionism and/or Arianism? Jenson acknowledges the theological significance of such questions and affirms that "as God the Son he must ontologically precede himself as Jesus the Son."[17]

Jenson's account of the second person's "eternal" priority to his birth as Jesus is determined by his narrative-theological interpretation of Jesus' role in Israel's story. As we have seen, Jesus the man surpassingly fills and fulfills Israel's son-relation to YHWH at the climax of covenant history. As Old Testament type is to New Testament antitype, so God's son Israel is to God's Son Jesus. As the antitypical Son of God, Jesus is at once a *creature,* a member of Israel, and a *dramatis dei persona,* a member of the Trinity. Jesus' divine nature is therefore identical with the fact that he uniquely fulfills the relational role of son that is embedded in the divine drama of salva-

---

[16]*ST* 2:99.
[17]*ST* 1:138. This assertion represents a theological development in Jenson's thought beyond *TI*. See *ST* 1:141n85.

tion.[18] What sort of divine preexistence, then, corresponds to the Jesus so characterized?

In order to lay the foundation for his answer to this question, Jenson describes two versions of eternity that Christian theology must reject as frameworks for understanding the Son of God's preexistence if it is to preserve the Bible's narrative christology. According to one version, which Jenson traces to Aristotle's view of time,[19] eternity is to be understood as the infinite extension of linear time in both directions. Interpreted according to this framework, the Son's preexistence would mean that he existed "in a time before the event of creation."[20] However, Jenson explains, the church quickly rejected the definition of eternity in terms of linear time because linear time can only be ascribed to creation.[21] As Augustine taught, "The world was not made in time but with time."[22] Because time is a *creature,* it "can have nothing to do with God."[23] According to the other version of eternity, which Jenson traces to Plato, eternity is to be understood "as sheer absence of time."[24] Jenson believes that the gospel requires us to reject this view of eternity as a framework for the Son's preexistence as well, for Israel's God is "blatantly temporal."

How, then, are we to understand Jesus' divine filial preexistence? Although Jenson's doctrine of eternity will occupy us more directly in the next chapter, his answer to the present question can be outlined in three steps. First, Jenson rejects the doctrine of the *logos asarkos,* that is, the doctrine of the *preincarnate* Word. In place of this doctrine, Jenson argues that God the Son preexists Jesus by virtue of God's self-determining act of election. Second, Jenson replaces the

---

[18] *ST* 1:77, 138.

[19] Ibid., 139.

[20] Ibid., 138.

[21] Ibid., 138-39.

[22] Augustine, *City of God,* Nicene and Post-Nicene Fathers 2: St. Augustine's City of God, Christian Doctrine (repr. Grand Rapids: Eerdmans, 1993), 11.6.

[23] *CD* 2.1:608.

[24] *ST* 1:139.

doctrine of the *pretemporal* Word with that of the Word's narrative preexistence. Third, in order to establish the Son's eternal preexistence to Jesus, Jenson appeals to a notion introduced in chapter two, that of the ontological priority of the future.

Jenson's first step in articulating the Son's preexistence is exegetical. He argues that we misinterpret texts referring to the Son's preexistence (e.g., Jn 1; Col 1) if we take them to suggest a two-stage existence of the Son, that is, a preincarnate stage followed by an incarnate stage. Such texts, Jenson insists, provide no warrant for a doctrine of a Word without flesh (*logos asarkos*). Jenson seeks to warrant his interpretation of such texts by appeal to the first rule of Christian exegesis: "Scripture interprets Scripture." According to Jenson, Jesus' statement in John 8:58, "Before Abraham was, I am," functions to identify the human Jesus with the preexistent Son in such a manner as to preclude any fleshless understanding of the one introduced in John 1:1 as "the Word."[25] "It is precisely the aggressively incarnate protagonist of this Gospel's narrative who says this of himself, and he puts his antecedence to Abraham in the present tense."[26] Understood along these lines, Jesus precedes Abraham in eternity *as* the human being who appears in Israel at the end of days.

This sort of eternal precedence is best understood, Jenson insists, as the consequence of God's eternal *decision* in the Spirit to exist as the Father of the man Jesus.[27] As noted already, for Jenson "God is a decision." And, as in the case of Barth, the divine decision in which God has his being is a decision that he makes *in relation to creatures*, specifically, in relation to the creature Jesus: God is "the decision made . . . in the confrontation between the man Jesus and his 'Father.'"[28] Consequently, "The triune God's eternity is precisely the

---

[25]Ibid. See Emmitt Cornelius, "St. Irenaeus and Robert W. Jenson on Jesus in the Trinity," *JETS* 55 (2012): 111-24.

[26]*ST* 1:139.

[27]Ibid., 139-41.

[28]*GAG*, 130.

infinity of the *life* that the Son, who is Jesus the Christ, lives with his Father in their Spirit."[29]

Jenson nevertheless argues that God's eternal decision to be the Father of the man Jesus is not enough to secure the Son's divine preexistence. According to Jenson, the personal identity of the Logos "must be somehow antecedent to his birth as man."[30] This leads us to the second step in his doctrine of Jesus' preexistence. According to Jenson, the Word's preexistence to himself as the son of Mary is not a *pretemporal* preexistence. It is rather his *historical* preexistence *as witnessed in Israel's Scriptures*. It is by virtue of his "active presence" in Israel's story as a "subsisting relation" to YHWH his Father that the second person of the Trinity eternally precedes his conception in Mary's womb.[31] More specifically, the Son preexists his birth to Mary in his *historically constitutive relation* to the Father who sends him to be the climax of Israel's filial story. His divine filial subsistence thus *precedes* his birth *in* the Father's founding historical commission of this temporal creature *toward* his birth.[32]

We are now prepared to appreciate Jenson's third step in articulating his doctrine of the Son's preexistence. According to Jenson, the primary way that Scripture establishes the Son's eternal prevenience to the gospel is not by appealing to preexistence at all: "Indeed, the logic of what one might call a founding 'postexistence' of Christ is more central in the New Testament than is the notion of 'preexistence.'"[33] Jenson finds specifically Pauline warrant for the ontological priority of the future. Building his argument on Romans 1:3-4, Jenson contends that Jesus' sonship is established in the "determination" made by the Father through the Spirit *in* the act of

---

[29] *ST* 1:141.
[30] Ibid.
[31] My explanation here follows Jenson's own refinement of the position he adopted in his *Systematic Theology*. See Robert W. Jenson, "Once More the *Logos Asarkos*," *International Journal of Systematic Theology* 13 (2011): esp. 132-33.
[32] This, at least, is what I take to be the point of Jenson's exceedingly brief refinement of his earlier position.
[33] *ST* 1:142.

raising Jesus from the dead.[34] According to Jenson, the Father's action in this regard can only mean that Jesus is divine:

> "Resurrection" is at a minimum of its meaning the location of the risen one's life in the future, and in a future that, because death is past, for it must be unlimited. But only God's future is unlimited; eschatological life can only be entry into God. In that Christ's Sonship comes "from" his Resurrection, it comes from God's future into which he is raised.[35]

Jesus' divine sonship ontologically *precedes* his birth in the line of David in that his human birth dramatically *anticipates* his divine birth from God in the resurrection event. And, according to Jenson's narrative ontology, "what obtains in *life* always comes from a future."[36] In summary, then, God's *decision* about how his story with Israel will end, a decision enacted *in* the resurrection of Jesus, determines not only how that story will end but also constitutes the "preexistence" of Jesus as God's eternal divine Son—"*Today* I have begotten you" (Ps 2:7).[37]

Jenson's reinterpretation of Jesus' divine filial preexistence represents one of the most controversial aspects of his trinitarian theology. We will have the opportunity to engage this controversy in later chapters. For the time being, it is instructive to observe several of the theological and hermeneutical moves that accompany Jenson's doctrine of the preexistent Son.

Three observations are worth noting. First, Jenson's understanding of Jesus' divine filial preexistence provides what is perhaps the most intense instance of his historicizing interpretation of God. Jenson's understanding of the preexistent Son reveals that, in his

---

[34]Ibid.

[35]Ibid., 143.

[36]Ibid.

[37]Compare Jenson's argument here with that of Eberhard Jüngel: "*God defines himself* when he identifies himself with the dead Jesus. At the same time he defines the man Jesus as the Son of God, as an old New Testament formulation puts it (Rom. 1:4). The kerygma of the Resurrected One proclaims the Crucified One as the self-definition of God." *God as the Mystery of the World: On the Foundation of the Theology of the Crucified One in the Dispute Between Theism and Atheism*, trans. Darrell Guder (Edinburgh: T & T Clark, 1983), 363-64, italics in the original.

theology, there is no doctrine which cannot be explained in terms of the temporal dynamics of God's relation to his people. Second, Jenson's understanding of Jesus' divine filial preexistence clarifies the significance of his eschatological orientation. Jenson's notion of the "founding postexistence of Christ" displays the extent to which eschatology not protology defines his historicized trinitarian theology insofar as he interprets the latter (i.e., divine filial preexistence) in light of the former (i.e., divine filial exaltation and enthronement). The definitive role played by eschatology at this point not only distinguishes Jenson's trinitarian thought from that of Barth, but also from that of Bruce McCormack, as we will see in chapter nine. Third, Jenson's eschatologically oriented, historicizing interpretation of Jesus' divine filial preexistence reveals the significance—and perhaps also the cost—of his predilection for biblical texts that emphasize the movement of creaturely rescue and exaltation over biblical texts that emphasize the movement of divine condescension and self-giving. For Jenson, God is preeminently identified by the acts of raising Israel from Egypt and Jesus from the dead. This predilection for texts that emphasize the movement of rescue and exaltation threatens to constrict the witness of the Christian doctrine of God to the full scope of the biblical identification of God. In the exodus narrative, for example, it is God's movement of coming down that materially precedes God's movement of bringing Israel up (Ex 3:8; Ps 113). Similarly, in the gospel it is the movement wherein the wealthy Lord impoverishes himself in the incarnation that materially precedes the movement wherein he enriches his impoverished people (2 Cor 8:9; Phil 2:6-11)—a point of architectonic importance for patristic christology. To the questions raised in the previous chapter regarding the adequacy of a thoroughly historicized interpretation of the biblical witness, we must therefore add questions about the viability of Jenson's hermeneutical predilection. Is something lost in the dogmatic description of God's identity when God's mighty act of raising Jesus from the dead overshadows God's gracious act of giving his only Son? We will return to this question in part two.

TOWARD A NARRATIVE-TRINITARIAN
THEOLOGIA CRUCIS ET GLORIA

For Jenson the fact that God raised Jesus from the dead is the sum of the gospel.[38] The resurrection is the event that constitutes *Jesus* as God's Son and therefore that constitutes God as *our* Father, and it does so because Jesus is our brother, the head of the *totus Christus*. In the remaining sections of this chapter, we will explore Jenson's interpretation of Jesus' death and resurrection as events within the being and life of the triune God.

Fundamentally, the resurrection is good news because God raised Jesus of Nazareth from the dead (and not, say, Shirley MacLaine). This explains why the gospel is necessarily tied to a particular set of narratives. *His* life is the one that was given over for us. *He* is the one who was raised to the right hand of the Father. *His* fellowship with the Father in the Spirit is what the saints will enjoy throughout eternity. And because this is the case, we must know *who* he is. Narratives are our primary means for making such an identification and thus for understanding the gospel.[39]

Jenson summarizes the Gospels' narrative identification of Jesus as follows. According to the New Testament, "Jesus was an itinerant prophet and rabbi, the content of whose message was the immediate advent of the Kingdom of God."[40] As a preacher of God's kingdom come, Jesus enacted God's future for his people by actualizing the promised eschatological blessings of healing, forgiveness of sin and fulfillment of the Law.[41] Faced with Jesus' word and deed, his contemporaries recognized only two alternatives regarding his identity:

---

[38] *ST* 1:12, 42.
[39] *ST* 1:170-78. In developing this argument, Jenson specifically opposes Bultmann.
[40] Ibid., 176.
[41] Ibid., 177.

"he was either indeed the Messiah and a unique Son, or a blasphemer."[42] Most of the ruling authorities concluded that the latter was the case and judged him accordingly. For his own part, Jesus, in answering the high priest's question, "Are you the Christ, the Son of the Blessed One?" (Mk 14:61 NASB) in the affirmative, brought on the event that would "put the implicit claim of his life and teaching to a final test."[43] Would he die for his people, thus sealing his vocation as Servant and therefore "the Man for Others"?[44] And would Israel's God, to whom Jesus had entrusted his life and on whose behalf Jesus claimed to act and speak, vindicate Jesus' identity as "the Son" in raising him from the dead?[45] The gospel is the claim that both questions have received the divine "yes."

In order to fully comprehend the meaning of God's "yes" in Jesus, the evangelical events of Jesus' crucifixion and resurrection must be interpreted. According to Jenson, we may rightly understand these events only if we interpret them strictly within the context of the biblical story line.

INTERPRETING ATONEMENT

As we have seen, the Old Testament Scriptures anticipate God's final confrontation with death. In continuity with the plot and *personae* of Israel's Scriptures, the Gospels portray Jesus' death as the dramatic climax of that anticipated confrontation: "the Son of Man must suffer many things" (Mk 8:31). Jesus' death had to happen, in Jensonian terms, by virtue of "dramatic necessity."[46] Furthermore, according to the New Testament witness, the dramatic necessity of Jesus' death is tied to the fundamental conflict of the Old Testament story line, namely, sin. In other words, Jesus' death had to happen in order to

---

[42]Ibid., 178.
[43]Ibid., 181.
[44]Ibid.
[45]Ibid.
[46]Ibid., 182-85.

achieve "reconciliation" between God and his sinful people.[47]

In Jenson's theology, reconciliation involves two things. First, Jesus' death achieves reconciliation in that his death occurs on behalf of others, that is, as a substitutionary event. Second, Jesus' death achieves reconciliation in that it overcomes sin, that is, as a victorious event.[48] How does this substitutionary victory *work* to accomplish reconciliation in Jenson's theology? Does the cross achieve penal satisfaction of God's just wrath? Triumph over demonic powers? Does it perhaps constitute a subversive model for a nonviolent social reality? Does it accomplish all of these or something else completely? Jenson is reticent to engage such questions because, in his eyes, all efforts to construct theories about how the atonement works are destined to fail. This is because, whether in Anselmian, Aulénian, or other theoretical form, traditional atonement theories end up stripping the story of Jesus' death from its narrative context and placing it within some other extrabiblical, and therefore alien, framework. While such frameworks purport to provide "the real significance" of God's interactions with his creatures,[49] they in fact blind us to the true contours of God's drama with Israel.[50]

Furthermore, such theories inevitably fail, according to Jenson, because they interpret what happens with Jesus on the cross in terms of "external" relations between God and humanity. Jesus' death becomes something one party must do *to* the other to make peace. The notion of an external relation is of course repugnant to Jenson's theological program.[51]

Contrary to such approaches to the atonement, Jenson urges us to see the crucifixion "as itself an event *in* God's triune life."[52] Viewed from this perspective, the atonement becomes

---

[47]Ibid., 184.
[48]Ibid.
[49]Ibid., 185-89.
[50]Ibid., 188.
[51]Ibid., 188, 75.
[52]Ibid., 189, italics mine.

the story of God's act to bring us back to himself at his own cost, and of our being brought back. There is no story behind or beyond it that is the real story of what God does to reconcile us, no story of mythic battles or of a deal between God and his Son or of our being moved to live reconciled lives. The Gospel's passion narrative is the authentic and entire account of God's reconciling action and our reconciliation, as events in his life and ours.[53]

Interpreting the atonement from this perspective does not reduce the theology of the cross to the status of bare assertion without explication. It does however require that explications of the cross's meaning be at once "more chastened" and "more daring" than the usual atonement theories.[54]

Jenson accordingly unpacks the meaning of Jesus' atoning death by addressing three questions. First, "Why did Jesus have to die?" Second, "How was Jesus' death a sacrifice?" Third, "How was this death a victory?"[55] To the first question, he responds: "The Crucifixion is what it cost the Father to be in fact—and not just in somebody's projected theology or ideology—the loving and merciful Father of the human persons that in fact exist."[56] In other words, the reason *why* the cross in fact happened and the meaning of *who* God in fact is are intrinsically related matters. Jenson explains this point by means of a theological commentary on the parable of the wicked tenants:

> We do not want to share in the Son's relation to the Father, we do not want there to be a Father; and that is why the one who said, "When you pray, say 'Our Father,'" had to die. The Father sends servant after servant and finally the Son. The vineyard-keepers kill each in turn; given the project that defines their lives, to have no one over them, they could not do otherwise. Who, then, delivers the Son to death? We can equally say: the Father does or we do.
>
> The eternal triune decision made at the Crucifixion and Resurrec-

---

[53]Ibid., 189.
[54]Ibid., 190.
[55]Ibid., 191.
[56]Ibid.

tion was between the parable as told, with a dead Son and slaughter of the vineyard-keepers, and raising a Son who insists rather on forgiving them.

Jenson goes on to explain the determinative nature of Jesus' life for the Father's identity. Faced with the fact of the Son's execution, the Father has two options: "The Father can have his Son and us with him into the bargain, or he can abolish us and have no Son, for there is no Son but the one who said, 'Father, forgive them.'"[57] That the Father raises the Son thus simultaneously establishes *what* the gospel's doctrine of salvation is and *what* the gospel's God is like: "the Father of Jesus Christ."[58]

Explicating Jenson's trinitarian *theologia crucis* at this point requires mention of the third *dramatis Dei persona*, the Holy Spirit. According to Jenson, the Spirit is the one who guarantees that the Father's abandonment of the Son on Golgotha nevertheless constitutes a *unified*—and therefore *triune*—act and not merely a betrayal or split in the divine life. How so? The Spirit is "the whirlwind" of the Lord's "*liveliness* that agitates whatever he turns toward."[59] He appears first in the Old Testament as the one who enacts the Lord's "historical agency through Israel's leadership" and who functions as "the agent of prophecy."[60] He appears finally as the one who marks off Jesus as Messiah, the one anointed to pour out this same Spirit on all flesh, again in fulfillment of prophecy.[61] The link between the Spirit and prophecy, Jenson insists, is not incidental. The Spirit's pivotal role in biblical prophecy signifies his essentially *eschatological* role in the triune life. Speaking of the threat Jesus' Godforsaken plight on the cross poses to the unity of the divine life, Jenson states:

---

[57]Ibid., 191.
[58]Thus Jenson states: "In knowing and willing Jesus, God knows and wills himself" (*TI*, 146).
[59]*ST* 1:86.
[60]Ibid.
[61]Ibid., 88.

Father and Son are one God even as the Father abandons the Son, in that the Spirit who will raise Jesus had come in advance—as Spirit, *anticipation* is his being—and "rested" on him from the moment of his dedication to this death, to be the bond of the triune love also in abandonment. Just so, this abandonment and its suffering become integral to what the Spirit means for the Father and the Son, and so to the Love that is God.[62]

The Spirit, whose role it is to pose God's own future by anticipating it,[63] thus liberates the Father to be the Father of *this* Son Jesus and frees Jesus to fulfill *this* particular role, the Servant-Son of the Father.[64] And so the Spirit, as the bond of love, constitutes the personal unity of the Godhead[65] by enabling the triune life to achieve dramatic coherence, even through the most profound conflict of that life.[66]

Just two steps remain in unpacking Jenson's doctrine of the atonement. The second question to be addressed is: "How was Jesus' death a sacrifice?" Jenson advises us to free ourselves of exclusively propitiatory understandings of sacrifice which, he asserts, "developed in theology only after little was any longer known about actual sacrificial practices."[67] A less truncated view requires that we define sacrifice as "any *prayer* spoken not only with language but also with objects and gestures, so that these latter are like the verbal prayer 'offered.'"[68] Understood in this way, the whole of Jesus' life, climaxing in his death, was an offering to God, attached to the request, "Father, forgive them."[69] According to Jenson, no deeper significance to this sacrifice need be gleaned because the resurrection proclaims that we have in fact been accepted on the basis of this sacrifice, as the one

---

[62]Ibid., 191, italics mine.
[63]On the relationship between the Spirit and possibility, see *TI*, 141.
[64]*ST* 1:156.
[65]Ibid., 158.
[66]Ibid., 160, on causality.
[67]Ibid., 192.
[68]Ibid.
[69]Ibid.

who was slain becomes the priest who administers the Holy Spirit in fulfillment of his messianic vocation.[70]

Finally, "How is Jesus' death a victory?" Again, Jenson rejects extratextual explanatory schemes in favor of a simple retelling of the gospel. The death of Jesus is a victory over the principalities and powers only because the one who opposed them in their religious and political forms was in fact raised to be God's Son. Jenson explains:

> It might have been that the power of demonic empire and religion— in Martin Luther's language, of "sword" and "the law," as these work in history to punish and to perpetuate our alienation—belonged to the constitution of being. It might have been that endless revanchism was the final meaning of fallen created history. But in that this terminally committed defier of the world's power is established as the Logos, is established as the Creator's meaning for his creation, it is not so. The bluster and disguises of this world's powers are become mere illusion. We need not fear them; we need fear only God, and just so are reconciled to him and one another.[71]

INTERPRETING RESURRECTION

Analyzing Jenson's theology of the cross has inevitably required us to speak of his theology of the resurrection. This is as it should be, for the events of Good Friday and Easter are integrally related as the two defining moments in "the infinite dramatic crisis and resolution" of the biblical narrative.[72] It is time, then, to turn from the event which defines the *way* God is (i.e., the cross) to a more direct focus on the event which determines *that* God in fact is (i.e., the resurrection).[73] In other words, we must determine what it means to say "he is risen" within the logic of Jenson's theology.

---

[70]Ibid.

[71]Ibid., 193.

[72]Ibid., 66.

[73]Jenson states: "The Crucifixion settled *who and what* God is; the Resurrection settled *that* God is" (*ST* 1:189). The crucified Christ is the subject of gospel discourse; resurrection is the predicate (*ST* 1:194).

When it comes to the resurrection, we may distinguish two questions: "Did it really happen?" and "What does it mean?"[74] Many modern discussions of the resurrection have focused almost exclusively on the former, admittedly vital (see 1 Cor 15), question.[75] While an affirmative answer concerning the actuality of Jesus' resurrection is important, the resurrection gains its significance from our answer to the second question, which concerns the meaning of Jesus' resurrection. What the resurrection means tells us why the resurrection matters. We turn now to the way in which Jenson answers to these two questions.

First, then, "Did it really happen?" Jenson rejects the modern temptation to reduce the historical actuality of the resurrection to the rise of the disciples' subjective experience of faith[76] and instead affirms the objective reality of the resurrection event. He does so with the help of his *Doktorvater*, Peter Brunner. Building on Brunner's discussion of New Testament resurrection appearances and their relationship to the disciples' "visions," Jenson states:

> By a vision, we ordinarily mean an event contained within the subjectivity of the visionary, whatever truth it may mediate; but in the case of the resurrection appearances the texts "provide absolutely no point of connection for the notion that the appearances were inward envisionings . . ." Nor indeed does Paul himself categorize his experience as an inner experience, but as an act of God to "reveal" (*apokalypsai*) something in any case there.[77]

What then actually happened? What does it mean? Jenson un-

---

[74]Carl Braaten, "The Reality of the Resurrection," in *Nicene Christianity: The Future for a New Ecumenism*, ed. Christopher R. Seitz (Grand Rapids: Brazos, 2001), 111.

[75]Two notable exceptions are N. T. Wright, *The Resurrection of the Son of God* (Minneapolis: Fortress, 2003); and Richard B. Gaffin Jr., *Resurrection and Redemption: A Study in Paul's Soteriology* (Phillipsburg, NJ: P & R, 1987).

[76]This, of course, is Bultmann's view of the resurrection. See his, "New Testament and Mythology," in *Kerygma and Myth*, ed. Hans Werner Bartsch, trans. Reginald H. Fuller (London: SPCK, 1964): "If the event of Easter Day is in any sense an historical event additional to the event of the cross, it is nothing else than the rise of faith in the risen Lord, since it was this which led to the apostolic preaching" (42).

[77]*ST* 1:196.

packs his answer in four propositions, three of which he draws from Brunner, the other being his own composition. The first proposition, which is Jenson's own, states: "The decisive difference between a living person and a dead one is that the former can *surprise* us as the latter cannot."[78] To be sure, Socrates might surprise us. However, it will only be because we learn something about his already completed life that we did not previously know.[79] In contrast to Socrates, the risen Jesus can surprise us because, as a living agent, he is able to do something new.[80]

Although the risen Jesus may surprise us, he will never disappoint us. Because his obedience unto death has determined his character once and for all as "the Man for others," we can be confident that his free actions toward us will always conform to this determinate character.[81] According to Jenson:

> Indeed, *fully* reliable love can *only* be the resurrected life of one who has died for the beloved ones. Contemporary society speaks much of "unconditional" love, and is always disappointed. If I commit myself in love, I may die of it. If I do not, my love remains uncertain; if I do, it is lost—unless I rise again. When the gospel proclaims actual unconditional love, it proclaims a specific, individual love, the love that is the actuality of the risen Jesus. No one else can love unconditionally as does the Lord.[82]

The remaining propositions concerning the meaning of Jesus' resurrection come from Brunner. The second states that "the Risen One is 'Jesus in the identity of his person.'"[83] According to Jenson, the identity of the crucified one and the risen one is that of the Logos.[84] He is the subject of both the crucifixion and the resurrection and

---

[78]Ibid., 198.
[79]Ibid.
[80]Ibid.
[81]Ibid., 198-99.
[82]Ibid., 199.
[83]Ibid.
[84]Ibid., 199-200.

thus provides the continuity of identity between the person who died and the "subsequent phenomenon" experienced by the disciples.[85] Because that which constitutes the identity between the crucified one and the risen one is the second person of the Trinity, certainty that the man raised from the garden tomb is the man killed only a few days earlier on Golgatha is a certainty available only to faith, which grasps "things not seen."[86] Ultimately, faith grasps the unified personal identity of Jesus by perceiving his essential unity with the one event that is God's life, an essential unity that is "the final object of faith."[87] In other words, the personal unity of the crucified and risen Jesus is constituted in the dramatic, eventful *coherence* of the one divine life itself, a life lived from the Father in the Spirit. Because the self-same Spirit of the Father rested on Jesus at his baptism *and* raised him from the dead, faith is assured of the identity between the one hanged and the one enthroned.[88]

Jenson's third proposition on the meaning of the resurrection states: "The risen one is 'neither the ghost of a dead man nor a dead man returned.' That is, the risen Jesus' life does not *continue on* from his death."[89] He is risen indeed. But he was not raised back into his former manner of existence, only to die again. As with the first proposition, the religious significance of the third is rooted in the fact that Jesus' death sealed his character once and for all. Thus, the life that Jesus pleads before the Father on our behalf is an already completed life, "the life lived from Mary's womb to Golgotha."[90]

Talk of Jesus' intercession before the Father leads to the fourth proposition, which speaks to the *location* of the risen Lord. According to Jenson, the life Jesus lives "he lives 'in the glory of God.'"[91]

---

[85]Ibid.
[86]Ibid., 200. Note Jenson's rejection of other candidates following Thomas Aquinas (*ST* 1:199).
[87]Ibid.
[88]Ibid.
[89]Ibid.
[90]Ibid.
[91]Ibid.

This means two things: first, Jesus dwells in the kingdom, the promised everlasting state envisioned by Old Testament prophets; second, Jesus dwells in God.[92] Because it is Jesus, the completed life of a human being, who dwells therein, not only is God's reality once and for all determined, so also is the future of creation.[93]

"GOD GIVES IT A BODY AS HE HAS CHOSEN"

Jenson insists on the objectivity of Jesus' resurrection. The risen Son of God lives objectively and personally, and not merely in the memory of the church. In order to fully appreciate the nature of this claim, one final issue requires our attention, namely, Jenson's understanding of Jesus' resurrection body. In his understanding of Jesus' resurrection body, we confront another one of Jenson's most controversial *theologoumena*.

Jenson's theology of the resurrection body of Jesus comes by way of an extended theological reflection on Pauline discourse about "the body of Christ," which he summarizes in a clear but controversial assertion. According to Jenson, "the only body of Christ to which Paul actually refers is . . . the Eucharistic loaf and cup and the church assembled around them."[94] This assertion, Jenson contends, is not a figure of speech. That the church is the body of Christ is a literal statement, a concept and not a trope.[95]

What does this mean? Answering this question requires attending to Jenson's theology of the body. Though Jenson departs from a position like that of Bultmann in insisting on the "objectivity" of Jesus' resurrection, he returns to a position very close to that of the Marburg *Neuetestamentler* when it comes to the nature of Jesus' resurrected body.[96] According to Jenson, a "body" is "simply the person

[92]Ibid., 200-201, 197.
[93]Ibid., 201.
[94]Ibid., 204.
[95]Ibid., 204-205.
[96]See Rudolph Bultmann, *Theology of the New Testament*, trans. Kendrick Grobel (New York: Charles Scribner's Sons, 1954), 1:193-200. Note, however, that in making the present point Jenson specifically cites the work of John A. T. Robinson, *The Body* (London: SCM, 1952).

him or herself, insofar as the person is an *object* for other persons and him or herself."[97] He continues:

> It is in that Paul is a body that persecutors can mark him as Christ's; it is in that Paul is a body that he can be seen and interrogated by one of his congregations, or be remote from this possibility; it is in that Paul is a body that he can discipline his own self. In Paul's ontology, such personal availability may or may not be constituted as the bodily entity moderns first think of as a "body"; for Paul, a "spiritual" body, whatever that may be, is as much or more a body as a biological body.[98]

Thus defined, to call the church "the body of Christ" is to identify the church as the *personal availability* of the Logos to himself and to us. Because the church can function as such as the body of the risen Christ, Christ needs no other resurrection body.[99]

How can it be that the church is the body of Christ in this literal, straightforward sense? The foundation for answering this question already lies before us. It *can* be the case that the church with her sacraments is the body of Jesus because, in Jenson's theology, what God *is* is determined by what God *wills* and *does*. Thus "to the question 'Who am I?'" the risen Lord answers, "I am this community's head. I am the subject whose objectivity is this community."[100] And because Christ intends that this is so, it is so. Christ's "self-understanding" in this regard "determines what is real."[101]

Surely one might ask: Does not the identification of Jesus' resurrection body with the church run counter to other Pauline descriptions of Jesus' relationship to the church? Jesus is not only the church's head. He is also the church's husband, and the latter description seems to presuppose a more robustly *personal* distinction between the two. Jenson acknowledges this potential objection and affirms: "We

---

[97] *ST* 1:205.
[98] Ibid.
[99] Ibid., 206.
[100] *ST* 2:215.
[101] *ST* 1:206.

may not so identify the risen Christ with the church as to be unable to refer distinctly to the one and then to the other."[102] The church must somehow be Christ's body, his personal availability to himself and to others, *and* his bride, his personal counterpart or "other."

To resolve the apparent difficulty posed by these two Pauline locutions regarding Christ's relationship to the church, Jenson appeals to the sociological distinction between *Gemeinschaft* ("community") and *Gesellschaft* ("society" or "association"). Jenson distinguishes the church as the *community* gathered around the sacraments from the church as the *association* that gathers around the sacraments in order to account for the distinction between Christ as head of his church and Christ as husband of his church.[103]

> The object that is the church-assembly is the body of Christ, that is, Christ available to the world and to her members, just in that the church gathers around objects distinct from herself, the bread and cup, which are the availability *to her* of the same Christ. Within the gathering we can intend Christ as the community we are, without self-deification, because we jointly intend the identical Christ as the sacramental elements in our midst, which are other than us.[104]

In other words, for Jenson, the same pattern that applies to the Servant and to the *totus Christus* in their individual and corporate modes of being applies also to the body of Christ, which the church simply *is*.[105]

Jenson's understanding of the body of Christ has met criticism from both Catholic and Protestant sources.[106] Though much of

---

[102]*ST* 2:213.

[103]See also ibid., 172.

[104]Ibid., 213.

[105]Aware of obvious Protestant concerns with such a construal of the Christ-church relationship, Jenson insists that his view preserves sufficient room for the possibility of church reform under the rubric of Christ's bodily *self*-discipline: "Churchly reform is the risen Christ's self-discipline in the Spirit" (*ST* 2:213).

[106]See, for example, Susan K. Wood, "Robert Jenson's Ecclesiology from a Roman Catholic Perspective," in Gunton, *Trinity, Time, and Church*, 178-87; and Ian A. McFarland, "The Body of Christ: Rethinking a Classic Ecclesiological Model," *International Journal of Systematic Theology* 7 (2005): 225-45.

the discussion surrounding Jenson's view is properly ecclesiological in nature, and therefore lies beyond the scope of the present
study, following John Webster we may identify two features of
Jenson's theology of Christ's resurrection body that are worthy of
comment, as they highlight some of the properly theological issues that we will have to address in later chapters. The first feature
is more methodological in nature. The second is more material and
substantive.

First, as Webster observes, Jenson's account of Christ's resurrection body "begins from observations about embodiment rather
from the identity of the agent of whom the metaphor is
predicated."[107] The question is: Is such a starting point legitimate,
given the unique identity of this agent and the unique nature of
this agent's relationship to the community that is his body? Along
these lines, we may also ask whether Jenson's understanding of the
"body" in fact follows his own methodological strictures, which require that we explicate theological concepts according to the inner
logic of the biblical narrative and not according to (what in the
final analysis appears to be) a generalized phenomenology of embodiment.[108] Second, acknowledging that the head-body image is
indeed a *relational* image, Webster worries nevertheless that Jenson's conception of the Christ-church relation does not adequately
account for Christ's primacy in relation to the church and therefore
for the unilateral nature of his creative agency in founding, sustaining and governing the church in its existence. Does conceptualizing the head-body relation as an internal relation do justice to
Christ's aseity on the one hand and to the "generativity" of Christ's
relation to his people on the other?

---

[107]John Webster, "'In the Society of God': Some Principles of Ecclesiology," in *The Domain of the Word* (London: T&T Clark, forthcoming), chap. 11.

[108]Mid-twentieth-century interpretations of the body in Paul, such as those of Bultmann and Robinson, have not survived thorough exegetical analysis. See Robert H. Gundry, *Soma in Bibli-cal Theology: With Emphasis on Pauline Anthropology* (Cambridge: Cambridge University Press, 1976).

CONCLUSION

We will return to critical questions such as these in part two. It is time, however, to draw the present chapter to a close. Having traced the way Jenson reads the biblical naming of God across the Old and New Testaments, and having identified many of the most significant hermeneutical and theological decisions that accompany this reading, we are now in a position to consider the material revisions and reconstructions to the Christian doctrine of God that Jenson proposes on the basis of his theological interpretation of Scripture.

5

THE TRIUNE IDENTITY

◆

INTRODUCTION

In Christian theology at least, doctrinal propositions apart from the exegetical arguments that they summarize are at best ambiguous.[1] Having analyzed the way Jenson reads the biblical naming of God, along with some of the most significant hermeneutical and theological presuppositions and entailments of this reading, we have tried to guard against potential ambiguity when it comes to his constructive theological proposal. With this discussion in place, we turn therefore to a more synthetic explication and analysis of Jenson's doctrine of the gospel's God.

As we saw in chapter two, Jenson's account of God according to the gospel requires a trinitarian metaphysics that is at once deconstructive and reconstructive. Our analysis of his proposal will accordingly unfold in two steps. First, we will consider the criticisms of traditional christological and trinitarian metaphysics that follow from Jenson's theological interpretation of Scripture. Second, we will consider the historicist trinitarian theology and metaphysics that Jenson proposes in keeping with his reading of the biblical identification of God by and with the story of his people. Before turning

---

[1]This is my paraphrase of John Behr's statement in "The Paschal Foundation of Christian Theology," *St Vladimir's Theological Quarterly* 45 (2001): "Conclusions without the arguments that lead to them are at best ambiguous" (115).

to this analysis, however, we will briefly review the rationale for metaphysical reflection internal to Jenson's hermeneutical and theological proposal.

ON METANARRATIVES AND METAPHYSICS

What sort of being does the gospel's God have? It might seem strange that a narrative theologian like Jenson would be so concerned to address the question of divine being.[2] What has Jerusalem's metanarrative to do with Athens's metaphysics? we might be tempted to ask. Much in every way, Jenson insists:

> Any doctrine which claims to open up to men the meaning and purpose of their lives is necessarily also a description of reality. The Christian Gospel is no exception. If it says to me that Jesus Christ is the center of everything it thereby says that everything has Jesus Christ at its center and so makes a decisive statement about the nature of what is real. It is not idle speculation but simply an unfolding of the concrete attachments of the Gospel to life, when we go on to ask what "everything" must be *like* to have Jesus Christ at its center. Therefore, theology as the science of this proclamation necessarily becomes a struggle with the old question of what things are really like.[3]

The seeming strangeness of Jenson's commitment to metaphysical reflection may follow from the (unwarranted) assumption that the field of "metaphysics" concerns "only positions materially consistent with those of the Greeks."[4] However, as we have seen, and as we will see more fully below, Jenson's devotion to metaphysical reflection is manifestly not a devotion to Greek metaphysics. The strangeness of this commitment may also follow from a perceived conflict with Jen-

---

[2]Indeed one of the characteristics of "narrative theology" has been a reticence to speak in this regard. See the criticism of Christoph Schwöbel, *God: Action and Revelation* (Kampen: Kok Pharos, 1992), 54-59. As noted in chapter two above, Murphy's analysis of Jenson fails to account for the ontological dimension of his narrative theology.
[3]*AO*, 112.
[4]*ST* 2:157.

son's commitment to explicating the Christian doctrine of God by means of interpreting the biblical names of God. However, Jenson's concern to reason metaphysically about God does not represent for him a separate enterprise from that of reading about God in biblical narrative. The former is instead the necessary entailment of doing the latter responsibly and meaningfully.

To see this we may recall Wittgenstein's famous remark: "Grammar tells us what kind of object anything is."[5] Of course, determining "what kind of object anything is" is an integral part of metaphysical reflection. On such an understanding, the hermeneutical enterprise is thus intrinsically metaphysical insofar as hermeneutics is the discipline attentive to the biblical "grammar" of identifying God and all things in relation to God. This is why theology is an intrinsically hermeneutical and metaphysical discipline for Jenson.[6] His desire to reason truly about the *being* of God is part and parcel with his desire to read the *story* of God well. Viewed in this light, then, the difference between reading well and reading poorly, and thus between good and bad metaphysics, is simply the difference between worship and idolatry, piety and blasphemy.[7] In the final analysis, metaphysical reflection belongs to the Christian doctrine of God because Holy Scripture names God as the one who *is* (e.g., Ex 3:14 LXX; Heb 11:6; Rev 1:4, 8) and because the church has been granted the gift of knowing God in accordance with the *truth* of his existence (Jn 17:3).

---

[5]Wittgenstein, *Philosophical Investigations*, 3rd ed., trans. G. E. M. Anscombe (New York: Macmillan, 1958), §373.

[6]On theology's hermeneutical, grammatical, and metaphysical modes, see *ST* 1:14-21.

[7]Commenting on the debate between Athanasius and the Arians, Frances Young states: "Athanasius is convinced that the difference between the Arian view and his orthodox interpretation is the difference between blasphemy and piety, between deceit and truth." *Biblical Exegesis and the Formation of Christian Culture* (Cambridge: Cambridge University Press, 1997), 41. For a fine discussion of the relationship between biblical exegesis and metaphysical reflection, see Matthew Levering, *Scripture and Metaphysics: Aquinas and the Renewal of Trinitarian Theology* (Oxford: Blackwell, 2004). For Jenson's reflections on the relationship between reading, metaphysics and idolatry, see *ST* 1:59-60.

REVISING GREEK RELIGION, REINTERPRETING BEING TO ACCOMMODATE THE GOSPEL

This being said, it is one thing to affirm *that* God is and quite another to explicate *who and what* God is like.[8] According to Jenson, the history of discourse about God's being presents three entry points for discussing this topic.

One approach, typical of Eastern Orthodoxy, accepts the ancient Greek concept of being and then seeks "to disengage God from some implications of this acceptation."[9] This method of disengagement often involves saying that God is "above" or "beyond" being. Another approach, exemplified by Martin Heidegger and Michael Wyschogrod, disallows entirely the application of "being" to God.[10] Yet, Jenson avers, "a straightforward doctrine of God's nonbeing must anyway be dangerous"[11] because it tends toward an ontology of violence: "Within the actual modern tradition, as it stems from Nietzsche and Heidegger, nonbeing is evoked as mere negativity, that is, as *violence* upon what is; Heidegger's fascism was no accident or coincidence."[12] The remaining approach, and the one which Jenson adopts, rejects the inherited Greek concept of being and pursues the path of metaphysical revisionism. Jenson explains: "We may shoulder the necessity, within the theological enterprise actually in course, of a concept of being and of its application to God, but *reinterpret being to accommodate the gospel,* and just by so doing say what it is for God to be."[13]

According to Jenson, the early Christian mission to the Greeks did much to "reinterpret being to accommodate the gospel."[14] Nicene trinitarianism is the church's greatest accomplishment in this regard,

---

[8]See Gregory of Nazianzus, *Oration* 28.5, in *Christology of the Later Fathers,* ed. Edward R. Hardy (Philadelphia: Westminster, 1954).
[9]*ST* 1:211.
[10]Ibid.
[11]Ibid.
[12]Ibid., 212.
[13]Ibid., italics mine.
[14]Ibid., 90, 212.

its "most decisive dogmatic achievement to date."[15] Nevertheless, in Jenson's judgment, Christian theology ever since has largely failed to *complete* the Nicene reinterpretation of Greek metaphysics.[16] Therefore, it is the task of Christian dogmatics today to finish the job of "revisionary metaphysics."[17] To do so requires that we purge the Christian theological imagination of every remnant of the god of the Greeks. Jenson is absolutely clear about the import of this task. Purgation is necessary because the god of Greek religion is "an exact antagonist of biblical faith."[18]

We may understand the nature of this antagonism by examining Jenson's theory of "religion." According to Jenson, "religion" represents humanity's attempt to give meaning to the otherwise "unplotted sequence" of temporal events. That which gives meaning to time constitutes a religion's view of "eternity." If that which gives meaning to time is believed to be a personal agent, someone capable of speaking and hearing, then a religion's "eternity" is a "god."[19]

For the religion of Greek antiquity, the lack of meaning perceived *in* temporal existence was perceived to be a problem *with* temporal existence.[20] Salvation in this situation was thus sought as a deliverance *from* time and its effects: change, suffering and death. On this scheme, if a "god" is to effect "salvation," he must be *timeless*—immune to time.[21] Moreover, a god whose identity is defined by his immunity to time must also be *immutable, impassible,* and *immortal,*[22]

---

[15]Ibid., 103.

[16]Ibid., 108; note his comments on Nicaea's failures in this regard.

[17]Jenson states: "The whole of my systematics is in one aspect an effort of revisionary metaphysics, aimed at allowing one to say things about God that scripture seems to require but that inherited metaphysics inhibits." Robert W. Jenson, "Response to Watson and Hunsinger," *Scottish Journal of Theology* 55 (2002): 230.

[18]*TI*, 57; see also *ST* 2:146.

[19]*ST* 1:55. Jenson's attempt to provide a general predicative meaning to the word *god* represents a modification of his Barthianism in a direction similar to that of Pannenberg. See Wolfhart Pannenberg, *Systematic Theology*, trans. Geoffrey W. Bromiley (Grand Rapids: Eerdmans, 1991), 1:66-73.

[20]*ST* 1:94.

[21]*TI*, 58; *ST* 1:94.

[22]*TI*, 57-63.

for the opposites of these attributes—change, suffering and mortal-ity—are things which happen *in* time and thus constitute the sources of human misery.[23] Timeless eternity, immutability, impassibility and immortality are of course mainstays in traditional Christian teaching about God. This longstanding tradition, however, represents for Jen-son a compromise between evangelical and Hellenistic theology, not a true reinterpretation of God's being in the light of the gospel. Though the problems with this conception of God are legion, they all may be traced to the fact that such a view of deity contradicts the fundamental Nicene-narrative grammar of Christian theology—that the gospel's God is identified by and with the "blatantly tempo-ral events" of the gospel's story.

Scripture's story of salvation is not about escaping *from* time *to* creation's timeless origin.[24] Scripture's story of salvation is rather about God's faithfulness to his promises *through* time in bringing his people *to* the promised future of the new creation. Moreover, this promised future is *better* than the past.[25] The new creation does not represent a return to Eden, but instead represents Eden's consum-mation.[26] In other words, the overarching plot of the biblical story line is "developmental" rather than "circular."[27]

This narrative feature comports with an almost universal ecumenical consensus regarding the nature of human salvation. Whether it be in a doctrine of deification or in a more modest doctrine of glorification, the church has taught with nearly unanimous consent that God's saving work in Christ brings redeemed humanity to a destiny that transcends

---

[23]*ST* 1:94.

[24]Ibid., 67.

[25]*ST* 2:12-15.

[26]Geerhardus Vos, *The Eschatology of the Old Testament*, ed. James T. Dennison Jr. (Phillipsburg, NJ: Presbyterian and Reformed, 2001), 73-76.

[27]According to Richard Pratt, *He Gave Us Stories: The Bible Student's Guide to Interpreting Old Testa-ment Narratives* (Phillipsburg, NJ: P & R, 1993), 185, a circular plot is one where "the closing returns to the situation" with which the story began. By contrast, a "developmental" plot is one where "the story ends by describing a different—though not opposite—state of affairs." For a discussion of how these different plot structures relate to different soteriological schemes, see Michael Root, "The Narrative Structure of Soteriology," *Modern Theology* 2 (1986): 149-50.

humanity's original Edenic state, a destiny which our first parents could have attained but did not reach because of sin.[28] For Christian "religion," then, salvation transcends the predicaments of temporality, not by extracting humanity from time, but by bringing humanity in and through time to time's appointed *telos*.[29] In this way, Christianity confesses that the gospel provides "dramatic coherence" to human existence.

Most importantly, in saving humanity God does not remain aloof from creation and time but instead comes to dwell *within* creation and time. The promise of Leviticus 26:12, "I will walk among you and be your God, and you shall be my people" points to the denouement of both the first and the second exodus (Ex 29:46; Rev 21:3). To summarize Jenson's argument: because God has chosen to be *our* God (temporal beings-toward-death that we are) in *this manner* (through a "developmental" story of salvation), the traditional understanding of the divine timelessness, immutability and so forth must be rejected. "He is a God to whom 'for us humans and for our salvation' belongs to his own . . . deity."[30]

Jenson finds further evidence of traditional theism's distorted view of divine being in its impact on the doctrines of Christ and Trinity. To his account of these distortions we now turn.

REVISING TRADITIONAL CHRISTOLOGICAL AND TRINITARIAN METAPHYSICS

Jenson argues that traditional understandings of the divine nature have led to an "incoherent"[31] and "contradictory"[32] christology at best and a heretical christology at worst.[33] On the one hand, Nicene Christians confess that the second person of the Trinity is the per-

---

[28]Eugene Rogers, *After the Spirit: A Constructive Pneumatology from Resources Outside the Modern West* (Grand Rapids: Eerdmans, 2005), 9.

[29]*ST* 2:350-52.

[30]Robert W. Jenson, "For Us . . . He Was Made Man," in *Nicene Christianity: The Future for a New Ecumenism,* ed. Christopher R. Seitz (Grand Rapids: Brazos, 2001), 77.

[31]Ibid., 78; *ST* 1:125.

[32]*ST* 1:94.

[33]See *TI,* 64-66.

sonal subject of the temporal events of the gospel story line—from womb to tomb. *He* was born. *He* suffered under Pontius Pilate. *He* was buried. *He* was raised. On the other hand, because of the failure to purge the Christian doctrine of God of its pagan corruptions, Christian theology has *also* insisted that the second person of the Trinity is timeless, immutable and impassible. Jenson calls such twofold christological discourse "paradox christology."[34]

According to Jenson, this "paradox christology is the only actual content of the 'two natures' christology . . . dogmatized at the Council of Chalcedon."[35] Such a Christology is finally "incoherent"[36] because it is unable to *synthesize* its two mutually contrastive forms of speech: it affirms both that the Son is timeless *and* temporal, impassible *and* passible, and so on.[37] The only coherent alternative for those committed to maintaining this twofold pattern of discourse is outright heresy. According to Jenson, christological heresy represents the attempt to resolve the dissonance of this twofold pattern of discourse either by softening the divine characteristics of Jesus or by softening the human characteristics of Jesus.[38] He explains:

> In each direction . . . the paradox can be softened in two ways: by fudging the predicate or fudging the copula. "The Impassible is passible" can be softened to "The Impassible is almost-passible" (Apollinaris!) or "The Impassible is closely but not entirely identified with the passible" (Nestorius!). . . . In the other direction, "The passible is Impassible" can be softened to "The passible is almost-Impassible" or to "The passible is almost identifiable with the Impassible." The first is traditionally labeled "subordinationism," the second "modalism."[39]

---

[34]Ibid., 63.
[35]Ibid., 64. Although Jenson considers Chalcedon a "failure" as an ecumenical council, he does believe it accomplished two noteworthy things. First, "it connected the trinitarian and christological discussions terminologically." Second, "it established the necessary dogmatic boundaries of christological interpretation and speculation," ruling out a merely Nestorian understanding of the union of Christ's two natures on one side and a Apollinarian *tertium quid* on the other (*ST* 1:132).
[36]Jenson, "For Us," 78.
[37]*TI*, 63-64; *ST* 1:125.
[38]*TI*, 64.
[39]Ibid.

The problem with such heretical attempts at coherence is that they inevitably "speak of God in just such a way that saws off our narrative limb, because they insist on so interpreting God 'himself' that no history can be told of him, so that the specific Christian identification of God cannot 'really' be true."[40] As Jenson says elsewhere: "It has been the open or concealed goal of each successive Christian heresy to shield Western antiquity's native concept of deity from the import of biblical narrative about God, that is, to protect deity from contamination by temporality's slings and arrows, above all from women's wombs or the tombs women tended."[41] In other words, the ultimate problem with traditional understandings of divine being, held in paradoxical form by the orthodox or in a consistent form by the heretics, is that it disables us from *reading* coherently the story of Jesus *as* the story of "God with us."[42]

The same problem confronts us in traditional trinitarian theology. Recourse to Jenson's theory of religion is again helpful in explaining the point. As we have seen, for Jenson *religion* refers to humankind's search for transcendent meaning amid time's disruptions. A *god* is an "eternal" being who grants such meaning by somehow transcending time's disruptions. According to Jenson, the distinctive feature of the biblical God is that he transcends time not by being immune to it but by being personally faithful to his promises in and through it.[43] Far from being characterized by immunity to time, therefore, God's sort of eternity is that of "temporal infinity."[44]

We will unpack this notion shortly. For our present purposes, it is necessary to observe that for Jenson the *taxis* of the *opera Dei ad extra* (the order in which all external divine works proceed from the Father, through the Son, in the Spirit) is an intrinsically *temporal* or-

---

[40]Ibid., 65.
[41]Jenson, "For Us," 83-84.
[42]See also *ST* 1:128-29.
[43]*ST* 1:210; *TI*, 141; *ST* 1:217.
[44]*ST* 1:217.

der.[45] The relations between Father, Son and Spirit that unfold in the economy of salvation are "either *temporal* relations or empty verbiage."[46] Traditional theism's failure with respect to trinitarian theology may be seen precisely at this point. And blame for this failure in the West must be imputed chiefly to Augustine of Hippo.[47]

For starters, Jenson faults Augustine for failing to grasp the basic Cappadocian distinction between *ousia* and *hypostasis*,[48] the distinction which enabled the Cappadocian fathers to acknowledge the aforementioned temporal *taxis* in the triune economy. As Jenson reads the Cappadocians, God's external works represent the unfolding event of *one ousia* by means of the mutually ordered, active relations of *three hypostases*.[49] "God," in this understanding, "picks out . . . the mutual action of Father, Son and Spirit."[50] Augustine, however, confessed: "I do not grasp what difference they intend between *ousia* and *hypostasis*."[51] Jenson traces Augustine's failure to grasp this distinction to his axiomatic commitment to a Platonic doctrine of divine simplicity, the doctrine which teaches that God is what God has[52] and which also therefore entails the proposition that "*no* sort of self-differentiation can really be true of" God.[53] But if there is no

---

[45] *TI*, 113-14, 140, following Barth.

[46] Ibid., 126.

[47] Blaming Augustine for Christianity's "loss" of the full trinitarian inheritance bequeathed to it by Nicaea is now commonplace. See, for example, the classic essay of Colin E. Gunton, "Augustine, the Trinity and the Theological Crisis of the West," *Scottish Journal of Theology* 43 (1990): 33-58. While Jenson's diagnosis of the Western/Augustinian failure is multifaceted (see *TI*, 114-38; *ST*, 1:110-15), his reading has been largely refuted in recent scholarly literature. See Sarah Coakley, "Persons in the 'Social' Doctrine of the Trinity: A Critique of the Current Analytical Discussion," in Stephen T. Davis et al., *The Trinity: An Interdisciplinary Symposium* (Oxford: Oxford University Press, 2004), chap. 6; Lewis Ayres, *Nicaea and Its Legacy: An Approach to Fourth-Century Trinitarian Theology* (Oxford: Oxford University Press, 2004); and Lewis Ayres, *Augustine and the Trinity* (Cambridge: Cambridge University Press, 2010).

[48] *TI*, 114; *ST* 1:111.

[49] *ST* 1:110.

[50] Ibid., 215.

[51] Augustine, *The Trinity*, trans. Edmund Hill (Brooklyn: New City Press, 1991), 5.10, cited in *TI*, 114.

[52] *ST* 1:112.

[53] Ibid., 111. As noted above (n. 47), Jenson's argument seems to rest at least in part on a misreading of Augustine. Jenson seems to conflate Augustine's rejection of *accidents* in God with a rejection of *relations* in God. But Augustine clearly states: "We do not say that the nature of the good is

self-differentiation in God, then there can be no temporal *taxis* in the *opera Dei ad extra* either. Instead, Christian theology must be governed by another rule: *opera Dei ad extra indivisa sunt* ("the external works of God are indivisible").[54] According to Jenson, this rule, at least as understood in the Augustinian tradition, renders the Bible's narrative revelation of the Trinity meaningless. So, for example, while we may "appropriate" Jesus' birth, suffering and death to the sent Son, "really" all three persons are indistinguishably operative in the incarnation.[55] Moreover (and here for Jenson is Western trinitarianism's most damning affirmation), *any* of the persons could have become incarnate.[56]

Given this understanding of the indivisibility of God's works *ad extra,* the *temporal* story of salvation can no longer account for the distinctions between the persons.[57] God's relations *to us* in the economy of salvation can no longer be viewed as constitutive of the relations that are internal *to his being*.[58] And so, for those who would nevertheless maintain some form of trinitarian faith, the distinctions must be sought in some *timeless,* unchanging reality, a reality that lies *behind* the biblical drama. Augustinian trinitarianism finds such a reality in its doctrine of the eternal processions.[59]

According to classical Augustinian trinitarianism, the personal distinctions between the three divine persons are rooted in eternal

---

simple, because the Father alone possesses it, or the Son alone, or the Holy Ghost alone; nor do we say, with the Sabellian heretics, that it is only nominally a Trinity, and has no real distinction of persons; but we say it is simple, because it is what it has, *with the exception of the relation of the persons to one another. For, in regard to this relation, it is true that the Father has a Son, and yet is not himself the Son; and the Son has a Father, and is not himself the Father.* But, as regards himself, irrespective of the relation to the other, each is what he has; thus, he is in himself living, for he has life, and is himself the life which he has." *City of God,* 11.10. See also *Trinity* 5.17, where Augustine develops the notion of relation as a useful category for speaking about God in relationship to creatures without admitting accidents in God.

[54]*ST* 1:111.

[55]*TI,* 126.

[56]Ibid., 127; *ST* 1:112; the affirmation is Peter Lombard's.

[57]*TI,* 125-27; *ST* 1:112.

[58]*TI,* 120.

[59]For a helpful introduction to this matter, see Edmund Hill, *The Mystery of the Trinity* (London: Geoffrey Chapman, 1985), esp. chaps. 9-11.

processions. The Father is "from" no one but is instead the *fons divinitatis*. The Son is eternally begotten of the Father and is by virtue of his eternal generation a distinct person from the Father. The Spirit eternally proceeds from the Father and the Son—as from one principle—and is by virtue of his passive spiration a person distinct from the Father and the Son.[60]

In Jenson's judgment, this relocation of the basis of trinitarian personhood from time to eternity constitutes "the most disastrous result" of Augustinian trinitarianism.[61] Why? If the temporal missions of Son and Spirit do not constitute their personhood, then they are merely *clues to* their "real" personhood. And what we have in the biblical narrative of the Trinity is not in fact the *Trinity*, but simply a temporal, changeable, and therefore ultimately *unreliable* reflection *of* the Trinity (because the intratrinitarian relations are *in fact* timeless and changeless).[62] In other words, the net result of traditional theism for trinitarian theology is the loss of any *biblical basis* for trinitarian theology.[63] As we saw in chapter three, Jenson repudiates any theological concept that in his judgment compromises the reliability of the biblical identification of God.

The distortions that traditional understandings of the divine being bring to christology and trinitarian theology may be best perceived by stepping back to view the economy of salvation as a whole. According to the traditional framework, the temporal missions of Son

---

[60]See Augustine, *Trinity* 4-7.
[61]*TI*, 125.
[62]Ibid., 127-28; *ST* 1:112.
[63]*TI*, 125-27; *ST* 1:112. Jenson, like Karl Rahner, also believes that this separation of the immanent from the economic Trinity, a separation required by the traditional theism's commitment to divine timelessness, etc., explains the irrelevance of the doctrine to everyday Christian piety. While the separation still provides for a way of distinguishing the three persons (i.e., the relations of origin), nevertheless, wedded to the rule concerning God's indivisible external works, this way of distinguishing the three persons evacuates trinitarian theology of its basis in biblical narrative, separates trinitarian theology from its soteriological relevance, and thus makes trinitarian theology something for the church to believe because revealed but never to understand. In other words, this way of distinguishing the divine persons makes the doctrine of the Trinity *irrelevant* (*TI*, 126-28, ix-x).

and Spirit bring about no change in God,[64] given his timelessness and immutability. Those missions only bring about a change in us.[65] Consequently, the narrative pattern followed in the temporal missions of Son and Spirit can only "really" be about *our* exit and return to the Father, who is our eternal and unchanging origin. The Son goes forth to be born of a woman and comes back a deified man. The Spirit is poured out on all flesh and draws back in his wake a deified humanity. Salvation on this scheme is eternal return. According to Jenson, it is precisely this narrative structure that explains the *exitus-reditus* structure of Thomas's *Summa theologiae*.[66]

Jenson believes that this version of the economy necessarily distorts the biblical story of salvation which, as we have seen, is a "developmental" story and not a "circular" one.[67] The triune economy does not put us back in the Garden of Eden, but pushes us forward into the new creation. Worst of all for Jenson, this view of the economy ultimately distorts the biblical story of *God*. The saving missions of Son and Spirit do not merely constitute a change in our hopeless estate, they constitute God as triune. As we have seen, the Bible's dramatic account of the economy of salvation is not simply a story about us. It is also a story about God. It is not only a story about "our journey away from and back to" God, but about "God's journey *with* us."[68]

For this and the aforementioned reasons, Jenson believes that traditional answers to the question about God's sort of being must be rejected. In its place, Christian theology must provide a constructive redefinition of God's being that better comports with the biblically narrated fact of God's journey with us.

---

[64]Augustine, *Trinity* 5.1.5.

[65]Augustine, *Trinity* 5.4.17.

[66]*ST* 1:60n102. For a discussion of the *exitus-reditus* structure of Thomas's *Summa theologiae*, see Brian Davies, *The Thought of Thomas Aquinas* (Oxford: Clarendon, 1992), 21. For an argument against seeing the *exitus-reditus* pattern as providing the structure of Thomas's *Summa theologiae*, see Rudi te Velde, *Aquinas on God: The 'Divine Science' of the* Summa Theologiae (Burlington, VT: Ashgate, 2006), chap. 1.

[67]Jenson of course knows that the Fathers believed in deification. I take it that his criticism concerns the *inconsistency* of the Fathers' "developmental" view of salvation with their view of God.

[68]*ST* 1:60n102.

REVISIONARY TRINITARIAN METAPHYSICS

Jenson pursues his constructive redefinition of being in dialogue with two of Christian theology's greatest thinkers on this subject, Thomas Aquinas and Gregory of Nyssa.

Jenson takes from Thomas what is perhaps his most famous revision of Aristotelian metaphysics, the distinction between essence and existence. For Jenson, Thomas's development of this distinction amounts to "one of intellectual history's most powerful and tantalizing ideas."[69] Thomas' distinction between essence and existence is the distinction between *what* a thing is and *that* a thing is. For creatures, the two are distinct. The concept of a creature—whether human or hobbit—does not entail its existence. For God, however, essence and existence are indistinct. This is what it means for Thomas to say that God is "simple." That God is and what God is are but one truth about him.[70]

Before attending to Jenson's development of Thomas's point, we must turn to Jenson's second interlocutor, Gregory of Nyssa. Jenson finds in Gregory's conception of divine infinity a resource for developing Thomas's thesis that God's essence is his act of existence. In particular, Jenson is attracted to the way Gregory "specifies God's triune being by disassembling the notion of being onto the logic of God's triunity and *so* enabling the notion's application to God."[71] Following Ekkehard Mühlenberg,[72] Jenson argues that Gregory understands *God* not to refer to an abstract substance *identically* possessed by each person of the Trinity and therefore *indivisibly* operative in the divine works *ad extra*. Rather Gregory understands *God* to refer to the *mutual activity* of the three persons who constitute God's one

---

[69] *ST* 1:213.

[70] For further discussion, see Davies, *Thought of Thomas Aquinas*, chap. 3; also David Burrell, "Distinguishing God from the World," in *Language, Meaning, and God*, ed. Brian Davies (London: Geoffrey Chapman, 1987), 75-91.

[71] *ST* 1:214.

[72] Ekkehard Mühlenberg, *Die Unendlichkeit Gottes bei Gregory von Nyssa: Gregors Kritik am Gottesbegriff der klassischen Metaphysik* (Göttingen: Vandenhoeck and Ruprecht, 1966).

life.[73] The being of God, according to this notion, is "a *going-on*...like a kiss or a train wreck."[74] Specifically, the being of God is the "going-on" of the three divine persons who *enact* their mutual divine life. The being of God is therefore an eminently *personal* phenomenon. "Being" is a function of "persons," *ousia* of *hypostases*.[75]

That God's being is constituted by the mutual interactions of the three persons explains Jenson's introduction of the term *identity* into Christian theological discourse. The term functions as a substitute for *hypostasis*,[76] the term traditionally used to describe the three "relations subsisting in God"[77] by which one trinitarian person is distinguished from another.[78] Jenson prefers the term *identity* because it suggests an additional nuance: a person's *choice in time* to be "this one and not another."[79]

Because we are talking of *divine* persons or identities, Jenson asserts that the being of their mutually enacted life must be *infinite*. He states:

> What Father, Son, and Spirit have from each other to be three identities of God, and what characterizes their mutual action *as* God, is limitlessness. What happens among them accepts no boundaries; nothing can hinder what they enact. If we label the triune action "love," then we must say: the Father's love can embrace whatever the Spirit's coming brings; the Son's love can endure whatever his Father sends him to do; the Spirit's creativity of love is inexhaustible. Just so, this love is *God* and not a creature.[80]

Such a conception of infinity in turn entails its own distinctive conception of eternity. Because God's limitlessness is established by and with the historical events of the exodus and the gospel, God's

---

[73] *TI*, 118-20; *ST* 1:214-15.
[74] *ST* 1:214.
[75] Ibid., 215; *ST* 2:96. See discussion below.
[76] See *ST* 1:106.
[77] *TI*, 106.
[78] *ST* 1:106.
[79] See *TI*, 110-11.
[80] *ST* 1:216.

eternity must be, as we have seen, a *temporal* infinity.[81] The transcendence of God, therefore, is not the transcendence *of* time itself, but of the *limitations* of time.[82] Jenson explains:

> What he transcends is not the having of beginnings and goals and reconciliations, but any personal limitation in having them. What he transcends is any limit imposed on what can he be *[sic]* by what has been, except the limit of his personal self-identity, and any limit imposed on his action by the availability of time. . . . The eternity of Israel's God is his faithfulness. He is not eternal in that he secures himself from time, but in that he is faithful to his commitments within time. At the great turning, Israel's God is eternal in that he is faithful unto death, and then yet again faithful.[83]

In Jenson's doctrine of eternity, the temporal structure of beginning, goal, and reconciliation *is* the very structure of God's being as Trinity. "The specificity of the triune God is not that he is three, but that he occupies each pole of time as *persona dramatis*."[84] The distinctions between past, present and future obtain in God *as* the identities of Father, Son and Spirit respectively. Moreover, because this structure is *God's*, it remains "unbroken," pure, and immeasurable:[85] "Nothing in God *recedes* into the past or *approaches* from the future."[86] Instead, "God *anticipates* his future and so possesses it."[87] And he does so because he *is* "Spirit."[88]

In sum, then, God *is* the infinite triumph of love and faithfulness that happens in the story worked out between the Father and the

---

[81]Ibid.

[82]Ibid., 216-17.

[83]Ibid., 217.

[84]Ibid., 89.

[85]Ibid., 217-18, following Barth.

[86]*ST* 2:35. Along with his commitment to creation *ex nihilo*, it is this qualification in particular (i.e., "Nothing in God *recedes* into the past or *approaches* from the future") that distinguishes Jenson's historicism from that of Hegel and process theology. Jenson's critics sometimes fail to appreciate this qualification.

[87]Ibid., 121.

[88]*TI*, 141.

Son in the Spirit.[89] His essence is *this* temporal, interpersonal act of existence. Having made this point, Jenson's revision of Augustinian trinitarianism is complete. God is not constituted triune by timeless relations of *origin*; God is constituted triune by temporal, narrative relations of *outcome*.[90] Jesus is constituted the Son, not because he is timelessly begotten of the Father, but because he is eschatologically raised by the God who sent him, the God who, in raising Jesus, constitutes himself the Father of this Son. The Spirit is constituted the Spirit, not because he timelessly proceeds from the Father and the Son, but in that he frees God to be the Father of Jesus and of Jesus' body the church, and vice versa.[91] In other words, God does not cohere in his being as the triune God by timelessly remaining who and what he always is. He coheres in his being as the triune God by temporally anticipating and remaining faithful to who and what he will be—our Father, through the Son, by the Holy Spirit.[92] The triune being of God is thus "constituted in *dramatic coherence*, it is established not from the beginning, but from the end."[93]

CHARACTERIZING THE BEING OF THE TRIUNE GOD

God is as God does in the triune story of salvation. His being *is* the dramatic plot initiated by the Father, carried out by the obedient man Jesus, and brought to perfection in the freedom of the Spirit who enables God to be our God. We conclude our summary analysis of Jenson's doctrine of God by discussing four predicates that characterize God's "plotted" sort of being or, as Jenson recently put it, that "ride the story's waves."[94] Because previous chapters have traced the

---

[89] *ST* 1:220-21.

[90] *TI*, 140; note similarity to position of Pannenberg, *Systematic Theology*, 1:318-24. Note that Jenson and Pannenberg cite each other for this point!

[91] See *ST* 1:160-61.

[92] See *ST* 1:157, 159, 216-27; *ST* 2:173.

[93] *ST* 1:66, italics mine; see also *ST* 1:159-60.

[94] Robert W. Jenson, "What Kind of God Can Make a Covenant?" in *Covenant and Hope: Christian and Jewish Reflections*, ed. Robert W. Jenson and Eugene B. Korn (Grand Rapids: Eerdmans, 2012), 12.

interpretive arguments on which these predicates are based, our discussion may be brief.

First, according to Jenson, the gospel's sort of God is an *event*:
"History occurs not only *in* him but *as* his being."[95] Because Jesus'
being is an historical one—one that is constituted *through* time
and *at* death—so is God's. For God just *is* the Father of Jesus
Christ by the dramatic occurrence of raising the dead Jesus by the
Spirit's power.

Second, the gospel's sort of God is thoroughly *personal,* and that
in two senses.[96] God is personal in the modern idealist sense of a
"subsisting *self*-consciousness."[97] More specifically, God's personhood is constituted in the threefold structure of the Father's *singular*
self-consciousness. The Father's "transcendental unity of appercep-
tion" perceives his objectified self (his "I") in the man Jesus and is
liberated to accept himself as the Father of Jesus by the Spirit.[98] God
is also personal in that his being is constituted by the dialogical, interpersonal relationships of his *three* subsistent social relations.[99] The
definition of *person* assumed here: "a person is one with whom other
persons . . . can *converse,* whom they can *address.*"[100] It should be
noted that Jenson's notion of the *interpersonal* subjectivity of the
three undermines the charge that Jenson collapses the three "into a
single Christomonadic subject."[101]

In other words, God is personal because the personal *ousia* of the
Father actually coheres in the subsisting modes of *self*-reflection (in
the Son) and *self*-affirmation (by the Spirit) rather than falling apart
and because the three *hypostases* remain faithful to each other over
the course of their mutually constitutive, interactive, communicative

---

[95]*ST* 1:221.
[96]Ibid., 222. See also 123.
[97]Here Jenson self-consciously follows a trajectory set by Augustine and (to Jenson's mind nearly)
perfected by Hegel: *TI*, 130-38.
[98]*ST* 1:120-21.
[99]Ibid., 117-19.
[100]Ibid.,117.
[101]Contra Brian K. Sholl, "On Robert Jenson's Trinitarian Thought," *Modern Theology* 18 (2002): 31.

relationships. Because God remains faithful to himself in both senses, his being is a hypostatic being.[102]

Third, the gospel's God "is a *decision*."[103] As the preceding discussion has demonstrated, God is personal in a radically voluntaristic sense. In the freedom of the Spirit, who is the Lord of possibility,[104] God the Father determines Jesus *as* the Son and thus reflexively determines himself *as* the Father of Jesus Christ. And so God *is* as God *decides*. This explains why the search for a list of divine "perfections" in Jenson's *Systematic Theology* is futile.[105] God's perfections are not timelessly true characterizations of the divine reality. Instead, God's perfections are simply the predicates we attribute to God as "speaking the gospel may from time to time require."[106] If anything, the one "unchanging" truth about God is that "God is himself the one absolute contingency,"[107] the contingency of his self-determining decision to be who and what he will be. Though Aristotle taught us to regard "liability to historical contingency . . . an ontological deficit," Jenson encourages us to consider it "an ontological perfection."[108] The Lord's *perfection* is his *freedom*[109] in the Spirit to become *our* loving Father in *this* Son Jesus. Furthermore, it is precisely God's *sort of freedom* that simultaneously requires us to affirm "*that* God could be otherwise the triune God" *and* forbids "us to say *how*."[110]

Fourth and finally, God according to the gospel "is a *conversation*."[111] The temporal infinity of the triune life unfolds in and by the distinctive *eloquence* of the trinitarian history. God *is* someone saying some-

---

[102] *ST* 1:222.
[103] Ibid.
[104] *TI*, 141. "Because God is the Spirit, anything can happen" (Jenson, "For Us," 82).
[105] But see Robert W. Jenson, "The Triune God," in *Christian Dogmatics*, ed. Carl E. Braaten and Robert W. Jenson (Philadelphia: Fortress, 1984), 1:79-191, esp. 181-91.
[106] *ST* 1:223.
[107] Jenson, "For Us," 77.
[108] *ST* 1:64.
[109] *TI*, 141.
[110] *TI*, 141, latter italics mine. But see now Jenson, "Once More the *Logos Asarkos*," *International Journal of Systematic Theology* 13 (2011): 131.
[111] *ST* 1:223.

thing to someone about something (Paul Ricoeur)—he *is* discourse. The matter *about* which the Father speaks is Jesus. *What* he says about him is, "This is my beloved Son," through the liberating power of the Holy Spirit.[112] Furthermore, Son and Spirit participate in the divine discourse as well, thus rendering the one God a glorious perichoresis of communication and communion.[113]

The good news, according to Jenson, is that we are invited to participate in the infinitely true, good and beautiful communication that *is* the triune life,[114] a communication that, in the end, is best described as "'pure' music."[115] The sinful dissonance of the story of God with his people is ultimately resolved in the harmony of the triune life, a harmony that is ordered to our deification. And just as the divine dramatic trialogue is finally best described under the aesthetic mode, so our deification is finally best described under the image suggested by Jonathan Edwards of "a society in the highest degree happy . . . sweetly singing to each other."[116] "The end" of God's triune saving ways "is music."[117] God *is* the beautiful harmony of our lives with his in Jesus by the Spirit.

CONCLUSION

In this and the preceding two chapters, we have surveyed the Jensonian theological landscape. In doing so, we have come to appreciate the hermeneutical and theological logic that undergirds Jenson's answer to the question regarding the relationship between God's being and God's evangelical action that governs the present study. Jenson's claim that the gospel's God must be identified by and with the events of the exodus and the evangel flows from a Nicene-narrative reading of the biblical names for God. This reading rests on the fundamental

---

[112]Ibid.
[113]Ibid., 223, 236.
[114]Ibid., 224-36.
[115]Ibid., 236.
[116]Jenson is quoting Jonathan Edwards (*ST* 2:369).
[117]*ST* 2:369.

hermeneutical judgment to grant primacy to the identification of God in the exodus, and also on the fundamental ontological judgment to interpret God's relationship with his people as a relationship that is "internal" to his being. As we have seen, this historicizing reading of the biblical narrative privileges eschatology over protology, as well as divine acts of rescue and exaltation over divine acts of condescending and self-giving, and results in the replacement of traditional trinitarian metaphysics with a revisionary trinitarian metaphysics that, to Jenson's mind, better accords with the gospel. Although much more could be said by way of summary analysis, it is required of a charitable reader not only to listen but also to exercise discernment. With this in mind, we turn therefore in part two to an evaluation of Jenson's theology of the gospel's God and to our own constructive response to the question of this study.

PART TWO

◆

TOWARD A CATHOLIC AND EVANGELICAL
ACCOUNT OF THE GOSPEL'S GOD

Following a lesson he credits to Barth's tutelage, Jenson's theology offers an "interpretation of God under rigorous obedience to the rule: God is in himself *precisely* what he is in the history between Jesus, and the one he called 'Father,' and us in their mutual Spirit."[1] In this lies one of his chief contributions to contemporary theology: Jenson demonstrates that a truly evangelical doctrine of the Trinity must account not only for the distinction between the *opera Trinitatis ad intra* and the *opera Trinitatis ad extra* but that it must also account for their positive relationship, even affinity. Jenson's theology presses us to show how the Trinity is the exemplary cause of the gospel.[2] And this pressure brings us back to the question that drives this book—the relationship between God's being Father, Son and Spirit and his covenantal self-determination to be our Father, through the Son, in the Spirit.

As I suggested in chapter one, our *quaestio* can be analyzed in terms of three distinct moments within God's unified movement of evangelical self-determination, moments that correspond to the three persons of the Trinity respectively. Accordingly, considering

---

[1]Robert W. Jenson, "Karl Barth," in *The Modern Theologians*, 2nd ed., ed. David F. Ford (Cambridge, MA: Blackwell, 1997), 31.

[2]See Karl Rahner's comments on Bonaventure in *The Trinity* (London: Burns and Oates, 2001), 10n5.

the relationship between God's being and God's evangelical self-determination requires us to consider the being of the triune God as the being of one who (1) eternally wills to relate to us as our God and Father, (2) executes that eternal will in history by becoming one of us through the incarnation of the Son, and (3) consummates that eternal will in the fellowship of the Holy Spirit. Put differently, we must consider how God's self-determining movement to *relate* to us, to *identify* with us, and to *perfect* us through fellowship with himself represents not the repudiation but the reliable expression of his trinitarian being.

The remaining chapters of this work will be devoted to dogmatic analysis of these three issues. In the present chapter, we will consider the relationship between God's being and his self-determination to become our Father. In chapter seven, we will consider the relationship between God's being and his self-determination to become a human being through the incarnation of the Son. In chapter eight, we will consider the relationship between God's being and his self-determination to perfect us in the fellowship of the Spirit. My approach in each instance will be one of indirect engagement with Jenson's construal of God according to the gospel. Rather than addressing his proposal point by point, I will sketch an alternative account of these three dimensions of God's evangelical self-determination, addressing critical points of divergence from Jenson's proposal along the way. Chapter nine will then take up Bruce McCormack's distinctly Reformed answer to our study's question, which is worthy of its own engagement in considering the relationship between the triune God and the gospel.

6

"A FATHER TO YOU"

God's Fatherly Self-Determination
in the Covenant of Grace

♦

"YOU, O LORD, ARE OUR FATHER":
RETRIEVING RELATIVE ATTRIBUTES

In the covenant of grace, God determines himself to be our God and Father: "I will be a father to you and you shall be sons and daughters to me, says the Lord Almighty" (2 Cor 6:18; also Ex 4:22; 2 Sam 7:14; Jn 20:17; Rev 21:7).[1] One of Karl Barth's greatest contributions to and conundrums for contemporary dogmatics concerns his observation that God's free decision in the covenant of grace to create, reconcile and perfect a people for himself says something not only about the status of human being but also about the status of divine being. When God freely determines that Israel and the church will be his people, he also freely determines to be God as their God. The question is: How does God's free self-determination to be our God affect his being? What sort of being must this God have who eternally wills to be the "friend and benefactor" of his creature?[2] As

---

[1]Johannes Wollebius: "The giving of the covenant of grace is the act by which God promises himself as a father in Christ to the elect, if they live in filial obedience." *Reformed Dogmatics,* ed. and trans. John W. Beardslee (Eugene, OR: Wipf & Stock, 2009), 117.
[2]*CD* 2.2:26.

we have already seen, Christian dogmatics after Barth continues to debate this issue with great passion and rigor.

Perhaps the first thing to stress is that the issue at stake here does not concern *whether* God freely enters into significant, self-determining relationships with his creatures. Indeed, as Augustine and Thomas both observe, God is constituted a king only insofar as he has a creaturely servant to whom he may relate as king.[3] The two terms of this relationship are mutually correlative. Only where both *relata* are present do we have a king-servant relationship. Moreover, because one party of this relationship is a temporal creature, God's *being* king is in some sense only ever a being in the act of *becoming* king in history. Indeed, the temporal *existence* of the creature is foundational to the temporal *relationship* between the creature and God.[4] "Certainly it happened to God in time to be . . . the lord of man," says Augustine.[5] For this reason, it is entirely appropriate to speak of God's "narrative identity." Holy Scripture proclaims the unfolding story of God's identity, the story whereby God becomes "our God."

Bruce Marshall resists ascribing events in the economy of salvation to God's identity because he is concerned that doing so makes those events necessary to God's identity and thereby robs them of their free and gracious character.[6] According to Marshall, we must differentiate between properties which "identify" God (i.e., those which allows us to distinguish God from other persons and things) and those which belong to God's "identity" (i.e., those which must be true of God for him to be God).[7] On this scheme, events in the

---

[3]Augustine, *Trinity* 5.17; Thomas Aquinas, *Summa theologiae* 1a.13. 7; see also 1a.34. 3 ad 2.

[4]Steven A. Long, *Analogia Entis: On the Analogy of Being, Metaphysics, and the Act of Faith* (Notre Dame, IN: University of Notre Dame Press, 2011), 71.

[5]Augustine, *Trinity* 5.17. Thomas's refutation of those who would deny the existence of a temporal relation between God and his creatures in *Summa theologiae* 1a.13.7 begins with a reference to the above cited passage from Augustine.

[6]Marshall, *Trinity and Truth* (Cambridge: Cambridge University Press, 2000), 26-28, 38-43, 261-65.

[7]Ibid., 26.

economy of salvation help us to identify God, but they do not belong to his identity.

Marshall's concern to preserve both the freedom of God and the gratuity of creation is certainly commendable. However, his distinction between "identification" and "identity," as he draws it, is not completely satisfying. The problem with this approach is that it employs a definition of identity that is stricter than the one we often presuppose in otherwise well-ordered speech about God and human persons. If "personal identity" provides the answer to the question, "Who is he/she?" then it seems awkward to deny that "our Father" is a legitimate answer to the question, "Who is God?" Though being "our Father" is not a property that must be true of God the Father in order for him to be God the Father (contra modalism), it does seem to be a property that belongs to his identity. "You, O Lord, are our Father, our Redeemer from of old is your name" (Is 63:16).

Marshall is certainly right that many of the properties that constitute someone's personal identity are necessarily true of that person. Some properties are "true of person *x* in order for him or her to be *x*."[8] Furthermore, not every property that is contingently true of a person is constitutive of his or her personal identity (e.g., waking up at 7:17 on Monday morning).[9] For this reason, it *is* legitimate to distinguish those properties by which we may "identify" a person from those which constitute a person's "identity." The problem remains, however, that Marshall's definition of personal identity seems too restrictive. Personal identity seems to include not only those properties which must be true of person *x* for him or her to be *x*, but also some properties which are *contingently* true of person *x*.[10] Personal identity seems

---

[8]Ibid. For purposes of the present discussion, it is not necessary to specify what it is that grounds the necessary properties of creatures.

[9]The example is Marshall's (ibid., 27). See also Boethius, *De trinitate* 4.44-53 in *The Theological Tractates and The Consolation of Philosophy*, trans. H. F. Stewart, E. K. Rand and S. J. Tester (Cambridge, MA: Harvard University Press, 1978), 20-21.

[10]Similarly Edwin Christian van Driel, *Incarnation Anyway: Arguments for Supralapsarian Christology* (Oxford: Oxford University Press, 2008), 97-98.

to include both natural and contingent properties.[11]

In the present context, a "contingent property" refers to a category broader than what is traditionally described as an "accident." Following Augustine, we may describe an accident as a contingent property "that inheres in a subject and that can be lost by a change of that reality to which it pertains, or something that inheres in a subject and that, though not lost, is capable of increase or decrease, or something that inheres in a subject and that, though inseparable from that subject, is lost through the destruction of that subject."[12] On this understanding, God has no accidents. However, also following Augustine, we may say that God has contingent properties which do not qualify as accidents.[13] Such properties do not refer to God's *being* but rather to God's *relationships* to those (contingent) beings which are external to his being (e.g., God's being "king").[14] To borrow the traditional idiom, God has "relative properties/attributes."[15]

An example of such a contingent but nevertheless identity-constituting property is "being married."[16] That *x* is married to *y* is a contingent property, not a natural one. It is not something that must be true of person *x* in order for him or her to be *x*. Nevertheless, if *x* is married to *y*, then "being married" is a property that belongs to *x*'s personal identity. Far from being an incidental feature of one's personal existence, marriage is an act of *self*-determination if ever there

---

[11]The language of divine "properties" is not without its liabilities in the doctrine of God. The divine perfections do not refer to something that God has but to the truth regarding who and what God is. However, as we will see, the language of divine properties is necessary in the doctrine of God, at least in certain cases, as biblical speech about the reality of God requires us to make affirmations that are *true* about God but which nevertheless do not refer to God in terms of his perfect *being* but rather in terms of the *relationships* that he perfects with his creatures.

[12]Roland J. Teske, *To Know God and the Soul: Essays on the Thought of Saint Augustine* (Washington, DC: Catholic University of America Press, 2008), 99-100. See Augustine, *Trinity* 5.3-5.

[13]See Augustine, *Trinity* 5.17.

[14]See further Teske, *To Know God*, chap. 5.

[15]Colin Gunton worries that "the effect of distinguishing between the absolute and relative attributes" is "the effective division of God's being from the persons of the Trinity." *Act and Being: Towards a Theology of the Divine Attributes* (Grand Rapids: Eerdmans, 2003), 92. I hope to demonstrate below that this is anything but the case.

[16]This example is particularly apt because marriage is a biblical type of God's covenant relationship with his people.

was one, for marriage is an act in which one commits oneself to a particular form of permanence in time (a key feature of personal identity), namely, that of faithfulness to one's word.[17] Moreover, faithfulness to one's marital bond is a form of personal identity that is invariably constituted *in relation to* another person. Being married, then, is a form of personal identity that is not natural but chosen, pertaining not to one's essence but to one's interpersonal relationships and binding obligations. Being married, on this description, is an instance of what we might call *covenant identity*.[18]

Acknowledging this point helps us better appreciate the issue at hand. When it comes to God's identity as "our God," the issue does not concern whether God can freely enter into binding relationships with his creatures or whether God has a narrative identity. In the covenant of grace, God pledges and gives *himself* to us, not simply a set of benefits and blessings that are external to God: *he* is our portion, our lot, and our inheritance (Ps 16:5-6).[19] In so doing, God constitutes himself as "our God." Moreover, this relationship of self-giving has a history. To paraphrase Augustine, certainly it happens in time that we receive the gift of having God as our God.

The issue, then, is not whether God enters into significant, self-determining relationships with his creatures. The issue is rather how those relationships affect his being. Does the fact that God's *narrative* or *covenant identity* (i.e., his identity as "our God") is constituted by faithfulness to his people through time entail that God's *being* is constituted by faithfulness through time, as Jenson repeatedly

---

[17]See Paul Ricoeur, *Oneself as Another,* trans. Kathleen Blamey (Chicago: University of Chicago Press, 1994), 118, 123-25. Jenson rightly emphasizes this dimension of the triune identity. See *ST* 1:217, 222, etc.

[18]The present analysis comports well with Gordon Hugenberger's widely accepted definition of covenant. According to Hugenberger, "A covenant, in its normal sense, is an elected, as opposed to natural, relationship of obligation under oath." *Marriage as a Covenant: Biblical Law and Ethics as Developed from Malachi* (Grand Rapids: Baker, 1998), 11. On this definition, a covenant thus involves: (1) a relationship (2) with a non-relative (3) that involves obligations and (4) is established through an oath (215).

[19]See Francis Turretin's rich discussion of the present point, *Institutes of Elenctic Theology,* trans. George Musgrave Giger, ed. James T. Dennison Jr. (Phillipsburg, NJ: P & R, 1992-1997), 2:180-81.

affirms?[20] According to Augustine and Thomas, God's self-determination to be king of the creature, though constituting a relationship
that does not hold apart from the history of the creature's existence
as servant, in no way affects the being of the God who so determines
himself to be the king of the creature. Augustine explains:

> Lord, says the psalm, you have become our refuge (Ps 90:1). God is
> called our refuge by way of relationship; the name has reference to us.
> And he becomes our refuge when we take refuge in him. Does this
> mean that something happens then in his nature, which was not there
> before we took refuge in him? No, the change takes place in us; we
> were worse before we took refuge in him, and we become better by
> taking refuge in him. But in him, no change at all. So too, he begins
> to be our Father when we are born again by his grace, because *He gave
> us the right to become sons of God* (Jn 1:12). So our substance changes
> for the better when we are made his sons; at the same time he begins
> to be our Father, but without any change in his substance.[21]

God's gracious relationship to his creature, in other words, is truly a
mutual, binding relationship.[22] Nevertheless, this relationship is one
wherein the ontological change brought about by that relationship is
wholly asymmetrical.[23] In this "mixed" relationship, God remains who

[20]See, for example, Jenson, "The Triune God," in *Christian Dogmatics*, ed. Carl E. Braaten and
Robert W. Jenson (Philadelphia: Fortress, 1984), 1:116.
[21]Augustine, *Trinity* 5.17. See also Peter Lombard, *The Sentences, Book 1: The Mystery of the Trinity*,
Mediaeval Sources in Translation 42, trans. Giulio Silano (Toronto: Pontifical Institute of Mediaeval Studies, 2007), 30.1; Jerome Zanchius, *De natura Dei* 1.10.9. Turretin states: "Relative attributes do not argue composition, but distinction. The formal nature of relations is not to be in,
but to be to. Nor do they superadd a new perfection to the essence, but only imply a habitude of
the essence to other things. Paternity and dominion do not render him another being, but in a
different manner dispose the possessor without superinducing a change in him" (*Institutes* 1:193).
[22]This point must be asserted, contrary to common misunderstandings regarding Thomas's denial
of a "real relationship" between God and the world (*Summa theologiae* 1a.13.7). For a clear refutation of this common misunderstanding together with a proper explanation of what Thomas
means in denying a real relationship between God and the world, see Merold Westphal, "Temporality and Finitism in Hartshorne's Theism," *The Review of Metaphysics* 19 (1966): 550-64; see
also Herbert McCabe, "Aquinas on the Trinity," in *Silence and the Word: Negative Theology and
Incarnation*, ed. Oliver Davies and Denys Turner (Cambridge: Cambridge University Press:
2002), 82-84.
[23]David Burrell, following Sara Grant, calls it a "non-reciprocal relation of dependence" in "Creation, Metaphysics, and Ethics," *Faith and Philosophy* 18 (2001): 213.

and what he is whereas the creature is changed, and that for the better.

As we have seen, Jenson fears that the "externality" of such a relationship between God and the world, requires a theology illumined by the gospel to sacrifice too much.[24] A God whose being remains unaltered by his relationship to the world, he fears, must also remain distant from the world and thus unable to move history forward to its blessed consummation in God. Such a God, Jenson believes, cannot be the God of Abraham, Isaac and Jacob. As our quote from Augustine suggests, however, this fear is unfounded. The fact that God's being remains unaltered in his relationship to his people does not necessarily mean that God is distant from his people or that he is unable to change his people. To put it in a slightly different way, saying "God is not necessarily related to his people" is not the same thing as saying "God is necessarily not related to his people." In fact, it is precisely the asymmetrical relationship between the being of God and the being of his people that determines the *sort* of change that God can bring about in his people by virtue of his self-determination to befriend and accompany them in the economy of salvation.

THE ETERNALLY RICH GOD AND
THE ECONOMY OF GRACE

To grasp the point, we may look to the theology of Irenaeus. Irenaeus is instructive on the present issue because of his consistent attention to Scripture's developmental economy of creation and salvation. According to Irenaeus, this economy has a goal, namely, "the growth of man into the immortality of God."[25] Moreover, time is essential to this economy because "only things which are subject to time can grow, and have the possibility of changing their mode of existence while remaining what they are by nature."[26]

---

[24]See *ST* 1:75.

[25]John Behr, *Asceticism and Anthropology in Irenaeus and Clement* (Oxford: Oxford University Press, 2000), 42.

[26]Behr, *Asceticism*, 43.

Irenaeus represents a striking contrast to Jenson on this issue precisely because he insists that one must understand both the necessity of temporal *change* in the creature and the *unchangeable* perfection of the Trinity if one is to understand properly the *nature* of the saving economy, which is the story of God with us. For Irenaeus, it is a first principle of the doctrine of creation that "in this respect God differs from man, that God . . . is always the same; but that which is made must receive both beginning, and middle, and addition, and increase" (see Ps 102:25-27). Later he states: "God is truly perfect in all things, himself equal and similar to himself . . . but man receives advancement and increase toward God."[27] Irenaeus thus distinguishes God, the unalterably perfect One, from the creature, who stands in need of God's perfecting work.

According to Irenaeus, moreover, God "is rich, perfect, and in need of nothing"[28] precisely insofar as he is the triune God.[29] Commenting on John 17:5, he states: "In the beginning, therefore, did God form Adam, not as if he stood in need of man. . . . For not alone antecedently to Adam, but also before all creation, the Word glorified his Father, as he did himself declare, 'Father, glorify thou me with the glory which I had with thee before the world was.'"[30] Because God is Father, Son and Holy Spirit, he stands in need of nothing from his creatures but remains forever rich, perfect and glorious in and of himself.

The doctrine of divine self-sufficiency, to which Irenaeus appeals, is deeply rooted in Scripture and tradition. The triune God is inherently rich, "the everlasting well of all good things which is never drawn dry."[31] To the gospel's "blessed God" (1 Tim 1:11) belong the immea-

---

[27]Irenaeus, *Against Heresies* 4.11.2; see also 2.2.4.
[28]Ibid., 4.14.1. On this theme in Irenaeus, see Eric Osborn, *Irenaeus of Lyon* (Cambridge: Cambridge University Press, 2001), 28-31.
[29]For an excellent exposition of the relationship between Trinity and aseity in Irenaeus, see D. Jeffrey Bingham, "Christianizing Divine Aseity: Irenaeus Reads John," in *Gospel of John and Christian Theology*, ed. Richard Bauckham and Carl Mosser (Grand Rapids: Eerdmans, 2008), 53-67.
[30]Irenaeus, *Against Heresies* 4.14.1.
[31]Heinrich Bullinger, *The Decades of Heinrich Bullinger: The First and Second Decades* (Cambridge: The University Press, 1859), 216.

surable fullness of greatness, power, glory, victory and majesty, an immeasurable fullness that God enjoys in and of himself (1 Chron 29:11; Ps 145:3; Jn 5:26; Rom 11:33-35).[32] The divine works *ad extra* are consequently the free and generous overflow of God's fontal plenitude (Ps 36:8-9; Jn 1:4; 5:21-25; Rom 11:33-36; Jas 1:17). Because all that humankind is and has comes from God, nothing that humankind offers to God enriches him in any way: God is not "served by human hands, as though he needed anything, since he himself gives to all mankind life and breath and everything" (Acts 17:25; see also 1 Chron 29:14, 16; Rom 11:35).[33] Indeed, if *per impossibile* God had a need, he would not tell us, for even then he remains rich enough to take care of himself (Ps 50:7-12; see also Is 40:16-17).[34]

For our present purposes it is important to observe that, according to Irenaeus, God's self-sufficiency does not isolate him from his people.[35] Instead, it is his self-sufficiency which explains the *kind of fellowship* that unfolds in the economy of salvation between God and his people. It is precisely God's identity as "the eternally rich God"[36] that constitutes the economy of salvation as an economy of radically superfluous grace, whereby God grants "communion with himself to those who stood in need of it . . . sketching out like an architect, the plan of salvation to those that pleased him."[37] The economy of salvation is one that flows from the all-sufficient, unchanging triune God of grace for the sake of the changeable creature's growth and enrich-

---

[32]For a recent statement of what it means for God to possess this immeasurable fullness of perfection "in and of himself," see John Webster, "Life in and of Himself: Reflections on God's Aseity," in *Engaging the Doctrine of God: Contemporary Protestant Perspectives*, ed. Bruce L. McCormack (Grand Rapids: Baker Academic, 2008), 107-24.

[33]See Anselm, *Proslogion*, trans. M. J. Charlesworth (Oxford: Clarendon, 1965): "He is the supreme good needing no other and is he whom all things have need of for their being and well-being" (103).

[34]*CD* 2.1:283.

[35]Compare with Jenson: "God is not personal in that he is triunely self-sufficient; he is personal in that he triunely opens himself" (*ST* 1:124).

[36]"The eternally rich God" is one of Barth's favorite descriptions of God. The description is drawn from the second stanza of Martin Rinckart's hymn, "Now Thank We All Our God." See Karl Barth, *Letters 1961-1968*, trans. Geoffrey W. Bromiley (Grand Rapids: Eerdmans, 1981), 176.

[37]Irenaeus, *Against Heresies* 4.14.1-2.

ment through union and communion with God.[38]

The *distinction* between an unchangeably blessed Trinity and a changeable creature thus determines the kind of *relation* that unfolds between the triune God and his creature in the covenant of grace.[39] Only because the triune God is wholly and absolutely sufficient unto himself can he be the author of an economy of grace.[40] Because the choice to create "was not motivated by any need of completion in the one who let it be" can creation be a work of "incomparable generosity."[41] Moreover, only because the creature is subject to change and growth can it be the recipient of an endless increase unto glory. It "takes time"[42] for the economy of salvation to unfold because it takes time for creatures to receive the fullness of blessing that flows from having the eternally rich God as "our Father."

The preceding discussion therefore suggests that Jenson's proposal operates on the basis of a false dilemma. As George Hunsinger observes, Jenson seems to equate "commitment with strong dependence, as if a metaphysically independent God could not freely commit himself to the world, or as if God's free commitment to the world necessarily made him dependent upon it for the constitution of his metaphysical identity."[43] Fortunately, as we have seen, these are not the only alternatives.

At this point it is also worth noting a systemic ambiguity in Jen-

[38]Behr, *Asceticism*, 37. See also Irenaeus, *On the Apostolic Preaching* 75.

[39]See Norris: "What makes God *different* from every creature—his eternal and ingenerate simplicity—is thus, for Irenaeus, precisely what assures his direct and intimate *relation* with every creature." R. A. Norris, *God and World in Early Christian Theology* (New York: Seabury, 1965), 70.

[40]Thus Paul Molnar, *Divine Freedom and the Doctrine of the Immanent Trinity: In Dialogue with Karl Barth and Contemporary Theology* (London: T & T Clark, 2002), 63, 72, 312, et passim.

[41]Robert Sokolowski, *The God of Faith and Reason* (Notre Dame: University of Notre Dame Press, 1982), 34; see also John of Damascus, *The Orthodox Faith* 2.2; Turretin, *Institutes*, 1:219-20.

[42]Eugene Rogers, *After the Spirit: A Constructive Pneumatology from Resources Outside the Modern West* (Grand Rapids: Eerdmans, 2005), 183; see also Osborn, *Irenaeus*, 168. Of course, creatureliness is not the *only* reason that the economy of salvation takes time. Sin affects the temporal economy as well, often *delaying* the reception of God's blessings. Consider Israel's forty years in the wilderness or the Danielic extension of Jeremiah's seventy years.

[43]George Hunsinger, "Robert Jenson's *Systematic Theology*: A Review Essay," *Scottish Journal of Theology* 55 (2002): 177. According to Jenson, an extrinsic relation between God and his creatures necessarily entails his immunity to the events of the gospel (see *ST* 1:75, 124).

son's proposal.[44] Jenson asserts that God determines who and what
he will be by determining to be the God of his people, and thus determines to realize his being along the same dramatic historical-
developmental axis as that of his people.[45] But he also affirms in certain places that God could or would have been the same God that he
is *apart from* his people.[46] These statements are difficult, if not impossible, to reconcile. The former assertion seems to bear the structural
weight of his theological system, whereas the latter seems to function
as a formally decorous, but—in terms of the system—meaningless,
add-on.[47] As Hart observes, if "the love that is the ground of creation
would without creation be fully actual in the triune life,"[48] then creation might *display* the fully actual love of the triune life—and, we
should add, it might provide an occasion for the *inclusion* of some of
its creatures within the fully actual love of the triune life, but creation
could never *determine* the fully actual love of the triune life.[49] If, as
Jenson suggests, the triune God *would* be the same God apart from
creation, then he *is* the same God apart from creation.[50]

More idiomatic for Jensonian discourse is his assertion that the
being of God is determined by the *decision* of God to be the Father of
the human Jesus through the Spirit, that God has in fact determined
to be in this way but that God could have determined to be in some

---

[44]Similarly David Bentley Hart, *The Beauty of the Infinite: The Aesthetics of Christian Truth* (Grand Rapids: Eerdmans, 2003), 162-63.

[45]*ST* 1:64-65.

[46]See, for example, ibid., 65, 141.

[47]As noted earlier, Jenson has recently conceded this point: "The sentence 'How would the Trinity have been the Trinity if God had not created a world, and there had therefore been no creature Jesus to be the Son, or had let the fallen creation go, with the same result?' is often taken for a real question. . . . In the past I have sometimes responded to the supposed question, saying that God would presumably have somehow been the same triune God that he is, but that we can say nothing further about that 'somehow.' I now think that even this response concedes too much to our unbaptized notion of time, by supposing that the collection of words quoted at the beginning of this paragraph actually makes a question which one can answer, however sparingly. It has now dawned on me that the putative question is nonsense, and so therefore is my previous attempt to respond to it." Robert W. Jenson "Once More the *Logos Asarkos*," *International Journal of Systematic Theology* 13 (2011): 131.

[48]*ST* 2:28.

[49]Hart, *Beauty,* 162.

[50]Ibid.

other way.[51] In this peculiar sense God's nature is *a se*—"from himself." "God is the subject who determines his own nature. . . . He himself determines what sort of being he is."[52] The ontological grounding for this view of self-existence is Jenson's understanding of divine "perfection," which consists in the "absolute contingency" of God's being.[53] God is perfect in that the contingent fact of his freely *willed* existence determines the *nature* of his existence.[54]

The problem with such a perspective is that if God's manner of being God is determined by his decision to be our God, then God's decision to be our God cannot be a decision to give God, for there is no antecedently existent God to be given.[55] One can have a developmental economy of salvation on Jenson's scheme where the history of the world is the drama of both God and the creature's quest for self-identity. But one cannot have a developmental economy of salvation on Jenson's scheme where the history of the world is the drama of triune *self-giving* for the sake of the creature's progress toward fellowship in the fully antecedent, fully realized triune *glory*. One cannot, in other words, truly have an economy of *grace*. The economy of salvation is not a pure gift on God's part if he does not have himself to give or if he has something to gain from the economy, that is, himself *Grace*, properly defined, must include within it a reference to God as both the absolute giver and the absolute gift and not merely a reference to the creature's receipt of unmerited favor. As Barth observes, "To say God is to say eternal benefit. . . . But in the covenant with man, as his God, he does not merely give out of his fulness. In his fulness he gives himself to be with man and for man. As the benefit which he is in himself, he makes himself the companion of man.

[51]For example, *ST* 1:215.
[52]*GAG*, 127.
[53]*ST*, 1:64; and Jenson, "For Us . . . He Was Made Man," in *Nicene Christianity: The Future for a New Ecumenism*, ed. Christopher R. Seitz (Grand Rapids: Brazos, 2001), 77.
[54]Jenson's view represents the creative reinterpretation (and reversal) of Thomas's understanding of divine simplicity as the identity of essence and existence.
[55]See Bruce D. Marshall, "*Ex Occidente Lux?* Aquinas and Eastern Orthodox Theology," *Modern Theology* 20 (2004): 33.

He does not merely give him something, however great. He gives himself, and in doing so gives him all things."[56]

There is an irony to Jenson's view, given his desire to vanquish any remnant of an unknown God from the shadows. According to his scheme, the gospel provides us with knowledge of what is only *a* particular instantiation of God. We know God as he *actually* is. What we do not, indeed cannot, know is the God who *possibly* could have been otherwise.[57] And here we must note that it is not a source of evangelical comfort that God's being could possibly have been otherwise. Only if God determines to be *for* his creatures in Jesus Christ the God that he unalterably and blessedly *is,* does the economy of salvation provide a gracious and true revelation of God in the fullness of his splendor.

"ONE AND THE SAME SIMPLE ACT": GOD'S FATHERLY WILL *AD INTRA* AND *AD EXTRA*

It is at this point that the doctrine of divine simplicity proves instructive for thinking about the nature of God's fatherly self-determination. Though some contemporary trinitarian theologians have questioned the coherence of divine simplicity with divine triunity,[58] historically it was the rejection of both doctrines that went hand in hand.[59] The doctrine of divine simplicity attempts to honor the name into which we are baptized: "the name of the Father and of the Son and of the Holy Spirit" (Mt 28:19; see also 1 Cor 8:6; Eph 4:4-6)—

---

[56]*CD* 4.1:40.

[57]*ST* 1:65.

[58]For example, Ted Peters, *God as Trinity: Relationality and Temporality in Divine Life* (Louisville: Westminster John Knox, 1993), 33. For a recent defense of the doctrine of simplicity against modern detractors, see Stephen R. Holmes, *Listening to the Past: The Place of Tradition in Theology* (Grand Rapids: Baker, 2002), chap. 4, "'Something Much Too Plain to Say': Towards a Defense of the Doctrine of Divine Simplicity"; and also Holmes, "A Simple Salvation? Soteriology and the Perfections of God," in *God of Salvation: Soteriology in Theological Perspective,* ed. Ivor J. Davidson and Murray A. Rae (Farnham: Ashgate, 2011), chap. 2. For Jenson's appropriation of divine simplicity, see *ST* 1:212-14.

[59]Turretin, for example, charges the Socinians with rejecting divine simplicity "for no other purpose than to weaken more easily the mystery of the Trinity" (*Institutes,* 1:191).

the name which proclaims that the Lord "is one and there is no other" (Mk 12:32; see also Is 42:8; 45:5-6, 14), and therefore that the only real distinctions within the one God are the distinctions between the three who share the singular being of the one God.[60] The doctrine of simplicity in turn also instructs us concerning the sort of perfection that characterizes these three who are one. Far from being an unrefined piece of Greek metaphysical thinking, the doctrine represents instead an intentional disassembling of Aristotelian categories in service of the biblical grammar of God.[61] The doctrine of divine simplicity teaches us how to speak of the one who radiates unmixed (1 Jn 1:5) and unchanging light (Jas 1:17) from the resources of his own intrinsic and indivisible life (Jn 1:4; 5:26; 14:6) and therefore forbids us from applying to God the composition and division that characterize the being of the creature.[62] In short, the doctrine of divine simplicity teaches us to confess that "God is simply and entirely God" (see Ex 3:14).[63]

How does the doctrine of divine simplicity inform our understanding of God's fatherly self-determination? Because God is not susceptible to composition or division, his will to be *God*—the "will of complacency" (whereby God delights in being the God he is) as well as that will's tripersonal expression in the *voluntas personalis* (whereby the Father delights in being the Father of the Son, and so

---

[60]For the role of divine simplicity within Augustine's trinitarian theology, see Lewis Ayres, *Nicaea and Its Legacy: An Approach to Fourth-Century Trinitarian Theology* (Oxford: Oxford University Press, 2004), chap. 15, esp. 372-83. For the role of divine simplicity in thirteenth- and fourteenth-century trinitarian theology, see Russell L. Friedman, *Medieval Trinitarian Thought from Aquinas to Ockham* (Cambridge: Cambridge University Press, 2010), chaps. 3-4.

[61]Thus explicitly Boethius, *De trinitate* 4.1-9, in *The Theological Tractates and The Consolation of Philosophy*, trans. H. F. Stewart, E. K. Rand and S. J. Tester (Cambridge, MA: Harvard University Press, 1978): "There are in all ten categories which can be universally predicated of all things, namely, Substance, Quality, Quantity, Relation, Place, Time, Condition, Situation, Activity, Passivity. . . . But when any one turns these to predication of God, all the things that can be predicated are changed" (17). It is worth emphasizing at this point that this rule also applies to the category of "substance" (see *De trinitate* 4.14-16)—so much for "substance metaphysics"!

[62]In Gregory of Nyssa's thought, divine simplicity functions especially to emphasize the *unmixed* nature of God's manifold perfections. See Andrew Radde-Gallwitz, *Basil of Caesarea, Gregory of Nyssa, and the Transformation of Divine Simplicity* (Oxford: Oxford University Press, 2009).

[63]Boethius, *De trinitate* 4.34 (19).

forth)—is not other than his will to be *our* God and Father.[64] Because "the will of God is the willing God himself," there can be "but one will of God," says Wilhelmus à Brakel.[65] "God wills himself and his creatures with one and the same simple act."[66]

Two consequences follow from this affirmation. First, there can be no God "behind" God the Father who does not yet will to be our God and Father. God's will is not secondary or adventitious to God's being. God's eternal *being* is an eternal *willing*. With Jenson, we must affirm that God's being is voluntive being through and through. Second, therefore, the only distinction we can make with respect to God's eternal fatherly will is the distinction between the *objects* of that will:[67] for the sake of the present discussion, God's eternal Son on the one hand, and God's creaturely children on the other. This distinction, however, is one that we must make.

With respect to the first object of his eternal fatherly will, the Father *naturally and necessarily* delights in being the Father of the Son. He does so naturally because, as Father, he is inherently generative, fecund and radiant.[68] He *is* "the Father of lights" (Jas 1:17) who by nature radiates "a coeternal, coequal and consubstantial splendor,"[69] a Son who is "the effulgence of his glory and the exact imprint of his being" (Heb 1:3, my translation).[70] The Father necessarily delights in

---

[64]On which, see Richard A. Muller, *Post-Reformation Reformed Dogmatics* (Grand Rapids: Baker, 2003), 3:453.

[65]Wilhelmus à Brakel, *The Christian's Reasonable Service*, trans. Bartel Elshout, ed. Joel R. Beeke (Grand Rapids: Reformation Heritage Books, 1992-1995), 1:112-13.

[66]Herman Bavinck, *Reformed Dogmatics*, trans. John Vriend (Grand Rapids: Baker, 2004), 2:233. Similarly, Turretin, *Institutes*, 1:193.

[67]Turretin, *Institutes*, 1:218; Brakel, *Christian's Reasonable Service*, 1:113.

[68]Bavinck, *Reformed Dogmatics*, 2:308-310.

[69]Bonaventure, *The Tree of Life* 1.1, in *Bonaventure—The Soul's Journey to God, The Tree of Life, The Life of Saint Francis*, trans. Ewert Cousins (Mahwah, NJ: Paulist, 1978), 126. See also Bonaventure, *Breviloquium*, Works of Saint Bonaventure, vol. 9 (St. Bonaventure, NY: The Franciscan Institute, 2005), 1.3.1-8.

[70]For the exegesis which maintains that Hebrews 1:3 entails an ontological claim regarding the Son, see Lane Tipton, "Christology in Colossians 1:15-20 and Hebrews 1:1-4: An Exercise in Biblico-Systematic Theology," in *Resurrection and Eschatology: Theology in Service of the Church, Essays in Honor of Richard B. Gaffin, Jr.*, ed. Lane G. Tipton and Jeffrey C. Waddington (Phillipsburg: Presbyterian and Reformed, 2008), 177-202; also John Webster, "One Who Is Son: Theological Reflections on the Exordium to the Epistle to the Hebrews," in *The Epistle to the*

being the Father of the Son because the Son is supremely delightful, "the first lovely thing that ever was."[71] Indeed, the title "beloved Son" refers not only to the second person's role in the economy of salvation but also to his status as the eternal object of the Father's love "before the foundation of the world" (Jn 17:24; see also Prov 8:30). Though natural and necessary, eternal generation nevertheless remains a free and spontaneous act insofar as the Father does not generate the Son due to external compulsion, against either his nature or his will, or due to internal indigence or defect.[72] The Father's eternal generation of the Son is *per modum naturae, concomitante voluntate*.[73] Thus states Bonaventure: "The supreme charity in the producer and the supreme goodness in that which is produced . . . necessarily include in themselves the will of complacency."[74]

What, then, of the second object of God's eternal fatherly will, that is, the creature he wills to adopt? The same Father who naturally and necessarily delights in being the eternal Father of the eternal Son, in the same eternal act of sovereign spontaneity, *contingently* desires to be the Father of his people as well. The latter contingent object of the Father's will logically presupposes the former necessary object of the Father's will insofar as the *possibility* of the Father's loving relation to us is inherent in the *actuality* of the Father's loving relation to the Son. In traditional terms, the Father's natural and necessary love for the Son is the exemplary cause of our adoption as creaturely sons and daughters. (In Barthian terms, we might say that the Father's natural and necessary love for the Son constitutes his "readiness" to love his

---

Hebrews and Christian Theology, ed. Richard Bauckham, Daniel R. Driver, Trevor A. Hart and Nathan MacDonald (Grand Rapids: Eerdmans, 2009), 69-94.

[71]Richard Sibbes, *A Description of Christ* in *Works of Richard Sibbes*, ed. Alexander B. Grosart (Edinburgh: Banner of Truth, 1979 [1862-64]), 1:11.

[72]Bonaventure, *Disputed Questions on the Mystery of the Trinity: An Introduction and Translation*, intro. and trans. Zachary Hayes, Works of Saint Bonaventure, vol. 3 (St. Bonaventure, NY: The Franciscan Institute, 1979), 7.a.1. See also Peter Lombard, *Sentences* 6.

[73]This is in contrast to the Father and the Son's eternal breathing forth of the Spirit, which is *per modum voluntatis, concomitante natura*. On the significance of both phrases, see Zachary Hayes, "Bonaventure's Trinitarian Theology in General," chap. 2 in Bonaventure, *Disputed Questions*.

[74]Bonaventure, *Disputed Questions* 7.a. 2.

creaturely children.)[75] Furthermore, the Father's natural and necessary love for the Son is the final cause of our adoption as well. The goal of the entire economy of salvation *ad extra* is that the Father's beloved Son might become preeminent as the firstborn among many brothers and sisters (Rom 8:29; Col 1:15-16; Heb 1:2), who are themselves destined for blessing "to the praise of his glorious grace . . . in the Beloved" (Eph 1:6; see also Jn 17:5, 24-26).[76]

Paul Molnar wonders: "If God's election has always taken place, how then can it be construed as a decision; does it not then become a necessity?"[77] The answer is that, while God's *act of willing* is eternal and necessary (the latter insofar as God's act of willing is never in potency but is pure actuality—there is no undeciding God), the *objects* of his will *ad extra* (including his self-determining relationship to those objects) are not ontologically necessary.[78] Rather, their existence is contingent on his free decision to enact them from among the infinite possibilities of his wise power. Moreover, God's free decision concerning these *ad extra* objects is one that he could have refrained from making and that could have been significantly different from the actual decision that he made, though not in a manner inconsistent with his perfect fatherly wisdom and goodness. Whatever decision God *could* have made concerning the objects of his decree, he *would* have made it as "the Father of lights," with whose radiant goodness "there is no variation or shadow due to change" (Jas 1:17). In this sense, then, God eternally but contingently wills the *ad extra* objects of his will.

Although the nature of God's free decree concerning all things

---

[75]*CD* 2.1:273, 280; *CD* 2.2:175; with Justin Stratis, "Speculating about Divinity? God's Immanent Life and Actualistic Ontology," *International Journal of Systematic Theology* 12 (2010): 20-32.
[76]Note: The distinction between objects of God's love that are "eternally natural/necessary" objects of his love versus those that are "eternally free/contingent" objects of his love is thus more precise than Torrance's (true but imprecise) distinction between God's being "always Father" versus his being "not always Creator," a distinction to which Molnar repeatedly appeals. See, for example, Paul Molnar, *Thomas F. Torrance: Theologian of the Trinity* (Farnham: Ashgate, 2009), 73.
[77]Molnar, *Divine Freedom*, 62.
[78]Turretin, *Institutes*, 1:220: "Although every volition in God is eternal, yet they ought not immediately to be called absolutely necessary. For what is necessary originally on the part of the principle can be free terminatively and on the part of the object." See also 1:193.

outside of God is a matter of perennial debate, I believe the position outlined above represents a consistent application not only of the doctrine of God but also of the doctrine of creation *ex nihilo.* If God could not have refrained from creating, then we are not dealing with a doctrine of creation but with a doctrine of emanation. Furthermore, if God could not have created a world significantly different from the world that he actually made, then the contingency of his creative act is violated—if this is the *best* of all possible worlds, then it is the *only* possible world.[79] With respect to the present topic, it seems to me also that understanding God's free decree in this manner is vital to preserving the distinction between the procession of creatures from God and the procession of the Son from the Father, a key feature of Nicene Christianity.

In summary, therefore, God's free self-determination to be our God and Father is not the choice of a blind and formless deity. Neither is it the necessary emanation of the divine being. God's free self-determination to be our God is his *fatherly* self-determination, the self-determination he freely makes *as* the one he unchangeably is: the eternal Father of the eternal Son. The covenant of grace, wherein God swears, "I will be a father to you" (2 Cor 6:18), is the free *and* fitting overflow of God's eternal fatherly love for the Son, the end of which is to include his elect children in God's eternal fatherly love for the Son, *soli Deo gloria.*

CONCLUSION

Question twenty-six of the Heidelberg Catechism asks: "What believest thou when thou sayest, 'I believe in God the Father, Almighty, Maker of heaven and earth'?" The answer is: "That the eternal Father of our Lord Jesus Christ . . . is for the sake of Christ his Son, my God and my Father."[80] That God is "the eternal Father of . . . his Son" and

---

[79]J. Martin Bac, *Perfect Will Theology: Divine Agency in Reformed Scholasticism as Against Suárez, Episcopius, Descartes, and Spinoza* (Leiden: Brill, 2010), 413-14.
[80]Cited from Philip Schaff, ed., *The Creeds of Christendom* (repr. Grand Rapids: Baker, 1996), 3:315.

that he is "my God and my Father" are both true statements about God's fatherly identity. However, they are true for different reasons. The first is naturally and necessarily true. The second is covenantally and contingently true. Moreover, rendering a clear *distinction* between these two identity descriptions enables us to grasp their proper *relation*. And it is their relation which indicates the supreme blessing of the covenant of grace: *What God is in himself as Father he wills also to be for us*[81]—not in order to perfect his fatherhood but in order to communicate and manifest his perfect fatherly goodness and glory to us.[82] In this sense, we may even say that God's perfection as Father *includes* the perfecting of his creaturely children as well.[83]

---

[81]Hart, *Beauty*, 158n5.

[82]See Thomas Aquinas, *Summa theologiae* 3.23.1 ad 2; Turretin, *Institutes of Elenctic Theology*, 1:219.

[83]"God's perfection includes his perfecting of creatures." John Webster, *Confessing God: Essays in Dogmatics II* (London: T&T Clark, 2005), 2.

7

IMMANUEL

THE SON OF GOD'S SELF-IDENTIFICATION
WITH HUMANITY IN THE INCARNATION

◆

INTRODUCTION

In the previous chapter we addressed the relationship between God's being and his eternal self-determination to be our God and Father. We turn now to a second issue that calls for critical examination, an issue that lies at the heart of Jenson's theological program, namely, the nature of God's free self-identification with the world in the Word made flesh. Here we will examine the relationship between God's being and self-determination in light of the execution of that self-determination in the incarnation of the Son of God. The questions now before us are: What sort of movement is this movement of the Son in the incarnation? And what sort of being corresponds to this movement?

THE INCARNATION AS A MOVEMENT OF SELF-GIVING
DESCENT AND "INCOMPARABLE GENEROSITY"

From the standpoint of the Christian confession, there can be no disputing the fact that the incarnation is indeed a movement. The incarnation is the Son's movement *from* the Father's side *to* Mary's womb with the result that he comes to exist among us in a new way—as a man.[1] The Word who was in the beginning with God and who was God (Jn 1:1) came "from the Father . . . into the world" (Jn 16:28) and "became flesh" (Jn 1:14). He "came down from heaven, and was incarnate by the Holy Ghost of the Virgin Mary." In order to properly understand the movement of the incarnation as a movement of divine grace, and in order to appreciate the being of the God who enacts this gracious movement, we may analyze the two poles of this movement, its "whence" and its "whither."[2]

With respect to the first pole of this movement, we must say that the Son comes into the world from the Father in order to fulfill the Father's eternal counsel regarding the adoption of his people: "In love he predestined us for adoption as sons *through Jesus Christ*" (Eph 1:4-5; see also 1 Pet 1:20). In Johannine terms, the Son comes *into* the world as one "consecrated" and "sent" on a mission (Jn 10:36) in order that those who receive him might receive "the right to become children of God" (Jn 1:12). The eternal act of self-determination whereby the Father wills to be our Father thus includes his appointment of the Son to be the Mediator between God and humanity, an appointment which belongs to what Reformed dogmatics calls the *pactum salutis*.[3] In this *pactum*, the Son *as Son* affirms the Father's eternal self-determination as well as his own role

---

[1] The movement of the incarnation is not a spatial one. Commenting on John 1:11, Thomas Aquinas states: "He [John the Evangelist] shows that the light which was present in the world and evident, i.e., disclosed by its effect, was nevertheless not known by the world. Hence, he came unto his own, in order to be known. The Evangelist says, unto his own, i.e., to things that were his own, which he had made. And he says this so that you do not think that when he says, he came, he means a local motion in the sense that he came as though ceasing to be where he previously was and beginning to be where he formerly had not been. He came where he already was," beginning "to be in a new way where he was before. . . . For he was there, indeed, by his essence, power and presence, but he came by assuming flesh." *Commentary on the Gospel of John, Chapters 1-5*, trans. Fabian Larcher and James A. Weisheipl (Washington, DC: Catholic University of America Press, 2010), 60-61.

[2] John Webster, "It Was the Will of the Lord to Bruise Him: Soteriology and the Doctrine of God," in *God of Salvation: Soteriology in Theological Perspective*, ed. Ivor J. Davidson and Murray A. Rae (Farnham: Ashgate, 2011), 26-27.

[3] For an introduction to the history of this doctrine, see Richard A. Muller, "Toward the *Pactum Salutis*: Locating the Origins of a Concept," *Mid-America Journal of Theology* 18 (2007): 11-65. For a recent discussion and defense of this doctrine, see Webster, "It Was the Will."

in that eternal self-determination.[4] In this sense, the Son too is the electing God.[5] The Son's eternal act of self-determination takes historical form in his filial obedience to the Father's counsel and appointment. Thus, when the Son comes into the world, he declares, "I have come down from heaven, not to do my own will but the will of him who sent me" (Jn 6:38).[6] With respect to the first pole of this movement, we must therefore say that the Son is a *personal agent* of the act whereby the Father's eternal counsel is fulfilled. The movement of the incarnation "is not something that *happens to* the Son, but which comes about by the very action of the Son himself."[7] He "*made himself* nothing" (Phil 2:7 NIV).

Simon Gathercole and others have criticized Jenson's understanding of the Son's preexistence precisely at this point.[8] While Jenson rightly asserts that "God the Son . . . must ontologically precede" his incarnation, it is not clear[9] whether the Son's entrance into Mary's

---

[4]Wilhelmus à Brakel asks and answers the relevant trinitarian question raised by the *pactum salutis:* "Since the Father and the Son are one in essence and thus have one will and one objective, how can there possibly be a covenant transaction between the two, as such a transaction requires the mutual involvement of two wills? Are we then not separating the Persons of the Godhead too much? To this I reply that as far as Personhood is concerned the Father is not the Son and the Son is not the Father. From this consideration the one divine will can be viewed from a twofold perspective. It is the Father's will to redeem by the agency of the second Person as Surety, and it is the will of the Son to redeem by his own agency as Surety." *The Christian's Reasonable Service,* trans. Bartel Elshout, ed. Joel R. Beeke (Grand Rapids: Reformation Heritage Books, 1992-1995), 1:252.

[5]For fuller discussion of what it means to say that the Son is the electing God, see Edwin Christian van Driel, *Incarnation Anyway: Arguments for Supralapsarian Christology* (Oxford: Oxford University Press, 2008), 101-3.

[6]Jn 6:38 and similar texts raise important questions regarding the unity of the divine will in its paternal and filial modes of existence, and also regarding the relationship between the will which the Son consubstantially shares with the Father and the will which he assumes by virtue of the incarnation. On the former issue, see Michael Allen and Scott Swain, "The Obedience of the Eternal Son," *International Journal of Systematic Theology* (forthcoming). On the latter issue, see Ivor Davidson, "'Not My Will but Yours Be Done': The Ontological Dynamics of Incarnational Intention," *International Journal of Systematic Theology* 7 (2005): 178-204.

[7]Simon Gathercole, "Pre-existence, and the Freedom of the Son in Creation and Redemption: An Exposition in Dialogue with Robert Jenson," *International Journal of Systematic Theology* 7 (2005): 46.

[8]See, for example, Gathercole, "Pre-existence," 46-47; and Paul Molnar, *Divine Freedom and the Doctrine of the Immanent Trinity: In Dialogue with Karl Barth and Contemporary Theology* (London: T & T Clark, 2002), 73-74, 80-81.

[9]Oliver Crisp wonders whether Jenson's notion of "founding post-existence" is even intelligible. See "Robert Jenson on the Pre-existence of Christ," *Modern Theology* 23 (2007): 35.

womb "from the eschatological future,"[10] a future determined by the
Father, enabled by the Spirit and anticipated in Israel, is sufficient to account for the Son's role as a personal agent of the incarnation.[11] If the
Son comes to Mary's womb from the future, then he might consent to
his place in the world *after* the fact of its occurrence, but he cannot be the
one whose will *determines* the fact of its occurrence[12]—that is, if Jenson
wishes to preserve the irreversible order of past, present and future, as he
clearly does.[13] On Jenson's scheme it seems that only the Father's will
determines the "whence" of all divine and creaturely occurrences.[14] The
problem is that this scheme seems to compromise not only the prevenience of the Son's personal agency with respect to the incarnation, but
also the unity of the Son's agency with that of the Father in determining
its occurrence (*opera Trinitatis ad extra indivisa sunt*).[15]

This being said, if we are to appreciate the full trinitarian depth of
the Son's personal agency with respect to the movement of the incarnation we must consider not only the manner in which the incarnation is an extension of the *pactum salutis,* we must also consider the
manner in which the incarnation is an extension of the Son's eternal
generation.[16] The mission of the Son to become incarnate is not the
point at which his divine sonship commences. The mission of the
Son to become incarnate is that which exhibits his divine sonship
and that which secures our creaturely participation in it. The order is

---

[10]Robert W. Jenson, "For Us . . . He Was Made Man," in *Nicene Christianity: The Future for a New
Ecumenism,* ed. Christopher R. Seitz (Grand Rapids: Brazos, 2001), 81.

[11]Jenson has recently conceded as much. See Robert W. Jenson, "Once More the *Logos Asarkos,*"
International Journal of Systematic Theology 13 (2011): 131.

[12]Hunsinger, "Robert Jenson's Systematic Theology: a review essay," *Scottish Journal of Theology* 55
(2002): 192; see also Hunsinger, "Election and the Trinity," 182-83, 193; and Edwin Christian
van Driel, "Karl Barth on the Eternal Existence of Jesus Christ," *Scottish Journal of Theology* 60
(2007): 54-55.

[13]See *ST* 1:218; *ST* 2:35.

[14]*ST* 1:114, 122-23, 218; *ST* 2:26-28; similarly Gathercole, "Pre-Existence," 50.

[15]Despite his rather severe criticisms of what he considers abuses of this ancient rule, it remains one
that Jenson affirms, as indeed any monotheist must. See *ST* 1:110.

[16]For a fuller dogmatic account of the eternal generation of the Son, see John Webster, "Eternal
Generation," in *God Without Measure: Essays in Christian Doctrine* (London: T & T Clark, forthcoming), chap. 3.

as follows: the eternal Father *has* an eternal Son; the eternal Father *sends* an eternal Son to become incarnate; as a consequence of the incarnate Son's obedience to his Father's commission, many sons and daughters are *brought* to glory.[17]

To insist on grounding the Son's temporal mission in his eternal procession is not to engage in empty speculation. It is rather to follow the instruction and direction of holy writ. The *ordo essendi* here described corresponds to the scriptural *ordo docendi,* thus obeying the rule that "in Christian theology the warrants of ontological necessity must finally be scriptural."[18] And the scriptural order here is crucial, instructing us that the Son's natural and necessary divine identity determines both the character and consequence of his contingent temporal mission.[19] Because he is the Father's perfect self-communication (Jn 1:1), dwelling at the Father's side (Jn 1:18), his mission can result in the revelation of the unseen God (Jn 1:18), and not simply the witness to a greater light (see Jn 1:8). Because he is God's proper/beloved Son, he is the Father's greatest gift in comparison to all other gifts that the Father gives (Rom 8:32; see also Gen 22:1-19) and the Father's supreme emissary in comparison to all other emissaries that the Father sends (Mk 12:1-12). Because he is the Son of God, his mission can result in the adoption of other sons and daughters (Gal 4:4-5), who may come to see and to share his filial repose at the Father's side (Jn 17:24-26), the repose he enjoyed "before the world existed" (Jn 17:5).

Jenson's counsel to collapse eternal filiation into temporal mission,[20] a counsel designed to secure the real presence of the second hypostasis in history, thus ironically threatens to rob that history of that which makes it distinctive as the history of the only-begotten

---

[17]The present point is developed at length in Allen and Swain, "The Obedience of the Eternal Son."

[18]Jenson, "Once More the *Logos Asarkos,*" 131.

[19]On the nature of eternal generation as a "natural and necessary" internal divine act as opposed to a "contingent" external act of the Trinity, see the previous chapter.

[20]Most recently: "The Father's sending and Jesus' obedience *are* the second hypostasis in God." Jenson, "Once More the *Logos Asarkos,*" 133.

Son. Apart from Jesus' metaphysically prevenient identity as God's beloved Son, we are unable to appreciate that which distinguishes his embassy from the embassy of the Father's other servants. Apart from his metaphysically prevenient identity as God's own/proper Son, we are unable to appreciate that which distinguishes his gift from the Father's other gifts. Apart from his metaphysically prevenient identity, we are unable to appreciate the ground and goal of our saving adoption. To put the point positively, Jesus' identity as God's only-begotten is what characterizes his saving action as properly divine filial action and not simply as the action of an otherwise ordinary historical agent.[21]

The point in all this is not that the Son must temporally precede his incarnation if he is to be the personal agent of its occurrence, for the Son is not temporal before the incarnation (see below). Nor is the point to establish a nonelecting Son "behind" the electing and elect Son.[22] The point concerns the *kind of movement* that the Son's incarnational act of self-determination is. According to Scripture, the "whence" of the incarnation is the Son's antecedently complete identity as the Father's only-begotten, not the eschatological fulfillment of his economic mission, and not a relation that subsists between the Father and historical Israel (or any member thereof). The incarnation is thus a movement of humble, self-giving descent, not of self-realization or self-constitution. The glorious Lord of creation, who must stoop even to behold heaven and earth (Ps 113:6), "came *down* from heaven" to assume the inglorious form of a servant. The Word became flesh *from* the glorious life of love he had with the Father "before the world existed" (Jn 17:5, 24; see also Jn 1:1, 14).

Only in understanding the "whence" of the incarnation in this way can we properly understand the "whither" of the incarnation. Because the Son comes to us from the antecedently rich life of the Trinity, this

---

[21]We will return to the relationship between the Son's eternal generation and his economic mission, and with Jenson's concerns about that relationship, toward the end of the present chapter.
[22]Recall our discussion of the simplicity of God's eternal will in the previous chapter.

coming may be understood as a personal act of free and condescending grace for the sake of humanity's enrichment and salvation.[23] "You know the grace of our Lord Jesus Christ, that *being
rich*, yet for your sake he became poor, so that you by his poverty
might become rich" (2 Cor 8:9, my translation). The Son comes
from the fullness of his life with the Father to the "emptiness" of
human existence (see Is 40:17), not that he might fulfill his own
being, but in order to fill *us* with all the fullness of God (Eph 3:19;
Jn 1:14, 16; see also Ex 34:6). "The Word became flesh," according
to Athanasius, "not for the sake of any addition to the Godhead"—
or as he later states, "not for the Word's own improvement"—"but
so that the flesh might rise again."[24] "He put on our flesh," says
Calvin, "in order that having become Son of Man he might make
us sons of God with him."[25]

Once again, we see that the distinction between an unchangeably blessed Trinity and a changeable world determines the kind of
relation that unfolds between the triune God and the world in the
drama of redemption. Only because the triune God is wholly and
absolutely sufficient unto himself can he be the author of an economy of grace. Only because the incarnation "was not motivated by
any need of completion" in the Word can it be an act of "incomparable generosity."[26] Only because he is *this* Son can he undertake a
movement of divine humiliation and obedience for the sake of
human exaltation and adoption.[27]

[23]So van Driel, *Incarnation Anyway*, 72-74.
[24]Athanasius, "The Letter of St. Athanasius to Epictetus Bishop of Corinth," in John McGuckin, *Saint Cyril of Alexandria and the Christological Controversy* (Crestwood, NY: St. Vladimir's Semi-nary Press, 2004), 387. See also McGuckin's comments on Cyril of Alexandria's understanding of the incarnational economy: "The Logos had no need whatsoever to appear as man. Two deduc-tions thus followed inevitably about the incarnation: firstly that it was an entirely free act of di-vine power, a Charis, or gracious act, of God. Secondly, that it was not for God's benefit but for mankind's" (184).
[25]I. John Hesselink, *Calvin's First Catechism: A Commentary, Featuring Ford Lewis Battles's Transla-tion of the 1538 Catechism* (Louisville: Westminster John Knox, 1997), 23.
[26]Robert Sokolowski, *The God of Faith and Reason* (Notre Dame: University of Notre Dame Press, 1982), 34.
[27]Cyril of Alexandria, "Scholia on the Incarnation of the Only Begotten," in McGuckin, *Cyril*, 305-6.

The relationship between the Son's eternal being and his self-determination to become incarnate may be summarized therefore as follows. The one who is by nature the effulgence of the Father's glory and the exact imprint of his being (Heb 1:3), graciously wills to become "like his brothers in every respect" (Heb 2:17)—to be born first of Mary's womb and later of the garden tomb—in order to realize the Father's purpose of "bringing many sons to glory" (Heb 2:10). The Son's contingent determination to become one of us flows out of his natural and necessary delight in being the eternal Son of the Father and out of his desire to include us in that delight as well: "I desire that they . . . may be with me where I am" (Jn 17:24). "He is not ashamed to call them brothers" (Heb 2:11). Because he desires that they may be with him where he is, because he is not ashamed to call them brothers, we must affirm that the radiant perfection of the eternal Son freely and graciously includes the incarnate history whereby he perfects the adoption of his brothers and sisters as well.

"THE MYSTERY OF GODLINESS" AND THE METAPHYSICS OF THE GREEKS

The movement of the incarnation is a movement of the Son from his fullness of glory at the Father's side to the inglorious humility of Mary's womb in obedience to his Father's commission. As a movement whereby the all-sufficient God relates to the world, the incarnation bears the character of all such movements, namely, "incomparable generosity." Nevertheless, while the incarnation is an instance in the history of God's relation to the world, it is not *merely* an instance in the history of God's relation to the world.[28] The incarnation is *sui generis*. It is a new thing, "the mystery of godliness" (1 Tim 3:16) that breaks into history in fulfillment of the Father's eternal resolve and that, in doing so, brings the history of the covenant which precedes it to its surprising yet necessary fulfillment. The incarnation

---

[28]Kathryn Tanner, *Jesus, Humanity, and the Trinity: A Brief Systematic Theology* (Minneapolis: Fortress, 2001), 7.

of the Son of God constitutes the "fullness" of time (Gal 4:4).

The incarnation is not merely another instance of the God-world relation because in the incarnation the Son does not merely *relate* to the world he created. He *enters* the world and becomes a member *of* that world.[29] More directly and precisely, the Son is in no way related *to* Jesus. He did not empower Jesus; he did not dwell in intimate fellowship with Jesus; he never came to or departed from Jesus. He did not and could not do any of these things because the eternal Son *is* Jesus. When the Son came to Mary's womb, he did not meet a human person in that hallowed space. When the Son came to Mary's womb, he assumed human nature in a manner that was not personally existent (anhypostatic) until he was conceived and that became personally existent (enhypostatic) only when he was conceived. "The Word *became* flesh" (Jn 1:14). And so the church confesses: Jesus is *unus ex trinitate*.

The declaration that the Word became flesh thus brings us beyond a discussion of God's free relation *to* the world to a discussion of God's free identification *with* the world "for us and our salvation." This declaration also brings us to the heart of Jenson's theological program. Here it is not sufficient simply to *distinguish* God's being from that of the creature. Here we must somehow account for the *union* of God's being with that of the creature in the incarnate person of his Son. Here we must account for the assumption of human nature by the Son of God.

The first rule of theological reflection on this matter is laid down in the angel's word to barren Sarah, a word later repeated to the Virgin Mary: "Nothing will be impossible with God" (Lk 1:37, citing Gen 18:14 LXX). As Gregory of Nyssa states, the Son's "descent to man's lowly position is a supreme example of power—of a power which is not bounded by circumstances contrary to its nature."[30]

---

[29]T. F. Torrance, *The Trinitarian Faith: The Evangelical Theology of the Ancient Catholic Church* (London: T & T Clark, 1995), 150; see also John of Damascus, *The Orthodox Faith* 3.11.

[30]Gregory of Nyssa, "Address on Religious Instruction," 24, in *Christology of the Later Fathers*, ed. Edward R. Hardy (Louisville: Westminster John Knox, 1954), 300-301.

Whatever we may wish to say about the being of the triune God must be governed by this rule: God *is* the sort of God who can do it.[31] With this rule in place, the question then becomes: What sort of one must this God be? What sort of divine being corresponds to the Son of God's act of becoming human?

As we have already seen, Jenson believes the tradition has failed to answer this question with consistency because it has followed Hellenism's bad metaphysical habit of identifying God by predicates such as timelessness, immortality, immutability and impassibility.[32] Because predicates such as these indicate an impassable gulf between divine and creaturely being, they render conceptually meaningless the Nicene claim that God *is* the man Jesus.[33] The way forward for thinking about the divine being, therefore, is to eschew "the metaphysical principles of the Greeks" for "the storytelling of the gospel."[34]

How should we respond to this line of argumentation? This is not the place to develop a full-scale *religionsgeschichtliche* argument about the relationship between early Christian theology and its surrounding Greco-Roman culture. Nor am I the one to mount such an argument. Nevertheless, several observations about the relationship between biblical and Greco-Roman theological thought can be made.

1. Jenson is correct to observe a convergence between biblical and Hellenistic thought in early Christian theology.[35] However, contra Jenson, the early Christian mission is not the root of this convergence.[36] An indispensable context for understanding the relationship between patristic and Greek theology is the much earlier meeting

---

[31]See Barth, "God can do this" (*CD* 4.1:187).
[32]*ST* 1:16, 94, 207-210. Jenson does not buy into a simple "Hellenization thesis" when it comes to the church's early theology. Jenson believes the early church made significant progress in "evangelizing" the metaphysics of its antecedent Greek culture. He just believes that this process of evangelization did not go far enough (see *ST* 1:90, 103-4, and the entirety of *ST* 1, chap. 6).
[33]*TI*, 65; *ST* 1:59, 102; Jenson, "For Us," 78.
[34]*ST* 1:112. Similarly, see J. R. Daniel Kirk, *Unlocking Romans: Resurrection and the Justification of God* (Grand Rapids: Eerdmans, 2008), 1-2.
[35]For a balanced assessment, see Eric Osborn, *The Emergence of Christian Theology* (Cambridge: Cambridge University Press, 1993).
[36]*ST* 1:16, 207.

between Jewish and Greek theology.[37] The patristic appropriation of
Hellenistic forms of theological discourse is best understood against
the backdrop of the prior appropriation of these forms of discourse
in the Judaism of the Greco-Roman era.

2. Contrary to Jenson's portrait,[38] the ancient Hellenistic culture met
by Judaism, and later by Christianity, presents no monolithic front with
respect to the ways it thinks and speaks about God.[39] For example, Paul
Gavrilyuk identifies "at least three competing views" held by ancient
Greek religious and philosophical thinkers concerning the question of
divine (im)passibility alone.[40] Furthermore, Greek theology is not exclusively preoccupied with "metaphysical principles" over against more
"personal" modes of discourse, including the use of proper names. Although Jenson acknowledges this point, he consistently argues that divine naming functions differently in Athens than it does in Jerusalem.
In Hellenistic religion, Jenson avers, proper names "are transcended at
higher levels of spiritual process in which the bonds of time loosen—as
therewith, of course, is transcended also their partnership in personal
discourse."[41] Walter Burkert, however, provides a different account of
the matter. Speaking of Greek popular religion, Burkert asserts:

> The Greek gods are persons, not abstractions, ideas or concepts; *theos*
> can be a predicate, but a divine name in the tellings of myth is a sub-

[37]So Adolf von Harnack, *Lehrbuch der Dogmengeschichte*, 5th ed. (Tübingen: J. C. B. Mohr [Paul Siebeck], 1931), 1:124-32. David T. Runia provides a helpful analysis of Harnack's view of the relationship between Jewish and Christian Hellenization in, *Philo in Early Christian Literature: A Survey* (Minneapolis: Fortress, 1993), 48-50. The now classic discussion of this matter is Martin Hengel, *Judaism and Hellenism: Studies in their Encounter in Palestine during the Early Hellenistic Period*, trans. John Bowden (Philadelphia: Fortress, 1981).
[38]See, for example, *TI*, 57-77; *ST* 1:94-100. Jenson, of course, possesses a more complete and nuanced understanding of Greek thought than his discussion of the divine attributes regularly displays. This makes it all the more puzzling that he fails to lend the same sympathy and patience to expounding the logic of the incommunicable attributes that he does (for example) to expounding Nicaea's identity statement that Jesus is the Son of God.
[39]Christopher Stead, *Philosophy in Christian Antiquity* (Cambridge: Cambridge University Press, 1994), 103. But see also p. 64, where Stead identifies Platonism as the "dominant tradition." See also Paul L. Gavrilyuk, *The Suffering of the Impassible God: The Dialectics of Patristic Thought* (Oxford: Oxford University Press, 2004), 21-36.
[40]Gavrilyuk, *Suffering*, 23.
[41]*ST* 1:47.

ject. We may say that the experience of a storm is Zeus, or that the experience of sexuality is Aphrodite, but what the Greek says is that Zeus thunders and that Aphrodite bestows her gifts. . . . The modern historian of religion may speak of "archetypal figures of reality," but in the Greek, locution and ideation is structured in such a way that an individual personality appears that has its own plastic being.[42]

Jenson's tendency to classify specific metaphysical judgments (e.g., impassibility) and specific modes of theological discourse (e.g., proper naming) with specific cultural forms of religion thus appears overly simplistic. The ancient world exhibits a theological diversity, both materially and formally, that spans the cultural and religious continuum.

3. Within the context of the broad diversity of theological standpoints that characterized Greek antiquity, predicates such as divine timelessness, immortality, immutability and so forth emerged among Greek "natural theologians." These devotees of right theological thinking strove for a theology that would accord with the divine "nature," not the mere "conventions" of popular religion.[43] Many Jews commended the Greek pursuit of right theological thinking and understood themselves to be the best exemplars of this pursuit. After all, it was to the Jews that God had revealed his nature as "the one who is" (Ex 3:14 LXX; see also Wis 13:1; 4 Ezra 8:7).[44] They had been given the knowledge of the true and living God (Jer 10:10; see also Jn 17:3; 1 Thess 1:9).[45] This perspective is manifested not only in what John J. Collins calls "Philosophical Judaism,"[46] but in other

---

[42]Walter Burkert, *Greek Religion,* trans. John Raffan (Cambridge, MA: Harvard University Press, 1985), 182-83. Cf. Jenson, *ST* 1:214.

[43]On this, see Werner Jaeger, *The Theology of the Early Greek Philosophers* (Oxford: Clarendon, 1947); Burkert, *Greek Religion,* chap. 7.

[44]Although the Septuagint's translation of the Tetragrammaton is highly debated today, it was considered an accurate revelation of the divine nature by Greek-speaking Jews, including at least some of those who wrote the New Testament. See, for example, Rev 1:4, 8; 4:8; 11:17; 16:5, with Sean M. McDonough, *YHWH at Patmos* (Tübingen: Mohr Siebeck, 1999). Disputed uses of the name include Jn 1:18 and Heb 1:3.

[45]For a helpful discussion of this theme as it appears in Paul's thought, as well as in Jewish antecedents, see Mark J. Goodwin, *Paul, Apostle of the Living God: Kerygma and Conversion in 2 Corinthians* (Harrisburg, PA: Trinity Press International, 2001).

[46]John J. Collins, *Between Athens and Jerusalem: Jewish Identity in the Hellenistic Diaspora,* 2nd ed.

forms of Judaism as well.[47] And though it is not a constant source of discussion in the apostolic writings, they too exhibit a conscious familiarity with the classical distinction between deities falsely so called by human convention and the one who is God "by nature" (Gal 4:8; see also 1 Cor 8:4-6; Heb 7:3).[48]

Along with the scriptural "language of Zion," Jews of the Greco-Roman period thus commonly used a wide variety of terms associated with Greek natural theology to describe Yʜwʜ, the one true and living God.[49] God is identified as uncreated, immortal, unchangeable, incorporeal, impassible, invisible, ineffable and eternally blessed.[50] This language, along with related concepts and patterns of speech, appears in the New Testament writings as well.[51]

4. Methodologically, the presence of this *theological language* in

(Grand Rapids: Eerdmans, 2000), chap. 5. See, for example, Aristobulus Fragment 4:8: "For it is agreed by all the philosophers that it is necessary to hold holy opinions concerning God, a point our philosophical school makes particularly well." James H. Charlesworth, *Old Testament Pseudepigrapha* (New York: Doubleday, 1985), 2:841.

[47]See, for example, Josephus, *Against Apion* 2.168, 180.

[48]Wolfhart Pannenberg, "The Appropriation of the Philosophical Concept of God as a Dogmatic Problem of Early Christian Theology," in *Basic Questions in Theology: Collected Essays*, vol. 2, trans. George H. Kehm (Philadelphia: Westminster, 1971), 136. Commenting on Gal 4:8, Augustine states: "Now when he says, *you were enslaved to beings that by nature are not gods,* he clearly shows that the one true God is God by nature. By this name the Trinity is understood in the depths of the most faithful Catholic heart." Eric Plumer, *Augustine's Commentary on Galatians* (Oxford: Oxford University Press, 2003), 183. On 1 Corinthians 8:4-6, see Paul Rainbow, "Monotheism and Christology in 1 Corinthians 8:4-6" (D.Phil. Thesis: Oxford, 1987). On the relationship between Heb 7:3 and Greek natural theology, see Jerome H. Neyrey, "'Without Beginning of Days or End of Life' (Hebrews 7:3): Topos for a True Deity," *Catholic Biblical Quarterly* 53 (1991): 439-55.

[49]For helpful summaries and catalogues of Jewish ways of speaking about God during this period, see especially: Rainbow, "Monotheism and Christology"; and Ralph Marcus, "Divine Names and Attributes in Hellenistic Jewish Literature," *Proceedings of the American Academy for Jewish Research* 3 (1931-32): 43-120.

[50]See, for example: *Apocalypse of Abraham* 17:8-10; *2 Baruch* 21:10-11; *2 Enoch* 33:4; *Sibylline Oracles* 3.10, 11-16, 593, 628-29, 717-18; 5.66; Josephus, *Against Apion* 2:166-68, 190; Philo, *Allegorical Interpretation* 2.33; *Sacrifices* 1.101.

[51]See, for example, Rom 1:20, 23; 1 Tim 1:11, 17; 6:15; Heb 7:3; 11:27; Rev 1:4. Although Paul's sermons in Acts do not trade very much in the specific *terms* of Hellenistic God-talk, they exhibit a number of common *conceptions and rhetorical patterns*. On the relationship between these sermons and the broader Greco-Roman world, see Eduard Norden, *Agnostos Theos: Untersuchungen zur Formgeschichte Religiöser Rede* (Stuttgart: B. G. Teubner, 1956); Robert Grant, *Gods and the One God* (Philadelphia: Westminster, 1986), 49-51; and Gerald F. Downing, "Common Ground with Paganism in Luke and in Josephus," *New Testament Studies* 28 (1982): esp. 550-59.

ancient Judaism, and later in the New Testament and early Christianity, must be distinguished from the *theological discourse* within which such language is employed. We must not fall into the trap of what Eric Osborn calls "philological stamp-collecting, which ignores the central principle that different words can mean the same thing and that the same words can mean different things."[52] Instead, we must pay attention to the overarching pattern of theological discourse within which such language is employed.[53] With this methodological principle in place, it becomes quite clear that ancient Judaism's wide and regular use of Hellenistic theological language often contradicts some of the fundamental tenets of Greek natural theology and serves instead to explicate and defend Judaism's distinctively monotheistic theology.

A few examples will substantiate this claim. First, the Jewish description of God as immortal, invisible, immutable and so on, functions as *a unique identity description* of YHWH, who alone is God, and not (as is sometimes the case in Hellenistic thought) as a generic category for "the divine," a category which might include many members.[54] Second, while the Jewish identification of God according to the aforementioned predicates functions to posit an *absolute distinction* between YHWH and his creatures,[55] these descriptions do not suggest an *ontological gulf or distance* between YHWH and his creatures

---

[52]Eric Osborn, *The Emergence of Christian Theology* (Cambridge: Cambridge University Press, 1993), 19n65.

[53]See E. P. Sanders, *Paul and Palestinian Judaism* (Philadelphia: Fortress, 1977), 12-18. Similarly, Larry Hurtado states: "One must always study a particular religious phenomenon in the overall 'pattern' of each religious movement, for the overall pattern may give to the phenomenon very different significance and meaning." *One God, One Lord: Early Christian Devotion and Ancient Jewish Monotheism* (Philadelphia: Fortress, 1988), 10.

[54]Richard Bauckham, "The Throne of God and the Worship of Jesus," in *The Jewish Roots of Christological Monotheism*, ed. Carey C. Newman, James R. Davila and Gladys S. Lewis (Leiden: Brill, 1999), 44-45. This is not to deny that there is a general tendency toward monotheism in Greek natural theology, on which see Michael Frede, "Monotheism and Pagan Philosophy in Later Antiquity," in *Pagan Monotheism in Late Antiquity*, ed. Polymnia Athanassiadi and Michael Frede (Oxford: Clarendon, 1999), 41-67.

[55]That is to say, these predicates identify what it means for God to be *uncreated*.

that must in turn be bridged by semidivine intermediaries.[56] According to Henry Wicks, the Jewish literature of this era almost universally portrays YHWH as "a God who is in unmediated contact with his
creation."[57] And this goes for those texts characterized by extensive
speculation regarding angels as well.[58] The divine king's absolute distinction from the world in no way compromises his intimate relation
to the world, but rather serves as its necessary condition.[59] Third,
while Jewish monotheism in the Greco-Roman period exhibits an
increasing tendency away from anthropomorphism, and thus an increasing tendency toward the kind of language currently under discussion, there remains nevertheless a healthy dose of anthropopath-
ism in the literature of this period.[60] I suggest that this particular
modulation of negative theology, constrained as it is by the scriptural
presentation of God as the incomparably transcendent one who nevertheless abounds in steadfast love and faithfulness toward his creatures, anticipates later patristic discussions of divine impassibility.[61]

As this brief sketch suggests, it is just too simple a historical pic-
ture to pit "the storytelling of the gospel" against "the metaphysical
principles of the Greeks," as Jenson repeatedly does. The Judaism
from which Christianity and the New Testament writings emerged
had long before this emergence confronted the metaphysical principles of the Greeks and, in this confrontation, had learned how to
appropriate many of the predicates of Greek natural theology in a
critical manner on the basis of its own distinctive monotheistic im-

---

[56]According to Jenson, "Antiquity's struggle to overcome the supposed gulf between deity and time
is discovered to be moot in light of the gospel" (*ST* 1:102). We should perhaps say that it had been
rendered moot already by Jewish monotheists.

[57]Henry J. Wicks, *The Doctrine of God in the Jewish Apocryphal and Apocalyptic Literature* (New York:
KTAV Publishing House, 1971 [1915]), 124.

[58]Wicks, *Doctrine of God*, 80, 115-19.

[59]For an especially helpful discussion of the present point, see N. T. Wright, *The New Testament and
the People of God* (Minneapolis: Fortress, 1992), 244-56.

[60]Wicks, *Doctrine of God*, 57-58, 79, 114, 122; J. L. Lightfoot, *The Sibylline Oracles: With Introduction, Translation, and Commentary on the First and Second Books* (Oxford: Oxford University Press,
2007), 35.

[61]See Gavrilyuk, *Suffering*.

pulse.[62] It is this situation, I suggest, which explains how 1 Timothy can extol the God of "the gospel" (1 Tim 1:11) as "the blessed and only Sovereign" (1 Tim 6:15), the "immortal" and "invisible" King (1 Tim 1:17). It is this situation which also explains how, much later, Origen can claim that it is "the doctrine of Jews and Christians which preserves the unchangeable and unalterable nature of God" against "those who hold impious opinions" about him.[63]

Before proceeding to the dogmatic implications of the present discussion, two further historical observations are in order. The first observation concerns what we might call the structural significance of the so-called incommunicable attributes within the edifice of patristic trinitarianism. Recent scholarship paints a portrait of the development of early trinitarianism that is rather different from the one painted by Jenson. As Gavrilyuk argues with respect to impassibility and as Ayres argues more broadly with respect to pro-Nicene theology,[64] the same tradition of biblical interpretation that confessed the Nicene dogma also confessed an understanding of the divine nature which included the incommunicable attributes.[65] Indeed, the immutability identity of the Son is a central feature of Nicene orthodoxy.[66] The doctrines of God's triunity and of God's uncreated being (as traditionally conceived) are thus *internally related* in the

---

[62]A full treatment of the relation/distinction between Judaism, Christianity, and ancient Greek metaphysics would have to include discussion of the doctrine of creation *ex nihilo*. For insightful reflections in this regard, see Janet Martin Soskice, "Athens and Jerusalem, Alexandria and Edessa: Is There a Metaphysics of Scripture?" *International Journal of Systematic Theology* 8 (2006): 149-62; and, more recently, Markus Bockmuehl, "*Creatio ex nihilo* in Palestinian Judaism and Early Christianity," *Scottish Journal of Theology* 65 (2012): 253-70.

[63]Origen, *Contra Celsum*, trans. Henry Chadwick (Cambridge: Cambridge University Press, 1980), 1.21. Origen cites Ps 102:27 and Mal 3:6 as biblical bases for this Jewish-Christian doctrine.

[64]Gavrilyuk, *Suffering*; Lewis Ayres, *Nicaea and its Legacy*, esp. chaps. 11-13.

[65]For further discussion of the way these divine perfections function within Pro-Nicene trinitarianism, see Luigi Gioia, *The Theological Epistemology of Augustine's "De Trinitate"* (Oxford: Oxford University Press, 2008); and Radde-Gallwtiz, *Basil of Caesarea*.

[66]See Gilles Emery, "The Immutability of the God of Love and the Problem of Language Concerning the 'Suffering of God,'" in *Divine Impassibility and the Mystery of Human Suffering*, ed. James F. Keating and Thomas Joseph White (Grand Rapids: Eerdmans, 2009), 28-34.

early church's theological vision.[67] If this reading is correct, then the burden remains on Jenson to explain how one can pull any single thread from the early church's trinitarian synthesis without unraveling the entire doctrinal tapestry.

The second observation concerns the ecumenical reception of Nicene Christianity. Adopting Jenson's interpretation would require us not only to conclude that the same tradition of gospel reasoning which gave us Nicaea's affirmation of the Son's identity with Jesus failed to recognize the striking incongruity of this affirmation with its concept of God. It would require us also to conclude that the ecumenical tradition of theology which received Nicaea—East and West, Roman Catholic and Protestant—also failed to recognize this striking incongruity. While such a situation is possible, it seems implausible. The *catholicity* of the traditional doctrine of the divine attributes must count more highly in its favor than Jenson permits.

"THE MYSTERY OF GODLINESS" AND
THE METAPHYSICS OF THE GOSPEL

The preceding discussion suggests that the choice between a Hellenized God and a historicized God—a choice repeatedly posed by Jenson—represents a false dilemma. It also suggests that there is another way of understanding the role of the incommunicable attributes in the church's confession than that offered by Jenson. We may find our way into such an understanding by recalling Gregory of Nyssa's earlier quoted statement regarding the nature of God as it is revealed by the incarnation, specifically his statement that the Son's descent to become man displays "a power which is not bounded by circumstances contrary to its nature."[68]

Gregory's statement represents a promising understanding of God's limitless, infinite being. God's being is "contrary to" that of his

---

[67]Contra, for example, *ST* 1:95, 101.
[68]Gregory of Nyssa, "Address on Religious Instruction," 24.

creatures in that it is not characterized by the limitations associated with creatureliness. Because God is "not a man" (Num 23:19; 1 Sam 15:29; Job 9:32), his "years have no end" (Ps 102:27; see also Job 36:26). He is uncontainable (1 Kings 8:27), immortal, and invisible (Rom 1:20, 23; 1 Tim 1:17). "His understanding is unsearchable" (Is 40:28). With the radiant and benevolent being of God "there is no variation or shadow due to change" (Jas 1:17; see also Ps 102:26-27). God's greatness is therefore quite literally unfathomable (Ps 145:3).[69]

Nevertheless, again following on Gregory's statement, this does not mean that God's limitless, infinite being is "bounded by" the limitations of creaturely being. Creaturely finitude is not a border that keeps God out. Nor is infinitude a distance that keeps God away.[70] Indeed, the eternal one is a "dwelling place" for his people throughout "all generations" (Ps 90:1-2). He is a God at once far off and near (Jer 23:23; Is 57:15; Ps 139). The infinitely exalted one stoops far down to raise the poor from the dust and the needy from the dunghill (Ps 113). Michael S. Horton aptly summarizes the logic of this and the preceding paragraph: "The focus of the biblical testimony seems to be on the proscription of any limitations on God's attributes, not of God's capacity to genuinely relate."[71]

Furthermore, God's limitless being does not imply that his being is indeterminate or impersonal due to its lack of finite objectivity, as Fichte supposed this sort of being must be.[72] This would only follow if the finite creature were the measure of personal being. Within such a framework, infinitude and personhood would be necessarily incompatible, infinitude representing an abstraction from the finite

[69]Dionysius, *The Divine Names* 1.2 in *Pseudo-Dionysius: The Complete Works*, trans. Colm Luibheid (New York: Paulist, 1987); John of Damascus, *The Orthodox Faith* 1.4.
[70]"God is trapped neither within nor outside the world." Eugene Rogers, *After the Spirit: A Constructive Pneumatology from Resources Outside the Modern West* (Grand Rapids: Eerdmans, 2005), 59.
[71]Michael Horton, *Lord and Servant: A Covenant Christology* (Louisville: Westminster John Knox, 2005), 47-48.
[72]See *ST* 1:215-17, 220; also Robert W. Jenson, "Creator and Creature," *International Journal of Systematic Theology* 4 (2002), 217.

determinacy that as such defines personal being. But, of course, one of the first principles of trinitarian theology is that the creature is not the archetype of personhood.[73]

A proper concept of God's infinite being, therefore, is not derived by contrasting or correlating it to creaturely being, by making God either the opposite or the analogue of the creature.[74] In this sense, Jenson is correct: "The finite/infinite conceptual pairing cannot as such fund the Creator/creature difference."[75] A proper concept of God's infinite being is instead derived from the self-manifestation of God's infinitely rich and perfect life within the sphere of creaturely being.[76] The prohibitions of the second commandment against imaging God after anything in heaven above or on the earth below (Ex 20:4; Deut 4:15-19) *follow* from the self-revelation of YHWH's unique and incomparable deity in the exodus (Ex 3–15). Similarly, the traditional prohibition against measuring God by creaturely standards (a prohibition that becomes pronounced in patristic debates concerning the nature of the Son's eternal generation from the Father) *follows* from the self-revelation of God's trinitarian being in the Word made flesh.[77]

God's infinity is not properly thought when naked reason reasons by itself (*ratio ratiocinans*), deriving a concept of infinitude comparatively, that is, by the simple negation of its own finitude or by the simple magnification of its own perfection (Feuerbach!). God's infinity is properly thought when faithful reason reasons according to the Word of God (*ratio ratiocinata*),[78] which "generously reveals a firm, transcendent beam, granting enlightenments proportionate to

---

[73]See Bavinck's discussion and critique of Fichte on this point in *Reformed Dogmatics*, trans. John Vriend (Grand Rapids: Baker, 2004), 2:46-47.

[74]Thus extensively Kathryn Tanner, *God and Creation in Christian Theology: Tyranny or Empowerment?* (Oxford: Blackwell, 1988).

[75]Jenson, "Creator and Creature," 217.

[76]Bavinck, *Reformed Dogmatics*, 2:130.

[77]See, for example, Athansius, *Orations Against the Arians* 1.15, in *The Trinitarian Controversy*, ed. William G. Rusch (Philadelphia: Fortress, 1980), 78.

[78]Bavinck, *Reformed Dogmatics*, 2:107-10.

each being, and thereby draws sacred minds upward to its permitted contemplation, to participation and to the state of becoming like it."[79] Understood in this way, God's infinitude is an essentially positive concept.[80] It is a way of speaking of the unbounded plenitude of God's self-manifesting, self-bestowing being in relation to the limitations of creaturely being.[81]

Such a conception of infinity requires us to confess: *Deus non est in genere*. While biblical reasoning requires us to affirm that finite creatures are "similar to God by reason of the divine image and likeness," it also requires us to observe that this similarity is a one-way street. We cannot affirm God's similarity to finite creatures "any more than we can say that man is similar to his own portrait."[82] "To whom then will you liken God, or what likeness compare with him?" Isaiah asks (Is 40:18). The required answer is: "no one" (Ex 8:10; Ps 40:5).[83] God is the unboundedly perfect archetype of all being and the generous fountainhead of all created beings, including their various classifications (Eph 3:15; see also Ps 94:8-10; Wis 13:3-5).[84] Therefore, God cannot be classified according to a general category of "beings." God and creatures are not infinite and finite versions of the same thing. Moreover, because God is in a class by himself, the difference/relationship between the infinite God and his finite creatures is not to be modeled after the way in which finite creatures are differentiated from/related to one another. God does not transcend the categories of finite beings in the way that finite beings transcend one another, "not in the way that oil floats on water, nor as heaven is above earth."[85]

This point holds several consequences for our understanding of

---

[79]Dionysius, *Divine Names* 1.2.

[80]Bavinck, *Reformed Dogmatics*, 2:160.

[81]An exceptionally beautiful discussion of God's infinity may be found in Katherine Sonderegger, "The Absolute Infinity of God," in *The Reality of Faith in Theology: Studies on Karl Barth Princeton-Kampen Consultation 2005*, ed. Bruce L. McCormack and Gerrit Neven (Bern: Peter Lang, 2007), 31-50.

[82]Dionysius, *Divine Names* 9.6.

[83]See John of Damascus, *The Orthodox Faith* 1.4.

[84]Dionysius, *Divine Names* 1.7; Thomas Aquinas, *Summa theologiae* 1a.4.2.

[85]Augustine, *Confessions*, trans. Henry Chadwick (Oxford: Oxford Univeristy Press, 1991), 7.10.16.

the incarnation.[86] We mention two for now. First, saying that the infinite God became a finite man is not the same thing as saying that a human being became a goat.[87] For a human being to become a goat, the human being would have to cease being human. It is not possible to be *both* a human being *and* a goat because humans and goats are mutually exclusive members of creaturely classifications.[88] However, this is not the case with God and humanity, for God is not in a class with his creatures.[89] Second, and more positively stated, because God is the infinite archetype of all perfection, and because he transcends all created beings in a unique manner, the incarnation is possible for God without necessitating a change in God. David Bentley Hart well summarizes the significance of this point:

> The absolute qualitative disproportion between infinite and finite allows for the infinite to appropriate and accommodate the finite without ceasing to be infinite; as all the perfections that compose a creature as what it is have their infinite and full reality in God, then the self-emptying of God in his creature is not a passage from what he is to what he is not, but a gracious condescension by which the infinite is pleased truly to disclose and express itself in one instance of the finite. Indeed, in this sense, to say God does not change in the incarnation is almost a tautology: God is not some thing that can be transformed into another thing, but is the being of everything, to which all that is always already properly belongs; there is no change of nature needed for the fullness of being to assume—even through self-impoverishment—*a* being as the dwelling place of its mystery and glory. Moreover, as human being is nothing at all in itself but the image and likeness of God, then the perfect dwelling of the eternal image and likeness of God—the Logos—in the one man who per-

---

[86]See more fully Sokolowski, *God of Faith and Reason,* chap. 4.

[87]I draw the illustration and argument in this and the following sentences from Herbert McCabe, *God Matters* (Springfield, IL: Templegate, 1991), 57-58.

[88]Even in C. S. Lewis's Narnia, one can only be *half* human and *half* goat.

[89]Thus McCabe: "A circle and a square make two shapes; a man and a sheep make two animals: God and man make two what?" (*God Matters,* 57).

fectly expresses and lives out what it is to be human, is in no sense an alien act for God.[90]

Of course, none of this *explains* the mystery of the incarnation, which must "always remain an unfathomable source of adoration."[91] To the announcement, "Nothing will be impossible with God" (Lk 1:37) corresponds the exclamation, "He who is mighty has done great things for me, and holy is his name" (Lk 1:49). Nevertheless, while this understanding of divine infinity does not explain the mystery of the incarnation, it does relieve to some degree "the burden of conceptual dissonance" which Jenson perceives in the traditional doctrine of the union of two natures.[92] For it helps us appreciate the fact that the union of two natures in the Son of God is not an attempt to construe "a unity between two distinct and metaphysically polar entities."[93] In relation to the infinitely perfect God, there can be no metaphysically polar entities. Indeed, when the Word became flesh, he assumed what was already "his own" (Jn 1:11).

"JESUS CHRIST IS THE SAME YESTERDAY AND TODAY AND FOREVER"

Before attending to some further consequences of the preceding discussion for the doctrine of the incarnation, we must address one specific application of divine infinity, namely, timeless eternity. This doctrine, of course, plays the role of chief antagonist in Jenson's theological program.[94]

Viewed from the perspective on divine infinity discussed above, God's timeless eternity should not be understood as the mere negation of time.[95] On certain traditional understandings of eternity at least, God's life does not lack the eventfulness of time but is in-

---

[90]Hart, *Beauty*, 357.
[91]Brakel, *Christian's Reasonable Service*, 1:511.
[92]*ST* 1:125.
[93]Ibid., 126.
[94]Ibid., 169.
[95]This point is rightly and repeatedly made by Jenson. See *ST* 1:94, 169, etc. See also *CD* 2.1, 610.

stead the paradigmatic instance thereof. Eternity is the application of the concept of *duration* to divine infinity:[96] "the complete possession all at once of illimitable *life*."[97] According to Holy Scripture, God's eternity lacks certain characteristics of *temporal* events, specifically, beginnings and ends (Ps 90:2; 102:27; 1 Cor 2:7; Tit 1:2-3; Heb 1:10-12; Jude 25).[98] But God's eternity lacks these things, not because it lacks eventfulness and duration, but only because God completely possesses the whole of his blissfully eventfull life "all at once."[99] "Jesus Christ is *the same* yesterday and today and forever" (Heb 13:8). Understood in this way, eternity is an essentially positive concept. And "timelessness" is simply the negation of finite limitations that must follow upon the apprehension of this positive concept.[100]

Thus construed, God's eternal being is not rightly regarded as a "persistence of the past," as Jenson charges. Strictly speaking, the concept of persistence does not apply at all to God, for "only events whose parts end persist."[101] Nor, for that matter, should it be said that God possesses the fullness of his life by means of anticipation, as Jenson avers. A God who must anticipate the fullness of his being

---

[96]Johannes Polyander, Andre Rivet, Antonius Walaeus and Antonius Thysius, *Synopsis purioris theologiae*, 6th ed., ed. Herman Bavinck (Leiden: Donner, 1881), 6.28.

[97]This, of course, is Boethius's definition, as cited in Eleonore Stump and Norman Kretzmann, "Eternity," in *The Concept of God*, ed. Thomas V. Norris (New York: Oxford University Press, 1987), 220, italics mine.

[98]Jenson understands Gregory of Nyssa to teach a doctrine of divine "temporal infinity." His reading is based in turn on the work of Ekkehard Mühlenberg, *Die Unendlichkeit Gottes bei Gregor von Nyssa: Gregors Kritik am Gottesbegriff der klassichen Metaphysik* (Göttingen: Vandenhoeck & Ruprecht, 1966), e.g., 113. However, Mühlenberg's interpretation has been decisively refuted by David L. Balás in his, "Eternity and Time in Gregory of Nyssa's Contra Eunomium," in *Gregory von Nyssa und Philosophie*, hrsg. Heinrich Dörrie, Margarete Altenburger, and Uta Schramm (Leiden: Brill, 1976), esp. 146-47. See, similarly, Morwenna Ludlow, *Gregory of Nyssa: Ancient and [Post]modern* (Oxford: Oxford University Press, 2007), 44-48. For further discussion of the scriptural material, see Brian Leftow, "Eternity and Immutability," in *The Blackwell Guide to the Philosophy of Religion*, ed. William E. Mann (Malden, MA: Blackwell, 2005), 48-77; and William Lane Craig, *Time and Eternity: Exploring God's Relationship to Time* (Wheaton: Crossway, 2001), 14-20.

[99]See Stump and Kretzmann, "Eternity," 220-25.

[100]Thus Burrell, "Distinguishing God from the World," 80.

[101]Leftow, "Eternity and Immutability," 57. A God who *persists* in his being is simply the inverse image of a God who *anticipates* his being.

is simply the inverse image of a God whose being persists. Neither is truly infinite. If the being of the triune God is indeed wholly realized (*actus purus*), then there can be no succession in God. He must *actually* possess the fullness of his life all at once.

Does such a conception of eternity imply a distance between God and the temporal world? Certainly not. For the eternal God is the creator, providential sustainer and perfecter of the temporal world. As is the case with every dimension of divine infinity rightly understood, eternity enables us to think of God's relation to the world as a relation in which he communicates his antecedently full and blessed life to the finite creature in order that the creature might in turn be "filled with all the fullness of God" (Eph 3:19). As Herman Bavinck states: "God's eternity does not stand, abstract and transcendent, above time, but is present and immanent in every moment of time. There is indeed an essential difference between eternity and time, but there is also an analogy and kinship between them so that the former can indwell and work in the latter."[102] As we have argued already, the latter takes time. The realization of God's eternal being, however, does not.[103]

INCARNATIONAL METAPHYSICS:
FOUR SUMMARY CONCLUSIONS

In light of the preceding argument, we may draw four summary conclusions regarding the relationship between God's infinite being and the event of the incarnation.

---

[102]Bavinck, *Reformed Dogmatics*, 2:163-64.

[103]What about Jenson's alignment of time's three poles with the three persons of the Trinity? This question should be distinguished from the question of whether there are beginnings, successions and ends in God. While the latter question requires a negative answer, the answer to the former question is not so clear, at least to me. There seems to be something theologically fitting about the Barthian-Jensonian *theologoumenon* that the Trinity is the paradigm of time's three dimensions, given that "first," "second," and "third" are real relations in God, eternally subsisting modes of God's one eternal life. I fear, however, that Jenson's particular construal of this *theologoumenon* runs the risk of compromising the consubstantiality of the three persons. If, as Jenson suggests, the three persons represent three different *poles* in God's temporally infinite life, do they not also represent three different *parts* of that life? And does not such a perspective run afoul of the *homoousion*, which requires us to understand eternity as a *common* property and not as a *personal* property? We may leave the preceding questions open for now.

First, the Word who was in the beginning with God and who was God (Jn 1:1) is not one thing among other things in the world. He is the Creator of "all things" (Jn 1:3; 1 Cor 8:6; Col 1:16) and as such is in a class by himself. *Deus non est in genere*. This means therefore (pace Jenson) that the Word *as such has no story*.[104] Story—including Jesus' story—cannot function as a "master-concept" that "comprehends both God and what is not God."[105] Story, together with temporal conflict, progression, crisis, and resolution, may indeed characterize the modality of creaturely being,[106] but it does not characterize the utterly complete being of the Word who is God (Heb 1:10-13).

Nevertheless, second, far from implying a distance between the Word and the world, the Word's distinct manner of transcending the world implies a distinct manner of intimacy with the world.[107] The world is "his own" (Jn 1:11). "In him all things hold together" (Col 1:17; Heb 1:3). The Word is not a story. But this does not mean that he is unrelated to the cosmic story of creation, redemption and consummation. The Word creates, sustains and perfects this story. The story of creation is "from him and through him and to him" (Rom 11:36; see also Col 1:16) who is its Alpha and Omega (Rev 22:13). Indeed, given the intimacy of the Word's sustaining and governing presence to creation, his eternal being might "better be imagined *inside* the becoming which time measures than *outside* it."[108]

Third, because the Word is not in a class with his creatures by virtue of his transcendence of all creaturely limitation and categorization, he is able to "cross the boundary" and *become* a creature. In doing so, he does not sacrifice his own being but instead brings the

---

[104]See Francesca Aran Murphy, *God Is Not a Story: Realism Revisited* (Oxford: Oxford University Press, 2007).

[105]*CD* 2.1:312.

[106]Thus Paul Ricoeur, *Oneself as Another,* trans. Kathleen Blamey (Chicago: University of Chicago Press, 1994).

[107]See Tanner, *Jesus, Humanity, and the Trinity,* chap. 1.

[108]Burrell, "Distinguishing God," 81; see also Dionysius, *Divine Names* 5.4; Bavinck, *Reformed Dogmatics,* 2:163-64.

fullness of his divine being to bear *in* his human existence.[109] "In him the whole fullness of deity dwells bodily" (Col 2:9; see also Jn 1:14, 16). Because creaturely being is no boundary to him, he can assume human nature as *his* being and by means of his human existence enact eternal salvation. "He who for us is life itself descended here and endured our death and slew it by the abundance of his life."[110] *He* is the sort of one who can do this.[111]

Fourth, then, as a consequence of the incarnation, we must insist that the Word *now has a story*, a story framed by birth and death, a story gloriously consummated in the Word's resurrection and ascension to the Father's right hand. Several implications follow from this assertion.

God's being is not, even dialectically, identified with his creature's mode of being.[112] "The form by which God, invisible in his own nature, became visible, was not God himself," says Augustine.[113] This applies to all of God's appearances in the creaturely sphere, including the incarnation. Flesh withers like grass (Is 40:6), but the Word of God remains forever (Is 40:8). "Nevertheless," Augustine continues, "it is *he himself* who was seen under that form."[114] As this applies to all of God's appearances in the creaturely sphere, so does it apply preeminently to the incarnation of the Word. The eternal Word *became* temporal, withering grass (Jn 1:14; see also Rom 8:3).[115] The Word's human body and soul are *his* body and soul and not mere theophany.

Consequently, the human story that unfolds from Jesus' birth, through his public ministry, to Gethsemane, Golgotha, and beyond the grave is nothing other than the human story *of the second person*

---

[109]For an able critique of modern kenotic christologies, see *CD* 4.1:179-83; also Oliver Crisp, *Divinity and Humanity* (Cambridge: Cambridge University Press, 2007), chap. 5.

[110]Augustine, *Confessions* 4.12.19; see also Gregory of Nazianzus, *Oration* 29.20.

[111]May we also say that only *the Son* can do this while remaining *who* he is? See John of Damascus *Orthodox Faith* 4.4.

[112]So Hunsinger, "Robert Jenson's Systematic Theology: a review essay," 179-80.

[113]Cf. *CD* 4.1:178.

[114]Augustine, *City of God* 10.13, italics mine.

[115]Jenson, "For Us," 83.

of the Trinity. Although the human form that the Son assumes is
not his natural form, it is nevertheless the (distinctly appropriate)
form of his ectypal self-revelation: His eternal birth from the Father is exhibited and extended in his birth from Mary (Lk 1:35),
and later in his birth from the dead (Col 1:18); his eternal filial
mode of being and acting from the Father is exhibited and extended in the mission that receives and enacts in filial obedience to
his Father (Jn 5:19-30);[116] his glory as the Father's beloved Son is
exhibited and extended in the economy as he undergoes baptism in
the Jordan (Mk 1:11), as he is transfigured on the mountain (Mk
9:7), and as he is enthroned at the Father's right hand as the firstborn among many brothers and sisters who are themselves destined
to behold and participate in the glory of the Father's beloved (Jn
17:24-26). These creaturely forms of the Son's existence are in each
instance "external" likenesses and images "of his internal essence"
because they are in each instance the creaturely forms of "the same
Son of God."[117]

This means that, contrary to Jenson's worst fears, the story of
Jesus is not merely a clue to the being of the triune God.[118] The
story of Jesus, as it unfolds in his filial relationship to the Father in
the power of the Spirit, is simply *the being of the triune God in the
temporal, self-manifesting, self-communicating execution of his eternal
resolve to become our God.*[119] Jesus is not a reflection of the Son of
God. He *is* the Son of God made flesh "for us men and for our salvation." In and through his "eloquent and radiant life,"[120] the unseen
God has now been fully and finally expounded in the sphere of
human history. In the incarnate Son of God, divine light shines in

---

[116]Again, see Allen and Swain, "The Obedience of the Eternal Son."

[117]Martin Luther, *The Three Symbols or Creeds of the Christian Faith,* in *Luther's Works,* vol. 34, ed.
L. W. Spitz (Philadelphia: Muhlenberg, 1960), 216-18.

[118]*ST* 1:59.

[119]Murphy provides a helpful discussion regarding how we may think of concepts such as "analogy," "expression" and "communication" from a trinitarian perspective in *God Is Not a Story,*
284, 317-19.

[120]*CD* 4.3:81.

the darkness and the darkness does not overcome it (Jn 1:5).

And here is perhaps the place to address more fully Jenson's worries regarding the traditional distinction between the trinitarian processions and missions. If we may follow Thomas Aquinas' version of the doctrine,[121] the distinction between procession and mission does not suggest the existence of two trinities, one timeless and unknowable, the other temporal and knowable.[122] Among other things, the distinction serves to underline two features that characterize God's relation to his people through Son and Spirit. The first concerns the sheer gratuity of God's presence to us through incarnation and indwelling. Here we must observe: Missions cannot simply be identified with processions (contra Jenson); otherwise, the missions are not movements of divine grace—new, unnecessary modes of God's personal presence in the world. The second feature concerns the astounding fact that in these temporal missions we are nevertheless dealing with God himself in the full depth of his triune identity.[123] Missions are not merely reflections or echoes of eternal processions. Missions are truly extensions *of* eternal processions *in time*, "the kindly Rays"[124] of God's immanent life shining forth on us. According to Thomas, the temporal missions of the Son and the Spirit "include" their eternal processions.[125] And because they include the eternal processions of which they are free extensions, the missions constitute the self-*communication* (i.e., "making common") of divine persons to temporal creatures.[126] In the missions of Son and Spirit, God graciously gives *himself*, as he eternally exists in his unchanging triune identity, in order that he might be truly pos-

---

[121]For an excellent exposition of Thomas on this point, see Gilles Emery, *The Trinitarian Theology of St. Thomas Aquinas,* trans. Francesca Aran Murphy (Oxford: Oxford University Press, 2007), chap. 15.
[122]Emery, *Trinitarian Theology,* 368.
[123]According to Emery, "Mission consists in the person's new way of being present . . . mission engages a *newness* and a real *presence* of the divine person who is sent"(*Trinitarian Theology,* 373).
[124]Dionysius, *Divine Names* 3.1.
[125]Thomas Aquinas, *Summa theologiae* 1a.43.2.
[126]Ibid., 1a.43.3.

sessed, known and enjoyed *by the creature*.[127] The missions are the means whereby the triune God "gives himself completely to us,"[128] Luther says. The fact that we as finite creatures cannot fully grasp this gift in no way detracts from the fact that the fullness of God has been, is being, and will be given to us by grace through the gospel (see Eph 3:14-19).

When it comes to Jesus, then, we are not forced to deal with two parallel stories of the Son, one eternal story above history and one temporal story in history, where the latter story is merely a reflection of the former story and where our minds are therefore always required to make the leap from the visible Jesus to the "real" Son, who functions as Jesus' transcendental form or condition.[129] When it comes to Jesus, we are dealing with the single story of God's only-begotten Son willingly made flesh in fulfillment of the Father's eternal resolve. There is no other story of God. And there is no other being of God than the being of the God who eternally and graciously wills to be our God, the God who can and does execute that will through the Word made flesh. In the story of Jesus we are dealing with "nothing other than the interior life of the triune God [made] visible (to the eyes of faith) in our history."[130]

Jesus' human story is not merely "instrumental" to God's eternal self-determination to be our God, a merely temporal surface that is tangentially related to God's triune life with us.[131] Jesus is the Son living out in human form his eternal relationship with the Father in the Spirit for our saving benefit.[132] And this human form of the

---

[127]Ibid. Emery states: "This gift is the grace through which a human being, made to the image of the Triune God, is lifted right up to objective participation in the procession of the Word and of Love" (*Trinitarian Theology*, 253).

[128]Martin Luther, *The Large Catechism*, in *The Book of Concord: The Confessions of the Evangelical Lutheran Church*, ed. T. G. Tappert (Philadelphia: Muhlenberg, 1959), 419-20.

[129]See Jenson's worries about Barth in *GAG*.

[130]McCabe, *God Matters*, 51.

[131]For a defense and proper explanation of what it means to say that the Son's human nature is "instrumental" to his person, see Thomas Joseph White, "Dyothelitism and the Instrumental Human Consciousness of Jesus," *Pro Ecclesia* 17 (2008): 396-422.

[132]Tanner, *Jesus, Humanity, and the Trinity*, 20; see also Tanner, "The Trinity and Politics," *Princeton*

Father-Son relationship is nothing other than the eternal object of God's gracious, self-determining will—that he become our Father and that we become his creaturely children *in and with the incarnate Son*. The incarnate Son is thus at once the human prototype of his people's filial relationship to the Father, the redeemer and guardian of that relationship, and the pledge of that relationship's final consummation in the Spirit.

CONCLUSION

All of the foregoing discussion is but a conceptual paraphrase of the reality announced in the fourth Gospel concerning the Word who was with God and who was God (Jn 1:1), who "became flesh" (Jn 1:14) in order to grant his own "the right to become children of God" (Jn 1:12), and who, having fulfilled his Father's commission on the cross (Jn 19:30), appeared to Mary Magdalene on Easter morning announcing: "I am ascending to my Father and your Father, to my God and your God" (Jn 20:17). More briefly put: The one who is Son by nature became his Father's creature by an act of incomparable generosity so that those who are creatures by nature might share in his filial relationship to the Father by grace.[133] The point of an evangelical metaphysics is nothing else but to explicate this wonderful exchange.

Seminary Bulletin 28 (2007): 141.

[133]Gregory of Nazianzus, *Oration* 30.8; Cyril of Alexandria, *Commentary on John,* in Norman Russell, *Cyril of Alexandria* (London: Routledge, 2000), 100-101.

8

"DELUGED WITH LOVE"

THE SPIRIT AND THE CONSUMMATION
OF TRINITARIAN FELLOWSHIP

◆

INTRODUCTION

There remains one final issue to address concerning the relationship between God's triune identity and his triune self-determination to be our God. The issue concerns the *telos* of God's self-determination for fellowship with us in the Holy Spirit.[1]

God's self-determination to be our God is consummated as he comes to dwell in the midst of his people: "I will walk among you and will be your God" (Lev 26:12; see also Ex 29:45). God's personal presence among his people is the "endorsement," "realization," and "sealing" of the covenant relation.[2] The divine indwelling presence is the great denouement of the Pentateuchal narrative[3] and of the gospel story as well: "When God, through Christ, gives the Spirit to human beings, it is the fulfillment of the greatest promise in which everything is summarized."[4] Jesus was sent from the Father that he

---

[1]See Eberhard Jüngel, *God's Being Is in Becoming: The Trinitarian Being of God in the Theology of Karl Barth*, trans. John Webster (Edinburgh: T & T Clark, 2001), 92.
[2]Rolf Rendtorff, *The Covenant Formula: An Exegetical and Theological Investigation* (Edinburgh: T & T Clark, 1998), 19, 59, 80-81.
[3]Walter Brueggemann, *Theology of the Old Testament: Testimony, Dispute, Advocacy* (Minneapolis: Fortress, 1997), 211-12.
[4]Boris Bobrinskoy, *The Mystery of the Trinity: Trinitarian Experience and Vision in the Biblical and*

might ultimately baptize his people with the Holy Spirit (Mk 1:8), constituting them a temple of the living God, the sacred locus of God's permanent covenantal presence (Jn 14:16-17; 2 Cor 6:16; Rev 21:3), and a chaste bride, the object of his devotion and delight (Eph 5:22-32; Rev 21:2). The electing love of the Father, executed through the gracious condescension and exaltation of the Son, is perfected in the fellowship of the Holy Spirit, by whose presence we are "deluged with love."[5]

The question which Jenson's theology puts before us is: How does God's consummation of fellowship with us in the Spirit relate to the eternal fellowship that exists between the Father and the Son in the same Spirit?[6] Having laid a foundation for addressing this question in the previous two chapters, our discussion will be brief.

MORE THAN "A BIT OF HEGELING"

According to Jenson, the Spirit's role in consummating our communion with the Father in the Son is strictly identical to his role in the Father-Son relationship. The event whereby the Spirit perfects divine fellowship with us is the same event whereby he perfects the Father's fellowship with his Son. That event is the cross and resurrection of Jesus Christ.[7]

The cross constitutes the length God has gone to execute his self-determination to be *our* Father.[8] Moreover, because the man Jesus is at once our brother and God's Son, the event of the cross constitutes

---

Patristic Tradition, trans. Anthony P. Gythiel (Crestwood, NY: St. Vladimir's Seminary Press, 1999), 75.

[5]Jonathan Edwards, *Charity and Its Fruits* (Edinburgh: Banner of Truth, 1969), 328.

[6]Our focus is limited to how the perfection of God's fellowship with us in the Spirit ("God with us") is related to God's eternal being. We must leave aside the question concerning the creaturely side of the God-human relationship, that is, the question of how the perfection of God's fellowship with us in the Spirit ("us with God") affects us. Addressing the latter question would prove a profitable critical angle on Jenson's soteriology and ecclesiology.

[7]See our summary of Jenson's view in chapter four.

[8]Jenson states, "The Crucifixion is what it cost the Father to be in fact—and not just in somebody's projected theology or ideology—the loving and merciful Father of the human persons that in fact exist" (*ST* 1:191).

the length that God has gone to *be* Father.[9] Because Jesus' identity is
intrinsically bound to that of a sinful people whose sin threatens to
thwart their relationship to God, the cross is not merely a test of
whether God will indeed be the merciful Father of sinners. It is also
a test of whether God will be the Father of Jesus Christ, the one who
is bound to sinners as their representative head. Jenson explains the
alternatives: "The Father can have his Son and us with him into the
bargain, or he can abolish us and have no Son, for there is no Son but
the one who said, 'Father, forgive them.'"[10] That the Father raises
Jesus thus realizes his eternal resolve to be our Father and to be the
Father of his Son Jesus Christ.[11]

Talk of the resurrection necessitates talk of "the Spirit of him who
raised Jesus from the dead" (Rom 8:11). Through the events of Good
Friday and Easter, the Spirit consummates God's fatherly relation to
Jesus and to his people. According to Jenson, the Spirit is able to do
so because he "is God as his and our future rushing upon him and
us."[12] As "the End of all God's ways,"[13] the Spirit poses to God his
own future *as* Father and thereby liberates God to be the Father of
Jesus and of the church.[14] The Spirit thus constitutes the triune identity in dramatic coherence, constituting it from the end and not
merely from the beginning.[15]

The Spirit's work is necessary in this regard because, according to
Jenson, the relationship between the Father and his Son Jesus, whatever else might have been, is one inherently threatened by opposition
and struggle against bondage. In dialogue with Hegel's *Phänomenol-*

---

[9]For a recent proposal with close analogy to Jenson on this point, see Neil B. MacDonald, *Metaphysics and the God of Israel: Systematic Theology of the Old and New Testaments* (Grand Rapids:
Baker, 2006), chap. 11.

[10]*ST* 1:191.

[11]*TI,* 146.

[12]*ST* 1:160.

[13]Ibid., 157.

[14]Ibid., 156.

[15]Ibid., 159-60. In Jenson's earlier work, he reassigned the role of "fount of the Trinity" from the
Father to the Spirit (*GAG,* 173). He did not stick with this particular locution, but the conceptual
force of this reassignment persists throughout his work.

ogie des Geistes,[16] Jenson argues that the two—in fact, *any* two—must always stand in tension with each other, must always live under the threat of mutual subjugation and alienation, always, that is, *unless* a third person comes to the rescue.[17] The Spirit's role on this scheme is to rescue the Father and the Son *from* a relationship of mutual subjugation and alienation *for* a relationship of mutual acceptance and love. The Spirit "is another who in his own intention liberates Father and Son to love each other."[18] In Jenson's theology, it is pneumatology which explains how God's intratrinitarian love *actually* prevails, whatever might have been.[19]

This description of the Spirit's role is difficult if not impossible to square with other statements in Jenson's theology (for example: "The love that is the ground of creation would without creation be fully actual in the triune life").[20] Taken as it stands, however, his proposal self-consciously turns the Western-Augustinian understanding of the Spirit's procession on its head.[21] No longer does the Spirit proceed as the hypostatic *fruit* of the rightly ordered relation of love that eternally exists between the Father and the Son.[22] According to Jenson's scheme, the Spirit proceeds as the personal *initiator and enabler* of a rightly ordered relation of love between a Father and a Son who "would have merely 'persisted' in deadlocked opposition" apart from his intervention.[23] In other words, the Spirit does not proceed *because* the Father and the Son perfectly love each other but *in order that* the Father and the Son might perfectly love each other: "The Spirit is

---

[16]See Jenson, *ST* 1:155n61.

[17]*ST* 1:155-56. See also Gary D. Badcock, *Light of Truth and Fire of Love: A Theology of the Holy Spirit* (Grand Rapids: Eerdmans, 1997), 247-48.

[18]*ST* 1:156, 158; see also *ST* 2:26, where the Spirit "frees the Father from retaining all being with himself" so that he can create a creaturely "other."

[19]Robert W. Jenson, "Identity, Jesus, and Exegesis," in *Seeking the Identity of Jesus: A Pilgrimage*, ed. Beverly Roberts Gaventa and Richard B. Hays (Grand Rapids: Eerdmans, 2008), 58.

[20]*ST* 2:28. But see now Jenson, "Once More the *Logos Asarkos*," *International Journal of Systematic Theology* 13 (2011): 131.

[21]See *ST* 1:156-61; see also Wolfhart Pannenberg, *Systematic Theology*, trans. Geoffrey W. Bromiley (Grand Rapids: Eerdmans, 1991), 1:309-19.

[22]See Thomas Aquinas, *Summa theologiae* 1a.37.2.

[23]Brian K. Sholl, "On Robert Jenson's Trinitarian Thought," *Modern Theology* 18 (2002): 33.

himself one who intends love . . . and *therefore* the immediate objects of his intention, the Father and the Son, love each other."[24]

THE SPIRIT AS ALPHA AND OMEGA OF
THE UNDIVIDED SAVING ECONOMY

We may appreciate Jenson's attempt to honor the Spirit's fully hypo-static being as a helpful corrective to Western trinitarianism's tendency to reduce that being to the mode of "fellowship" between the Father and the Son or to the "power" of the divine purpose in its operation *ad extra*.[25] However, this appears to be a case where the proposed cure is worse than the disease.

It is simply not necessary to sacrifice the inherent and inviolable perfection of the Father-Son relation in order to magnify the Spirit's personal density. To be sure, Christian dogmatics must account for the Son's experience of abandonment by the Father on the cross, an experience expressed in the cry of dereliction (e.g., Mk 15:34).[26] But this experience of abandonment should not be conceived as evidence of a general principle that three are better than two, as Jenson's use of Hegel's model would suggest. (In fact, it is unclear how employing Hegel's "Master-Slave" model in this context does not constitute a violation of Jenson's own rule that we interpret the atonement strictly in light of its location within the biblical narrative and not in light of an

---

[24]*ST* 1:158, italics his; see also Robert Jenson, "You Wonder Where the Spirit Went," *Pro Ecclesia* 2 (1993): 300. Contrast Jenson's position here with that of Thomas: "To say that the Holy Spirit stands to the Father and to the Son as a principle of their loving . . . is altogether impossible" (*Summa theologiae* 1a.37.2).

[25]Thus, "You Wonder," 298, 300, 302; *ST* 1:154-55. Jenson seeks to address a fault that he detects in Barth's trinitarian theology but that is also, in his judgment, characteristic of the broader Augustinian tradition. For similar accounts to that of Jenson, see Badcock, *Light of Truth*, 191-92; and Eugene Rogers, *After the Spirit: A Constructive Pneumatology from Resources Outside the Modern West* (Grand Rapids: Eerdmans, 2005), 141. For a more positive interpretation of Barth on this matter, see George Hunsinger, *Disruptive Grace: Studies in the Theology of Karl Barth* (Grand Rapids: Eerdmans, 2000), chap. 7.

[26]For a fine articulation of the Son of God's impassible suffering, see Thomas Weinandy, *Does God Suffer?* (Notre Dame: University of Notre Dame Press, 2000), chap. 8. See also many of the essays in James Keating and Thomas Joseph White, eds., *Divine Impassibility and the Mystery of Human Suffering* (Grand Rapids: Eerdmans, 2009).

alien conceptual scheme.)[27] Nor should the Son's experience of abandonment be conceived as evidence of even a potential disjunction in the divine life.[28]

Jesus' experience of abandonment on the cross should be understood instead as the extension of his willing, personal descent into the abyss of God's curse on God's people (Phil 2:6-8; Gal 3:13), the farthest reach on "the way of the Son of God into the far country" (Barth). Moreover, this descent should be understood as the Son's fulfillment of the vocation given him by the Father in the *pactum salutis.* "God sent forth his Son" (Gal 4:4). And the Son was "obedient to the point of death" (Phil 2:8). Consequently, whatever may be said about Jesus' cry on Golgotha—and silent awe may be the most theologically appropriate response to this mystery—Christian dogmatics must acknowledge the cross to be the consummate expression of the *undivided saving purpose of the Father and the Son.*[29] The cross fulfills the Father's determination to be our God. "It was the will of the LORD to crush him" (Is 53:10). "This was the Lord's doing" (Mk 12:11). And the cross fulfills the Son's filial obedience to the Father's appointment and plan. "I have come to do your will, O God" (Heb 10:7; see also Phil 2:8). "I do as the Father has commanded me, so that the world may know that I love the Father" (Jn 14:31). The cry of dereliction—and the cries of Gethsemane which precede it—do not therefore represent even the possibility of contradiction or conflict in God.[30] They express the costly fulfillment of the undivided triune plan and purpose, which includes the incarnate Son's *willing* assumption of an experience toward which he, as a sin-

[27]See *ST* 1:188-90.
[28]Jenson's theology of the cross is an attempt to walk the fine line between asserting the *possibility* of a rupture in the triune life while denying the *actuality* of such a rupture (contra, for example, Moltmann). See Jenson, "Identity, Jesus, and Exegesis," 56-58.
[29]See Barth's discussion in *CD* 4.1:185-92.
[30]Gary A. Anderson offers penetrating reflections on the ways that God's unswerving, impassible, saving purpose incorporates rather than excludes the contingencies and conflicts of human history in his, "Moses and Jonah in Gethsemane: Representation and Impassibility in Their Old Testament Inflections," in Gaventa and Hays, *Seeking the Identity of Jesus,* 215-31. See also Jenson's essay in the same volume, "Identity, Jesus, and Exegesis," 58.

less human being, must be *naturally averse,* namely, the crushing burden of God's wrath.[31]

Understood in this light, the Spirit's role vis-à-vis the events of Good Friday and Easter cannot be to reconcile an otherwise alienated Father and Son. The Spirit's role must instead be cast in relation to their undivided saving purpose. The Spirit does not appear in the economy as one who must reconcile an otherwise alienated Father and Son. He characteristically appears in contexts where the supreme love and unity of the Father and the Son are on display. Thus, when Jesus descends into the Jordan to be baptized in fulfillment of his Father's will (Mt 3:15), the Spirit descends from heaven signifying the Father's delight in his beloved Son's obedience (Mt 3:16-17; Is 42:1). Similarly, when Jesus rejoices in the Father's "gracious will" to hide his counsel from "the wise" and to reveal it to "little children," he does so "in the Holy Spirit" (Lk 10:21). Jesus obediently offers himself to the Father on the cross "through the eternal Spirit" (Heb 9:14), and the Father expresses effectual approbation for Jesus' obedience by vindicating him, through the same Spirit, in the resurrection (Rom 1:4; 1 Tim 3:16).[32] Within this economy, the Spirit rushes forth in the mutual, impassible and undivided resolve of the Father and the Son to include treacherous creatures within their eternal bliss.

We must add also that the Spirit empowers the consummation of this undivided resolve of the Father and the Son as one who is an eternal party to this resolve. According to Paul, "the Spirit searches ... the depths of God" (1 Cor 2:10), the depths which concern God's secret decree "before the ages" regarding the crucifixion of "the Lord of glory" (1 Cor 2:7-8). The Spirit, with the Father and the Son, is thus *both* Alpha and Omega in relation to the saving economy of the

---

[31]Maximus the Confessor, Opuscules 3 and 7, in Andrew Louth, *Maximus the Confessor* (London and New York: Routledge, 1996), 193-98 and 180-91 respectively. See also Ivor Davidson, "'Not My Will but Yours Be Done': The Ontological Dynamics of Incarnational Intention," *International Journal of Systematic Theology* 7 (2005): 178-204.

[32]For further discussion of the Spirit's role vis-à-vis the Son's faithful execution of his Father's mission, see Bobrinskoy, *Mystery,* 76-100.

cross: the incomprehensible, untutored author and executor of God's eternal decree (see Is 40:13-14).

PERFECTLY SUPERFLUOUS

The Spirit does not enable the perfect union of the Father and the Son in love. The Spirit expresses the perfect union of the Father and the Son in love. He does not proceed due to some lack or limitation in the Father-Son relation, a lack or limitation that he must overcome. He proceeds in the Father's infinite ocean of delight in the Son, and, if we accept the *filioque*, in the Son's infinite ocean of delight in the Father.[33]

Does such a view reduce the Spirit to the status of impersonal bond between the Father and the Son, as Jenson and many others worry? Not if we follow Eugene Rogers and identify the Spirit as the *witness* of the love that exists between the Father and the Son.[34] The notion of witness accounts for the Spirit's identity as the *third* person of the Trinity: "A witness is irreducibly a third, tied to the two, but giving its own testimony." The notion of witness also accounts for the Spirit's identity as the third *person*: "A witness can be the bond of love between the Father and the Son *in Person* and not as an inanimate chain."[35] As witness, the Spirit is a genuinely personal agent who "seals" the Father's love for the Son and the Son's love for the Father.[36] In this regard, he *adds* to their love, not by filling a deficit in that love but rather by searching out, celebrating and confirming the fullness of that perfect love.[37] "The logic" of the

---

[33]See William Desmond, *Hegel's God: A Counterfeit Double?* (Aldershot: Ashgate, 2003), 116; Matthew Levering, *Scripture and Metaphysics: Aquinas and the Renewal of Trinitarian Theology* (Oxford: Blackwell, 2004), 194-95; and Emery, *Trinitarian Theology*, 249-58.

[34]Rogers, *After the Spirit*, 141. For the Spirit's role as witness, see Jn 15:26; Acts 15:8; Rom 8:16; Heb 2:4; 10:15; etc. Jenson also appeals to the Spirit's role as witness in his (quite different) construal; see *TI*, 147-48.

[35]Rogers, *After the Spirit*, 141.

[36]See T. C. O'Brien, who says the Spirit "is their Love as the impress and seal of their love for each other." In "The Holy Spirit: Love (1a.37, 1 & 2)," Appendix 2 in Thomas Aquinas, *Summa theologiae*, vol. 7 (New York and London: McGraw-Hill, 1976).

[37]Rogers, *After the Spirit*, 67.

Spirit's sealing activity in this regard "is not the logic of productivity, but the logic of superfluity."[38]

Such an understanding of the Spirit's personal character is not the fruit of empty speculation, unrelated to the economy of salvation. We know these traits belong to the Spirit's distinctive personal character because the fatherly love he seals *to* us (Rom 5:5) and the filial love he awakens *in* us (Rom 8:15; see also Mk 14:36) are nothing other than a creaturely fellowship in the *same* love shared by the Father and the Son "before the foundation of the world" (Jn 17:24-26; also Jn 1:1).[39] Because he is "the Spirit of [God's] Son," he is able to replicate the archetypical love of the Father and the Son in God's adopted children by including them within the circle of that love: "Because you are sons, God has sent the Spirit of his Son into our hearts, crying, 'Abba! Father!'" (Gal 4:6). In doing so, the Spirit acts according to his own hypostatic character.

It is relevant to note at this point one further, and ironic, accompaniment of Jenson's pneumatological revision. Not only does Jenson's construal of the Spirit strike against the inherent perfection of the Father-Son relation, it also strikes against the possibility of other properly related pairs. Just as in Jenson's thought the Spirit no longer proceeds as the personal bond of perfect communion between the Father and the Son, so is he unable to effect communion between other peacefully related dualities, such as the divine and human natures of Christ (on Jenson's scheme, the two natures must be "transcended" in a higher personal synthesis)[40] or the Logos and his body (on Jenson's scheme, the Logos must leave behind the body born of

---

[38]Ibid., 71.

[39]The Belgic Confession, article 9, states: "All this we know, as well from the testimonies of Holy Writ as from their operations, and chiefly by those we feel in ourselves." In Philip Schaff, ed., *The Creeds of Christendom* (repr. Grand Rapids: Baker, 1996), 3:390.

[40]*ST* 2:173. While I am very much indebted to Jenson for his Cyrilline emphasis upon the unity of Christ, I worry that his preference for the language of a hypostatic union "from two natures" over against Chalcedon's "in two natures" (*ST* 1:131-32) indicates a material departure from the church's dogmatic christology. For a more sanguine reading of Jenson on this point, however, see Tee Gatewood, "A Nicene Christology? Robert Jenson and the Two Natures of Jesus Christ," *Pro Ecclesia* 18 (2009): 28-49.

Mary's womb and laid in Joseph's tomb for a new mode of "embodiment" in his gathered church).[41] Jenson's revision is ironic because it ultimately reveals a failure to excise a false, contrastive view of the God-world relation from his theology. He has instead *dramatized* this false view, making it a moment in the story of God and creation, a moment which the Spirit must *transcend*. But *Aufhebung* is not the same thing as the Spirit's *koinonia*.

The Spirit does not bear the burden of overcoming (even potential) *personal* differences between the Father and the Son. And neither does he bear the burden of overcoming the *ontological* differences between God and creation. There is no inherent "distance" between Father and Son that he must overcome by enabling a higher synthesis of the two. Nor is there a distance between Creator and creature that he must overcome, whether in the case of history more generally or in the case of the hypostatic union more particularly. Instead, the Spirit acts as the one whose personal character it is to "cross" or "traverse" such differences (not distances!) "in love." He lovingly binds the two together, whether it be the Father and the Son, the Creator and his creatures, or the Word and his flesh, in a fellowship that does not "abrogate" their differences but that rather affirms and embraces them in their natural affinities.[42]

THE SPIRIT OF GOD AND OF THE GOSPEL

What, then, is the Spirit's role in relation to God's triune being and self-determination to be our God? The sketch of an answer looks something like this: The Spirit overflows in the fullness of the Father and the Son's natural and necessary love, in a procession that is *per modum voluntatis, concomitante natura*. As the one who proceeds in the fullness of the Father and the Son's mutual love, the Spirit exhib-

---

[41]*ST* 1:201-6.
[42]Desmond, *Hegel's God,* 118, for quotes in this and the preceding sentence. For helpful reflections on the way a trinitarian pneumatology enables us "to conceive a created world that is external to God and which does not yet exclude interrelationship," see Colin Gunton, *The Triune Creator: A Historical and Systematic Study* (Grand Rapids: Eerdmans, 1998), 141-44.

its the inexhaustible nature of that love and in so doing constitutes hypostatically the "readiness" of the Father and the Son to include us within that love as well.[43] The eternal, mysterious procession of the Spirit from the Father and the Son is therefore the deepest "foundation" of all the saving benefits which he distributes to us, and supremely "of all our distinct communion with him and our worship of him."[44] Because *he* is eternally welcome in the fellowship of the Father and the Son, *we* too may be welcomed into the fellowship of the Father and the Son.

The Spirit who flows forth in the mutual love of the Father and the Son fathoms the possibilities and purposes of that love. In one simple act of divine freedom, the Spirit who affirms and participates in that mutual love thus affirms the eternal and utterly superfluous plan to include us as participants within that mutual love. In this way, the Spirit adds his seal to the *pactum salutis*, which reaches its goal *ad extra* as he sheds abroad in time that which he searches out in eternity: God's eternal love for his Son and for his people in and with the Son.

As the agent who immediately effects the incarnation, the Spirit empowers the Son's personal assumption of human nature in Mary's womb (Lk 1:34-35).[45] Throughout the course of Jesus' earthly life, the Spirit "enables the incarnate Christ to be himself—to be who he

---

[43]See Emmanuel Durand, "A Theology of God the Father," in *Oxford Handbook of the Trinity*, ed. Gilles Emery and Matthew Levering (Oxford: Oxford University Press, 2011), 383-84.

[44]John Owen, *Communion with the Triune God*, ed. Kelly M. Kapic and Justin Taylor (Wheaton, IL: Crossway, 2007), 360.

[45]The Spirit is the agent who immediately effects the incarnation in the same way that he is an agent of all external (and hence undivided) operations of the Trinity, that is to say, as the one by whom the acts which proceed from the Father through the Son are brought to their perfection. See Gregory of Nyssa, *An Answer to Ablabius: That We Should Not Think of Saying There Are Three Gods*, in *Christology of the Later Fathers*, ed. Edward R. Hardy (Louisville: Westminster John Knox, 1954), 262. Though I am open to being persuaded, I am not yet convinced that a "Spirit christology" like that of John Owen provides the conceptual key to a coherent Reformed and catholic christology and thus to describing the Spirit's agency in this regard. For an articulate account of such a christology, see Alan Spence, *Inspiration and Incarnation: John Owen and the Coherence of Christology* (London: T & T Clark, 2007). For its potential problems, see Oliver D. Crisp, *Revisioning Christology: Theology in the Reformed Tradition* (Farnham, Surrey: Ashgate, 2011), chap. 5.

is as the presence of God in properly human form among us."[46] This divine enablement includes equipping Jesus with all of the graces necessary for growth in wisdom (Lk 2:52) and obedience (Heb 5:8), as well as with the leadership required for executing his divinely given mission (Mk 1:12; Lk 4:1-21). In these ways and others, the Spirit progressively enables Jesus to become a truly perfected human being (Heb 5:9), the paradigm for a renewed filial humanity (Gal 3:26-28).[47]

Having enabled the completion of Jesus' earthly mission through his self-offering to the Father on the cross (Heb 5:9; 9:14), the Spirit becomes the immediate agent of Jesus' resurrection (Rom 1:4; 1 Tim 3:16) and thereby ushers the incarnate Son into the glorious destiny appointed for humanity from the beginning of creation (see Heb 2:5–4:13). As the Gospel of John makes clear, the glory that the Son inherits is not new for the Son *as* Son. He returns to the glory he had with the Father "before the world existed" (Jn 17:5). Nevertheless, the glory that the Son inherits *is* new in that he now enjoys that glory *as the incarnate head of the new humanity,* "the firstborn from the dead" (Col 1:18) and the "firstfruits" of the final eschatological harvest (1 Cor 15:20).[48] By the Spirit's power, the Son realizes humanity's eschatological perfection, becoming the "spiritual" man (1 Cor 15:42-49).[49]

---

[46]Davidson, "Not My Will," 200-204.

[47]The progressive perfection of Jesus' humanity is a special emphasis in Reformed christological thinking. See Bavinck, *Reformed Dogmatics,* trans. John Vriend (Grand Rapids: Baker, 2004), 3:311-13; also R. Michael Allen, *The Christ's Faith: A Dogmatic Account* (London: T & T Clark, 2009).

[48]For further discussion, see Richard B. Gaffin, *Resurrection and Redemption.* See also Bavinck, *Reformed Dogmatics,* 3:432-36.

[49]The contrast between the "natural" human and the "spiritual" human in 1 Corinthians 15 is not a contrast between "embodied" human and "disembodied" human. According to 1 Cor 15:44, Christ inherits a "spiritual *body.*" The contrast is between man in his original state and man in his eschatological, perfected state. See Gordon Fee, *God's Empowering Presence: The Holy Spirit in the Letters of Paul* (Peabody: Hendrickson, 1994), 262-69; also Bavinck, *Reformed Dogmatics,* 2:564-88. For the Spirit's role in Jesus' human and therefore *temporal* development and growth in grace, see Wilhelmus à Brakel, *The Christian's Reasonable Service,* trans. Bartel Elshout, ed. Joel R. Beeke (Grand Rapids: Reformation Heritage Books, 1992-1995), 1:506.

Moreover, the same Spirit by which the incarnate Son inherits eschatological glory guarantees the eschatological glorification of God's elect children as well (Eph 1:13-14; see also 1 Cor 15:48-49; Phil 3:21). Indeed, the Spirit guarantees *our* eschatological glory because of *his* eschatological glory. And here is another reason why we must distinguish more sharply than Jenson does between Christ's personal body and Christ's ecclesial body: "Because Christ's humanity is the pathway by which we receive the Spirit, his humanity must be fully transformed by the Spirit in order for it to spill out and over to others."[50] And so, having transformed Christ's glorious body, and by means of the ministry of "the gospel of the glory of Christ" (2 Cor 4:4), the Spirit causes Christ's glory to overflow in the formation of a renewed humanity in order that it may be "exalted, not as God or like God, but to God, being placed at his side, not in identity, but in true fellowship with him, and becoming a new man in this exaltation and fellowship."[51]

The Spirit thus "blazes a trail through time on the way to the kingdom":[52] birthing, nourishing and perfecting the *totus Christus*, head and body. Ultimately, the perfecting of the Spirit's economic activity involves welcoming God's children to share with him in the antecedently perfect love of the Father and the Son, world without end (see Rev 22:17). The Spirit's perfect fellowship in the eternal love of the Father and the Son thus includes his perfecting of our fellowship in that love as well.[53]

CONCLUSION

Jonathan Edwards's meditations on heaven as a world of love provide a fitting conclusion to the present chapter:

---

[50]Kathryn Tanner, *Christ the Key* (Cambridge: Cambridge University Press, 2010), 171.

[51]*CD* 4.2:6; see also 100-101.

[52]The language here is Willem Van Asselt's, summarizing Johannes Cocceius's view of the Spirit's role in the economy of creation and redemption. *The Federal Theology of Johannes Cocceius (1603-1669)* (Leiden: Brill, 2001), 193.

[53]See again Thomas, *Summa theologiae* 1a.37.2, for a more general statement of this principle.

There, even in heaven, dwells the God from whom every stream of holy love, yea, every drop that is, or ever was, proceeds. There dwells God the Father, God the Son, and God the Spirit, united as one, in infinitely dear, and incomprehensible, and mutual, and eternal love. There dwells God the Father, who is the father of mercies, and so the father of love, who so loved the world as to give his only-begotten Son to die for it. There dwells Christ, the Lamb of God, the prince of peace and of love, who so loved the world that he shed his blood, and poured out his soul unto death for men. There dwells the great Mediator, through whom all the divine love is expressed toward men, and by whom the fruits of that love have been purchased, and through whom they are communicated, and through whom love is imparted to the hearts of all God's people. There dwells Christ in both his natures, the human and the divine, sitting on the same throne with the Father. And there dwells the Holy Spirit—the Spirit of divine love, in whom the very essence of God, as it were, flows out, and is breathed forth in love, and by whose immediate influence all holy love is shed abroad in the hearts of all the saints on earth and in heaven. There, in heaven, this infinite fountain of love—this eternal Three in One—is set open without any obstacle to hinder access to it, as it flows for ever. There this glorious God is manifested, and shines forth, in full glory, in beams of love. And there this glorious fountain for ever flows forth in streams, yea, in rivers of love and delight, and these rivers swell, as it were, to an ocean of love, in which the souls of the ransomed may bathe with the sweetest enjoyment, and their hearts, as it were, be deluged with love![54]

---

[54]Edwards, *Charity and Its Fruits* (Edinburgh: Banner of Truth, 1969), 327-28.

GRACE AND BEING

Bruce McCormack on the Gospel's God

♦

INTRODUCTION

In this chapter we return to the broader discussion of trinitarian theology after Barth, and to one of the principal participants in this discussion, Bruce L. McCormack, Charles Hodge Professor of Systematic Theology at Princeton Theological Seminary. McCormack is the leading contemporary proponent of the "inconsistency thesis" described in chapter two. Over the past decade or so, he has initiated a highly controversial and constructive proposal regarding the relationship between God's being and self-determination. McCormack's essay in *The Cambridge Companion to Karl Barth* ignited widespread debate among contemporary Anglo-American Barth interpreters not only about how best to interpret Barth but also about how best to appropriate Barth in constructive dogmatics.[1] McCormack's subsequent publications have further demonstrated the importance of the present topic to a proper understanding of

---

[1]Bruce L. McCormack, "Grace and Being: The Role of God's Gracious Election in Karl Barth's Theological Ontology," in *The Cambridge Companion to Karl Barth*, ed., John Webster (Cambridge: Cambridge University Press, 2000), 92-110; republished in McCormack, *Orthodox and Modern: Studies in the Theology of Karl Barth* (Grand Rapids: Baker, 2008), chap. 7. See also the discussion in chapter two.

the gospel's God.[2] Our study would be incomplete therefore without some interaction with his work.

It is worth observing at the outset that McCormack's proposal is still in its provisional stages of articulation, if not development. With the exception of a handful of articles and essays, most of McCormack's writings on our topic to date have been directly concerned with interpreting Barth, or else with defending his interpretation of Barth against its critics, and only indirectly with elaborating his own constructive position.[3] Consequently, we still await the full complement of exegetical, historical and conceptual argumentation that will accompany a straightforward dogmatic account of his thesis. In recent years, McCormack has delivered a number of distinguished lectures series that promise to provide a more complete dogmatic foun-

---

[2]Besides the essays included in *Orthodox and Modern,* see Bruce L. McCormack, "The Ontological Presuppositions of Barth's Doctrine of the Atonement," in *The Glory of the Atonement: Biblical, Historical, and Practical Perspectives: Essays in Honor of Roger Nicole,* ed. Charles E. Hill and Frank A. James III (Downers Grove, IL: InterVarsity Press, 2004), 346-66; "Karl Barth's Christology as a Resource for a Reformed Version of Kenoticism," *International Journal of Systematic Theology* 8 (2006): 243-51; "The Actuality of God: Karl Barth in Conversation with Open Theism," in *Engaging the Doctrine of God: Contemporary Protestant Perspectives,* ed. Bruce L. McCormack (Grand Rapids: Baker 2008), 185-242; "'With Loud Cries and Tears': The Humanity of the Son in the Epistle to the Hebrews," in *The Epistle to the Hebrews and Christian Theology,* ed. Richard Bauckham, Daniel R. Driver, Trevor A. Hart and Nathan MacDonald (Grand Rapids: Eerdmans, 2009), 37-68; "God *Is* His Decision: The Jüngel-Gollwitzer 'Debate' Revisited," in *Theology as Conversation: The Significance of Dialogue in Historical and Contemporary Theology: A Festschrift for Daniel L. Migliore,* ed. Bruce L. McCormack and Kimlyn J. Bender (Grand Rapids: Eerdmans, 2009), 48-66; "Divine Impassibility or Simply Divine Constancy? Implications of Karl Barth's Later Christology for Debates over Impassibility," in *Divine Impassibility and the Mystery of Human Suffering,* ed. James F. Keating and Thomas Joseph White (Grand Rapids: Eerdmans, 2009); "Election and the Trinity: Theses in Response to George Hunsinger," *Scottish Journal of Theology* 63 (2010): 203-334; "Let's Speak Plainly: A Response to Paul Molnar," *Theology Today* 67 (2010): 57-65; "Why Should Theology Be Christocentric? Christology and Metaphysics in Paul Tillich and Karl Barth," *Wesleyan Theological Journal* 45 (2010): 42-80; "Karl Barth's Version of an 'Analogy of Being': A Dialectical No and Yes to Roman Catholicism," in *The Analogy of Being: Invention of the Antichrist or the Wisdom of God?* ed. Thomas Joseph White (Grand Rapids: Eerdmans, 2011), 88-146; "The Doctrine of the Trinity After Barth: An Attempt to Reconstruct Barth's Doctrine in Light of His Later Christology," in *Trinitarian Theology After Barth,* ed. Myk Habets and Phillip Tolliday (Eugene, OR: Pickwick, 2011), 87-118. An important earlier study that anticipates many of his later doctrinal moves may be found in Bruce L. McCormack, *For Us and Our Salvation: Incarnation and Atonement in the Reformed Tradition,* Studies in Reformed Theology and History 1 (Princeton: Princeton Theological Seminary, 1993).

[3]See McCormack, *Orthodox and Modern,* 265.

dation to his constructive claims.[4] When these lecture series are published, a fuller account of his doctrine of God will be possible, as will a more intelligent response.[5] It is also worth noting that McCormack's arguments have undergone some degree of modification over the course of debate—particularly with respect to the character of divine freedom, and this too must qualify our engagement as tentative in nature.

With these observations in view, the aim of the present chapter is as follows: to summarize the main lines of McCormack's proposal regarding the relationship between God's being and self-determination, and to offer a response to that proposal, in dialogue with other responses that have already appeared. The goal is not to assess McCormack's reading of Karl Barth, but rather to engage McCormack's own constructive dogmatic claim regarding "the subject matter to which he [Barth] bore witness," namely, the being of the gospel's God. As McCormack rightly insists: "It is to that subject matter that we must direct our attention, not to Karl Barth as an end in himself."[6]

TOWARD A REFORMED EVANGELICAL HISTORICISM

McCormack's proposal is quite simple. If Barth's identification of Jesus Christ as the electing God is to be taken with utter seriousness, then God's triune identity must be viewed as the (logical not temporal) consequence of his eternal election to be our God in the covenant of grace. According to McCormack, the eternal act in which God gives himself to be *our* Father, through the Son, in the Spirit is the act in which God gives himself his being *as* Father, Son and Spirit. God's eternal act of grace determines God's eternal act of being.[7] This eternal act of divine self-determination in turn grounds

---

[4]These include the T. F. Torrance Lectures at the University of St. Andrews in 2008, the Croall Lectures at the University of Edinburgh in 2011, and the Kenneth Kantzer Lectures in Revealed Theology at Trinity Evangelical Divinity School in 2011.
[5]McCormack's article, "Karl Barth's Christology as a Resource," provides a brief introduction to his T. F. Torrance Lectures.
[6]McCormack, "Election and the Trinity," 224.
[7]See McCormack, *Orthodox and Modern*, 265-66.

the historical movement whereby God reconciles humanity to himself through the humiliation and exaltation of Jesus Christ and guarantees that this historical movement truly corresponds to God's being. Put differently, the "economic Trinity" (i.e., God in the history of revelation and reconciliation) corresponds to the "immanent Trinity" (i.e., God in himself) because the immanent Trinity is nothing other than the ontological precondition of the economic Trinity: God in his eternal and exclusive resolve to be our God by virtue of the election of grace.[8]

Intrinsic to McCormack's understanding of divine election is a historicized understanding of divine being. McCormack seeks to extend the historicizing trajectory, initiated by Barth and continued by theologians like Jenson, through translating the two natures of Christ into the twofold history of a single divine-human subject.[9] McCormack's evangelical historicizing is distinguished from that of many of his Lutheran contemporaries, however, in its commitment to preserving what he regards as two essential features of a Reformed christology: (1) the abiding, absolute distinction between Christ's two natures; and (2) the identification of the Mediator in his theanthropic unity as the "subject" of christology rather than "the [second] *hypostasis* as such."[10] The first feature blocks the so-called *genus majestaticum* of Lutheran christology (which posits a communication of divine attributes directly to the human nature of Jesus)[11] and leads instead to a more robust defense of the *Logos asarkos* than is found in his historicizing Lutheran counterparts, whose focus tends to be on the man Jesus qua man as the second hypostasis of the Trinity.[12] The

---

[8]McCormack, "God *Is* His Decision," 59; "Election and the Trinity," 217; *Orthodox and Modern*, 187, 266.

[9]McCormack, *Orthodox and Modern*, 222, 232.

[10]McCormack, *For Us and Our Salvation*, 16. See also "Karl Barth's Christology as a Resource," 247-48.

[11]McCormack, "Karl Barth's Christology as a Resource," 247.

[12]See chapter two. This, of course, is not an exclusively Lutheran tendency. Jürgen Moltmann, a Reformed theologian, is also less than secure in his affirmation of Christ's two natures. See Moltmann, *The Crucified God: The Cross of Christ as the Foundation and Criticism of Christian Theology*, trans. R. A. Wilson and John Bowden (Minneapolis: Fortress, 1993), 244-46; and *The Trinity*

second feature enables McCormack to emphasize both the fully
human nature of the Mediator's life and experience, including his
complete dependence on the Holy Spirit throughout his ministry,[13]
and also the unity, indeed *correspondence*, between the Christ's divine
nature/history and his human nature/history since the two never
exist in isolation from Christ's "composite person."[14] Because the
subject of his Christology "is not finally the Logos *simpliciter*, but the
Logos made human,"[15] the eternal *divine* being of the Son of God
must be conceived as an eternal being-toward his *human* incarnation,
suffering and death, as a being that is susceptible to human suffering
and death.[16] The Mediator's eternal deity, in this scheme, is nothing
other than the necessary ontological precondition for his historical
humanity.[17] Accordingly, though distinct from and transcendent of
his human nature, the *Logos asarkos* never exists in abstraction from
his human nature but is always *ensarkos*, whether by anticipation in
election as the *Logos incarnandus* (i.e., the to-be-incarnate Logos) or
by realization in history as the *Logos incarnatus* (i.e., the incarnate
Logos).[18] This is what it means for McCormack to affirm with Barth
that God's "deity *encloses humanity in itself*."[19]

McCormack's Reformed understanding of God's evangelical self-
determination results in a more pronounced protological emphasis
in his doctrine of the Trinity than is found in Jenson's doctrine, which

and the Kingdom: The Doctrine of God, trans. Margaret Kohl (Minneapolis: Fortress, 1993), 120-21.
[13]McCormack, "With Loud Cries and Tears," 38-46. For further discussion of this stream of modern Reformed christology, see Alan Spence, *Inspiration and Incarnation: John Owen and the Coherence of Christology* (London: T & T Clark, 2007).
[14]See McCormack, "With Loud Cries and Tears," 41-51.
[15]McCormack, *For Us and Our Salvation*, 34.
[16]Though he rejects the *genus majestaticum*, McCormack affirms the *genus tapeinoticum* ("Karl
   Barth's Christology as a Resource," 247, 250-51). It should be noted that this Christology explains how McCormack can affirm death *in* God while repudiating the death *of* God. God, in the
   theanthropic person of the Mediator, embraces a fully human experience of death and thereby
   overcomes it ("For Us and Our Salvation," 34; "Karl Barth's Christology as a Resource," 247, 250;
   "With Loud Cries and Tears," 55-56).
[17]McCormack, "Election and the Trinity," 217. See also McCormack, *Orthodox and Modern*, 187.
[18]McCormack, *Orthodox and Modern*, 266-67.
[19]Karl Barth, *The Humanity of God* (Atlanta: John Knox Press, 1960), 50, italics in the original.

exhibits a more pronounced eschatological emphasis. In terms of a different set of tradition-historical labels: Whereas Jenson's historicized Trinity tends in a more "Dominican" direction, focusing on the trinitarian persons in light of their *fully realized* (*eschatological*) *relations*, McCormack's historicized Trinity tends in a more "Franciscan" direction, focusing on the trinitarian persons in light of their (*pretemporal*) *productive origin in the Father,* who is the personal fountain from whom the other two persons spring forth in the eternal act of divine self-determination.[20] For Jenson, identifying God as Trinity involves identifying the Father as the one who eschatologically raises the man Jesus in the Spirit to be his Son. For McCormack, however, identifying God as Trinity involves identifying the Father as the one who eternally begets the Son in the act of commissioning him to be the incarnate Mediator and who eternally breathes the Spirit in the act of commissioning him to empower the Mediator with everything necessary to accomplish his reconciling work.[21] The eternal processions thus flow from the eternal missions.[22]

McCormack's doctrine of the triune God is ultimately driven by two christological desiderata. The first desideratum is epistemological in nature and concerns the quest to limit our knowledge of God exclusively to the sphere of that which is revealed in the history of Jesus the God-man. McCormack believes that traditional theism failed to meet this requirement insofar as it derived its doctrine of God "metaphysically"—that is to say, by attempting to speak of God

---

[20]These two tendencies are discussed in Friedman, *Medieval Trinitarian Thought from Aquinas to Ockham* (Cambridge: Cambridge University Press, 2010), chap. 1. Needless to say, these two tendencies are not developed in historicizing directions by medieval theologians and therefore do not exhibit the protological and eschatological features described above. Moreover, both the Franciscan tendency and the Dominican tendency affirm the importance of relations of origin and relations of opposition in defining the nature of the trinitarian persons. The difference between these two tendencies is one of emphasis and concerns that which is *foundational* to the constitution of the trinitarian persons.

[21]McCormack, "The Doctrine of the Trinity After Barth," 111-12; "Karl Barth's Christology as a Resource," 249; *Orthodox and Modern*, 194.

[22]The significance of identifying McCormack's trinitarian theology as "Franciscan" will be demonstrated in due course.

by speaking of something else (whether the cosmos in ancient thought or the human person in modern thought), rather than deriving its doctrine of God christologically—that is to say, by speaking of God solely on the basis of God's *self*-revelation in Jesus Christ.[23] The second desideratum is ontological in nature and concerns the quest to define the being of God exclusively in terms of that which makes possible the history of Jesus the God-man.[24] The doctrine of God under this principle is controlled by the question of *Church Dogmatics* 4.1: *Quo iure Deus homo?* By what right or inner law of the divine being did God become a man?[25] What must be true of God if God can "live a human life, suffer and die without undergoing change on the level of his being?"[26] In McCormack's judgment, even Barth reveals inconsistency in the answers he provides to this question, affirming for example a *Logos asarkos* that exists independently of his self-determination to be the God-man Jesus Christ,[27] rather than limiting the being of the *Logos asarkos* exclusively to that which makes possible the *Logos ensarkos*.[28] According to McCormack, both desiderata may be satisfied within a hermeneutical circle that posits a historicized christology as the epistemological basis for a doctrine of the electing God and a doctrine of the electing God as the ontological basis for a historicized christology.[29] Anything beyond this hermeneutical circle, he fears, amounts to unwarranted "speculation" and threatens to introduce a "metaphysical gap" between God's being and his evangelical self-determination.[30]

---

[23]McCormack, "Why Should Theology Be Christocentric?" 64; "The Actuality of God," 186-88. For a similar line of argument, see Gunton, *Act and Being*.
[24]McCormack, *Orthodox and Modern*, 187, 267; "God *Is* His Decision," 57, 62, 64.
[25]*CD* 4.1:184.
[26]McCormack, "Why Should Theology Be Christocentric?" 73. See also *Orthodox and Modern*, 187.
[27]For example, *CD* 4.1:52.
[28]McCormack, "Election and the Trinity," 220-21; *Orthodox and Modern*, 193-94.
[29]Compare with what McCormack says about the hermeneutical relationship between Barth's doctrine of election in *CD* 2.2 and his later christology of *CD* 4: "Christology is the epistemological basis of election, and election is the ontological basis of Christology" ("Karl Barth's Version," 90).
[30]The twin worries about (1) "speculation" (or "abstraction") and (2) the introduction of a "metaphysical gap" between God's being and self-determination seem to be the corresponding negative epistemological and ontological alternatives to satisfying McCormack's twin christological desid-

QUESTIONS OF DOGMATIC COHERENCE
AND CORRESPONDENCE

As noted above, McCormack's proposal has evoked a number of responses. Many of these are primarily concerned with his interpretation of Barth, and thus with matters that lie beyond the scope of the present study. Insofar as these responses do focus more directly on the constructive dogmatic dimension of McCormack's proposal, they tend to be concerned not only with the coherence of his constructive claim, but also with its correspondence with certain fundamental features of trinitarian orthodoxy.

With respect to McCormack's understanding of the "subject" of election, some have questioned whether it is coherent to affirm at one and the same time that Jesus Christ is the *subject* of God's primal decree and that he is the *consequence* of God's primal decree.[31] If Jesus the God-man only exists as a result of God's electing grace, it is unclear how he can be the cause of electing grace. It seems that McCormack is saying: "Jesus Christ elects [i.e., constitutes himself] to be Jesus Christ."[32] McCormack's response is to suggest that, as in the case of Barth, the *theologoumenon* "Jesus Christ is the electing God" is *christological* shorthand for what is actually a *trinitarian* statement about God's evangelical self-determination. Because God's triunity consists in his being "one divine subject in three modes of being," it

---

erata. See, for example, "Election and the Trinity," 208, 209, 210, 212, 213, 214, 215, 216, 217, 219, 222.

[31]See Edwin Christian van Driel, "Karl Barth on the Eternal Existence of Jesus Christ," *Scottish Journal of Theology* 60 (2007): 54-56. See also George Hunsinger, "Election and the Trinity: Twenty-Five Theses on the Theology of Karl Barth," *Modern Theology* 24 (2008): 196n7: "The idea that 'God gives himself being' . . . seems unintelligible."

[32]Van Driel, "Karl Barth on the Eternal Existence," 55. Someone might respond to the coherence challenge by suggesting that McCormack's critics are begging the question, presupposing an unevangelized metaphysics perhaps, where subjects must precede their acts of existence rather than being constituted in their acts of existence. However, this response seems misplaced. As Kevin Hector explains: "McCormack does not think that God's determination to be God-with-us is *subjectless*, since that would render the determination a matter of fact rather than will, such that the God so determined could *not* be otherwise—not freely, at any rate." Hector, "Immutability, Necessity, and Triunity: Towards a Resolution of the Trinity and Election Controversy," *Scottish Journal of Theology* 65 (2012): 67n9.

is strictly speaking the divine subject *in his first mode of being* who initiates the self-determination to be our God in the covenant of grace and who, as the logical consequence of that self-determination, begets the *Logos incarnandus* and breathes forth the Spirit of Jesus.[33]

While this response may satisfy the criterion of coherence, some wonder whether it fails to satisfy the more significant criterion of correspondence with Nicene orthodoxy. McCormack's claim that the subject of election precedes that subject's second and third modes of being, who eternally proceed as a consequence of election, seems to the mind of some critics to entail either modalism or subordinationism.[34] This claim seems to entail modalism insofar as the subject of election is not, strictly speaking, identical with the Father. The subject of election seems instead to be *a fourth mode of the divine subjectivity* that only begins to exist as Father as a consequence of election when he generates the Son and breathes forth the Spirit.[35] This claim seems to entail subordinationism insofar as the subject of election either *possesses capacities* (e.g., existing independently of the decree of election) that the second and third persons do not possess or *performs actions* (e.g., issuing the decree of election) that the second and third persons of the Trinity do not perform.[36] We will consider these charges in order.

The modalism charge appears to presuppose what I have (admittedly, rather loosely) described above as a "Dominican" trinitarian logic, where persons are constituted fundamentally by *relations of opposition*. According to this logic, the first person of the Trinity *is* Father only insofar as he *stands in relation* to the second person of the Trinity *as Father*. On such a scheme, to posit the existence of the subject of election (even logically) prior to his fatherly relation to the sec-

---

[33]McCormack, *Orthodox and Modern*, 270-72.
[34]See Hector's helpful discussion of these two charges in "Immutability, Necessity, and Triunity," 66-68, 78-81.
[35]Thus, for example, Edwin Christian van Driel, *Incarnation Anyway: Arguments for Supralapsarian Christology* (Oxford: Oxford University Press, 2008), 100-101.
[36]Thus, for example, Hunsinger, "Election and the Trinity," 192-93.

ond person of the Trinity is thus to introduce a fourth mode of divine subjectivity, a mode that cannot be identified as Father, Son or Holy Spirit because it does not yet stand in any person-constituting relation to the other persons prior to the decree of election.

One potential response to this line of criticism is to observe that McCormack's doctrine of the Trinity does not seem to reflect a "Dominican" logic.[37] Rather, as we have already seen, it seems to reflect (at least implicitly) a "Franciscan" logic.[38] According to a Franciscan logic, the persons of the Trinity are not constituted fundamentally by *relations of opposition*. They are constituted fundamentally by *relations of origin*. Consequently, while having a son is the *consequence* of first person's fatherly identity on a Franciscan model, it is not what *constitutes* the first person's fatherly identity. What constitutes the first person's identity as Father is not his having a son. What constitutes the first person's identity as Father is his "innascibility," his being *unemanated* from any other divine person. Moreover, innascibility on this scheme is not merely a negative property (i.e., signifying the first person's lack of being emanated from someone else), as it is on a Dominican model. Innascibility on this scheme is a positive property, signifying the first person's *inherent capacity* to beget the Son and to breathe forth the Spirit. Innascibility here means "primity" or "fontal plenitude." In McCormackian terms, innascibility thus refers to the Father's inherent capacity to initiate the covenant of grace, to generate the Son and to spirate the Spirit. And because "primity" is what characterizes the Father as Father—both (logically) *before* the acts of election and active generation and (logically) *after* the acts of election and active generation—McCormack's view acquits itself of modalism.

What, then, about the charge of subordinationism? Does McCor-

---

[37]See the alternative but analogous line of response offered by Hector, "Immutability, Necessity, and Triunity," 80.

[38]McCormack does not himself appeal to these labels, but they do seem to fairly capture the implicit principles of his argument. See, for example, McCormack, "Doctrine of the Trinity After Barth," 112-13 with n70.

mack's view accord capacities and actions to the Father that it does not accord to the Son and the Spirit? Consider, first, the criticism that McCormack accords certain *divine actions* (in this case, election) to the Father that he does not accord to the Son or the Spirit. According to this criticism, McCormack's view illicitly subordinates the Son and the Spirit to the Father by inhibiting their full participation in the decree of election. On this view, critics suggest, the decree of election cannot be understood as "an inner-trinitarian decision"; it can only be understood as "a decision legislated autonomously by the Father."[39] This is a potentially damning critique, as it rests on the sound trinitarian principle that all *divine* works (from their internal basis in election to their external execution in creation, providence, redemption, and consummation) are *undivided* works and therefore that *every* divine person necessarily participates in *every* undivided work: *opera Trinitatis ad extra indivisa sunt*. Is McCormack's view susceptible to this criticism?

Not necessarily. A McCormackian notion of the Father's innascibility/primity does not require that the Father is the sole *agent* of the decree of election. It only requires that the Father is the sole *initiator* of the decree of election. The decree of election (along with the processions of the Son and the Spirit as its logical consequence) flows freely *from* the Father/fountain of all. However, because God in his fatherly mode of being communicates all that he is and does to his second and third modes of being, save his innascibility/primity, the decree of election may be understood as flowing *from* the Father-fountain *through* the sent/begotten Son *in* the sent/spirated Spirit.[40] And therefore, while the Father is the sole initiator of the decree of election, he is not the sole agent of election. Insofar as the Son and the Spirit freely enact the missions in which they proceed, they are free coagents with the Father of the eternal act of divine self-determination in which God constitutes himself as our God. Moreover,

---

[39]Hunsinger, "Election and the Trinity," 192-93.
[40]See McCormack, *Orthodox and Modern*, 196-97.

because the decision of election and the trinitarian processions occur within one eternal moment, the first person only precedes the other persons according to *who* he is (i.e., his mode of being), not according to *what* he is (i.e., ontologically) or *when* he is (i.e., temporally).

Things become a bit more complicated however when we consider, second, the criticism that McCormack accords certain *divine capacities* to the Father that he does not accord to the Son or the Spirit. According to this version of the subordinationism charge, the Father and the Son appear to be *non*-consubstantial because the Father is metaphysically *necessary* (i.e., his existence is not contingent on the decree of election), whereas the Son is metaphysically *contingent* (i.e., his existence is contingent on the decree of election).[41] One strategy for defending McCormack against this criticism is to construe metaphysical necessity and metaphysical contingency as distinctive personal properties of the Father and the Son respectively.[42] However, this strategy seems problematic because personal properties do not modify the *kind of being* that the persons share; personal properties concern the distinctive *modes* of being in which the persons share the kind of being that they share. In other words, for the Father and the Son to be *consubstantial* requires (at a minimum) that they share *the same kind of existence* in accordance with their distinctive personal properties.[43] If the Father is metaphysically necessary (i.e., not contingent on the decree of election), then the Son must also be metaphysically necessary (i.e., not contingent on the decree of election), even while he receives his metaphysically necessary being from the Father who begets him. Or, if the Son is metaphysically contingent (i.e., contingent on the divine decree), then the Father must also be metaphysically contingent (i.e., contingent on the decree of election), albeit as the Father/fountain of this metaphysi-

---

[41]Again, see Hunsinger, "Election and the Trinity," 192. Cf. Hector, "Immutability, Necessity, and Triunity," 78-79.
[42]Thus Hector, "Immutability, Necessity, and Triunity," 79.
[43]Given monotheism, consubstantiality requires not only that the Father and the Son share the same kind of divine existence, but that they also share one divine being.

cally contingent kind of existence. The question then is: Can Mc-Cormack's doctrine of the triune God sustain this requirement of consubstantiality?

MCCORMACK'S DEVELOPING DOCTRINE
OF DIVINE FREEDOM

In order to address this question, it is helpful to consider the ways in which McCormack's understanding of divine freedom has developed in recent years. In earlier writings on this topic, McCormack seems to suggest that an evangelically appropriate conception of divine freedom includes the following elements: *With respect to God himself,* (1) God is free to determine for himself both *what* he is (i.e., the divine nature) and *who* he is (i.e., the divine processions); but (2) God is not free to determine *whether* he is (i.e., the divine existence).[44] While God's freedom to shape his nature and his processions protects God's capacity to determine himself for the economy of grace, the necessity of God's existence apart from the economy protects the gracious nature of the economy. According to McCormack, "'*God* would be God without us' would be a true statement and one whose truth must be upheld at all costs if God's grace is to be truly gracious."[45] *With respect to things outside of God*: (1) God is free to decide *whether or not* to create, and (2) he is also free to decide *what sort of world* to create. McCormack asserts: "God need not have created this world; God might have chosen to create a different world or to have created no world at all."[46]

How does this view of divine freedom fare in relation to the aforementioned requirement of consubstantiality? Not very well. This view seems to admit a distinction between the status of the Father's existence, which is not logically contingent on the decree of election ("God would be God without us," McCormack affirms) and the sta-

---

[44]McCormack, *Orthodox and Modern*, 274, 296-97.
[45]Ibid., 274.
[46]Ibid., 297.

tus of the Son's existence, which is logically contingent on the decree of election. And this distinction of status seems to entail the non-consubstantiality of the Father and the Son.

McCormack's more recent writings on this topic reveal a somewhat different conception of divine freedom. This conception of divine freedom does seem to fare better vis-à-vis the requirement of consubstantiality, although it raises other concerns. On this account, an evangelically appropriate conception of divine freedom includes the following elements: *With respect to God himself*: (1) God is free from all external or internal constraints. No external compulsion drives God to choose as he chooses. No internal deficit or need drives God to choose as he chooses.[47] (Note: This element of divine freedom seems to be implicit in McCormack's earlier writings as well and therefore does not appear to be an innovation.) (2) God is not free to determine *what* he is (i.e., his nature) or *who* he is (i.e., his processions) if that freedom is understood to be "a choice between alternatives."[48] God's freedom rather consists in his *power* to determine, without external or internal constraint, both *what* he is (i.e., his nature) and *who* he is (i.e., his processions) *in the economy of grace*.[49] In other words, positively speaking, God's freedom consists in his unhindered capacity to be the triune God "'for us' and to be God in no other way."[50] (3) Consequently, the only alternative to God's freedom to be God for us is not another manner of being or another mode of existence. The only alternative to God being our God, according to this conception of divine freedom, is God's *nonexistence*: "God's freedom is finally the freedom to exist—or not to exist."[51] I do not take divine nonexistence as a real possibility in Mc-

---

[47]McCormack, "Election and the Trinity," 223.
[48]Ibid.
[49]Ibid.; also "Let's Speak Plainly," 60-61. According to McCormack: "*Freedom* in God is not a *choice* among options. It is rather the *power* to do all that is in God to do" ("Let's Speak Plainly," 60).
[50]McCormack, "Let's Speak Plainly," 61.
[51]McCormack, "Election and the Trinity," 223.

Cormack's metaphysical scheme. I take it rather as a *per impossibile* counterfactual statement, that is, as a statement emphasizing the utter impossibility of God being God in any other way than the way he has willed and revealed himself to be in the covenant of grace, that is, our Father, through the Son, in the Spirit.[52] *With respect to things outside of God*: If we have understood correctly McCormack's view of God's freedom *ad intra*, then it appears that God's freedom *ad extra* consists in his unhindered ability to enact his will to create *this world and this world alone*.

How does this more recent conception of divine freedom fare in relation to the requirement of consubstantiality? Recall that the problem with McCormack's earlier conception of divine freedom is that it seemed to admit two different sorts of being within God: the sort of being enjoyed by the Father, whose manner and mode of his existence are contingent on the decree of election, but whose fact of existence is not contingent on the decree of election; and the sort of being enjoyed by the Son and the Spirit, whose manner, mode *and* fact of existence are contingent on the decree of election. McCormack's more recent conception of divine freedom does not seem to face this problem. On this conception, the manner, mode and fact of all three persons' existence are absolutely contingent on the decree of election. The only alternative to this manner, mode and fact of existence is not the existence of the Father (even as a logical possibility) apart from the Son and the Spirit. The only alternative to the being of the triune-God-for-us is the nonexistence of the triune God, which (I take it) is not a real possibility at all. In other words, all three persons share the same kind of existence—one that is wholly contingent on the decree of election, and in this sense "free," and one that is wholly determined by the decree of election, and in this sense

---

[52]One good reason for this interpretation is that McCormack seems quite strongly committed to the thesis that God is *actus purus*. Of course, a God who chooses between two *possibilities* (in this case, existence or nonexistence) is anything but *pure* actuality. Such a God instead would be the actualization of one possibility over against another.

"necessary," since it is the only decision regarding the triune existence that lies within God to make.

BEING AND GRACE

Up to this point, we have concerned ourselves primarily with the implications of McCormack's proposal regarding God's triune being *ad intra*. I have argued that his proposal, on a certain reading at least, does not necessarily expose itself to the charge of modalism or subordinationism.[53] It is time now to consider some of the implications of McCormack's proposal regarding God's triune being *ad extra*. The question before us concerns whether or not McCormack's thesis is able to preserve the free and gratuitous nature of the economy, and of God's relation to the economy. Some critics are concerned that, by tying God's triune existence to God's decree of election, McCormack's thesis falls prey to the error of Hegelian theogony, at once robbing the economy of its gracious status and rendering God dependent on the world.[54] Once again, addressing this concern requires that we appreciate McCormack's developing doctrine of divine freedom.

Recall that McCormack's earlier conception of divine freedom sought to preserve the contingency of the economy, and of God's relation to it, by describing the economy as contingent in two ways. On this conception, the economy is contingent (1) insofar as God is free either to initiate or not to initiate the economy; and (2) insofar as God is free to initiate an altogether different economy. McCormack's more recent conception of divine freedom, however, no longer admits these two features of contingency. On the more recent conception, the economy is contingent only in the sense that it proceeds on the basis of (i.e., contingently on) God's will, a will whose

---

[53]Similarly Hector, "Immutability, Necessity, and Triunity."
[54]This concern is pressed rather forcefully by Paul Molnar. See, for example, Molnar, *Divine Freedom*, 61-64; and Molnar, "*Orthodox and Modern:* Just How Modern Was Barth's Later Theology?" *Theology Today* 67 (2010): 55-56.

freedom is not defined by its capacity to choose alternative econo-
mies or to choose no economy at all but rather in its capacity to enact
this economy and this economy alone without external or internal
constraint. On this conception, God is free *ad extra* in that he is free
for this economy and this economy alone. The question before us
therefore is: Does this more recent conception of divine freedom
compromise the gratuitous nature of the economy, and of God's relation to the economy?

Much of our answer to this question will be determined by what
dimensions of freedom we consider requisite to the will of God in its
external orientation. Does the preservation of God's freedom *ad
extra* require that God be free to create or not to create? Does it require that God be free to create different worlds? Or does it require
only that God creates the one world that he creates without internal
or external constraint? While I am inclined to insist on all three dimensions of divine freedom in relation to the economy,[55] as McCormack's earlier view did, there is a substantial tradition of Reformed
thought, traceable to Jonathan Edwards,[56] that believes only the last
dimension of divine freedom is required in order to preserve God's
free relation to the economy.[57] Such a view simultaneously maintains
(1) that this is the best of all possible worlds (and consequently that
this world is the *only* possible object of God's wise and sovereign
decree *ad extra*) and (2) that the God-world relation is nevertheless
wholly asymmetrical: God being the absolutely sovereign creator, redeemer and consummator of all things, the world being absolutely
dependent on God's sovereign creating, redeeming and consummating activity. In a view such as this, God's free relation to the world is
not necessarily compromised. All that God is and does, he is and
does in and of himself. And all that the world is and does, it is and

---

[55]See chapter six.
[56]Richard Muller discusses Edwards's modulation of divine freedom *ad extra* in relation to the
broader Reformed tradition in "Jonathan Edwards and the Absence of Free Choice: A Parting of
Ways in the Reformed Tradition," *Jonathan Edwards Studies* 1 (2011): 3-22.
[57]See William L. Rowe, *Can God Be Free?* (Oxford: Oxford University Press, 2004).

does from, through and to God. To the extent therefore that Mc-
Cormack's conception of God's free relation to the world belongs to
this tradition of reflection, it is immune to the charge of theogony.
Edwardsean necessitarianism is of a different species than Hegelian
necessitarianism.[58]

I believe that, though not a species of Hegelian theogony, Mc-
Cormack's understanding of God's trinitarian being *ad extra* nevertheless suffers structurally in an important regard. The problem lies
at the heart of his constructive thesis and concerns his claim that
"the works of God *ad intra* (the trinitarian processions) find their
ground in the *first* of the works of God *ad extra* (viz., election)."[59]
Why is this a problem?

Addressing this question requires attending to one of the most
fundamental insights of Nicene trinitarianism, namely, the "distinction between two modes of deriving from God."[60] Nicene trinitarianism distinguishes between two modes of proceeding from God:
the *internal processions* of the Son and the Spirit, which belong to
God's being, and the *external processions* of creatures, which do not
belong to God's being. As the preceding discussion demonstrates,
McCormack has no interest in abolishing this fundamental trinitarian distinction between created and uncreated being, nor does he
appear even inadvertently to have done so. McCormack is interested,
however, in revising the traditional understanding of the *relationship*
between these two modes of proceeding from God. And this is
where the problem lies.[61]

While the *distinction* between these two modes of proceeding
serves to protect the deity of the Son and the Spirit, and also the

---

[58]Note also that, according to McCormack, God's triune identity is wholly realized within his
primal decree and not along the historical axis of that decree's fulfillment, and this fact also distinguishes McCormack's proposal from more robustly Hegelian alternatives (see McCormack,
Orthodox and Modern, 190-91).

[59]McCormack, *Orthodox and Modern*, 194, italics in the original.

[60]*ST* 1:102.

[61]See Hunsinger, "Election and the Trinity," 192.

creatureliness of the creature, the *ordered relationship* between these two modes of proceeding serves to establish the utter gratuity and glory of the trinitarian economy *ad extra*. Without rehearsing the argument of chapters six through eight, two brief points can be made. First, in terms of the gratuity of the economy: Because the procession of creatures from God "follows" the processions of the Son and the Spirit from God, the procession of creatures may be understood as a matter of "incomparable generosity."[62] God's perfect processional fecundity *ad intra* is what makes the procession of creatures from God *ad extra* utterly unnecessary and gratuitous in character.[63] While the economy of creation is free on McCormack's construal (in the sense described above), it is not utterly gratuitous *in relation to God's triune life*. In fact, quite the opposite is the case: The procession of creatures is the *reason/explanatory cause* for the processions of the Son and the Spirit. *Because* God elects the covenant of grace, he generates the Son and breathes forth the Spirit. Second, in terms of the goal of the economy, because, on a traditional understanding, the procession of creatures does not "ground" the processions of the Son and the Spirit, the covenant of grace does not bear the explanatory weight for the constitution of the Trinity, as it does in McCormack's construal. Instead, the covenant of grace bears the evangelical glory of announcing our inclusion within God's triune life through the utterly gratuitous (not self-constituting) divine missions. The covenant of grace is not the occasion for begetting the Son and breathing the Spirit. The covenant of grace is the occasion for bringing many sons and daughters into the antecedently perfect glory of the triune God.[64]

This, then, is my major criticism of McCormack's proposal to date.

---

[62]Sokolowski, *God of Faith and Reason*, 34.

[63]See Thomas Aquinas, *Summa theologiae* 1.32.1.3. For an instructive discussion of the distinction/relation between internal and external processions in the theology of Thomas Aquinas, see Gilles Emery, *The Trinitarian Theology of St. Thomas Aquinas*, trans. Francesca Aran Murphy (Oxford: Oxford University Press, 2007), chap. 14.

[64]Thomas Aquinas, *Summa theologiae* 3.23.1.2.

Although his proposal can affirm what Barth calls "the special truth" of the Christian message, namely, that "the divine being and life and act takes place *with* ours," it cannot affirm with Barth that "it is *only as* the divine takes place that ours takes place."[65] While positing this irreversible relationship between the *opera Trinitatis ad intra* and the *opera Trinitatis ad extra* may not be the only way of preserving Nicene trinitarianism, I believe it is the only way of preserving the proper evangelical relation between God's triune being and God's triune grace, and thus of enabling us to see the eternally rich and triune God as the fountain from which God's gracious turn toward us in the gospel flows, and toward which it runs.

---

[65] *CD* 4.1:7, italics mine.

CONCLUSION

◆

10

CONCLUDING REFLECTIONS
ON THE QUESTION

◆

In drawing this book to a close, it is worth reflecting on the argument of the preceding chapters. The present study has engaged a question posed to contemporary theology by the trinitarian theology of Karl Barth: What is the relationship between God's being Father, Son and Spirit and the evangelical events whereby God realizes his self-determination to become our Father, through the Son, in the Spirit? We have addressed this question by considering the answers provided by two theologians self-consciously committed to extending the historicizing impulse of Barth's trinitarian thought, Robert Jenson and Bruce McCormack. Both Jenson and McCormack seek to translate the claims of trinitarian orthodoxy into a historicist key, not in order to accommodate those claims to the exigencies of modern culture but in order to provide what they perceive to be a more faithful witness to the gospel. In both instances, historicizing trinitarian orthodoxy involves conceptualizing God's triune identity in terms of an agent who freely projects and enacts his identity in the sovereign act of turning to the world in Jesus Christ. In Jenson's theology, God's sovereign act of self-projection and enactment "happens" along the historical axis of the exodus and the evangel, though it is possessed by anticipation from the moment of its free self-origination. In McCormack's theology, God's sovereign act of self-projection and enactment occurs within God's primal, pretemporal decree and determines the course of historical events that flow there from. It is their commitment to preserving what they consider to be the substance of trinitarian orthodoxy, as well as their emphasis on the free and sovereign nature of God's self-enactment, that distinguishes both theologies from Hegelian theogony,[1] as well as from other less dogmatically responsible historicizing approaches.

Although the proposals of Jenson and McCormack succeed in varying degrees in preserving the claims of trinitarian orthodoxy—in my judgment, Jenson's radical Lutheran, eschatologically oriented theology is less secure vis-à-vis Nicene trinitarianism and Chalcedonian christology than is McCormack's Reformed, protologically oriented theology. I do not believe either proposal adequately preserves the proper evangelical relation between God's triune being and the events of the gospel. If evangelical theology is to account for the pure gratuity of the relation between God and the divine acts of election, incarnation, and indwelling, God's triune identity must be wholly actual, not just *de facto* but *de jure,* prior to the act wherein he gives himself to us and welcomes us into his trinitarian bliss. Any notion of divine self-realization seems to compromise the biblical portrait of divine self-giving in the covenant of grace. The point, it must be emphasized, is not to *separate* God's being from the historical events of the gospel.[2] It is, rather, to properly construe the nature of the *relation* between God's being and those events as a relation of incomparable generosity. In describing the evangelical relation between God and the gospel along these lines, we thus discover not only a proper characterization of the being of the gospel's God *in se*; we also discover a proper characterization of the God who works *pro nobis*

---

[1]Again see Karl Barth, *Protestant Theology in the Nineteenth Century*, trans. Brian Cozens and John Bowden (Grand Rapids: Eerdmans, 2002), 406.

[2]Recall, for example, our discussion of divine simplicity in relation to the divine willing in chapter six.

not "in order to supply his wants" but "in order to communicate to others the abundance of his perfection." In the specific evangelical case of adoption, wherein God the Father sovereignly realizes his purpose to become our God and Father through the missions of the Son and the Spirit, God does not act in order to constitute his natural paternity, filiation and spiration but in order to communicate "the likeness of natural sonship . . . to men."[3]

I am aware that there is more than a little irony in the fact that the present study finds in the evangelical historicist proposals of McCormack and Jenson less satisfying answers to the questions posed by Barth's trinitarian theology than the answers that can be gleaned from the theologies of Irenaeus, Augustine, Peter Lombard, Thomas Aquinas, and Bonaventure (though the role of Francis Turretin and his fellow Protestant scholastic theologians in the preceding discussion is perhaps less surprising). My argument of course has not been that an evangelical theology of the gospel's God should ignore the question that Barth's theology puts before us—far from it. Although this question is addressed indirectly throughout the history of trinitarian thought in discussions of the relationship between the Father's will and the Son's eternal generation, and also in discussions of God's relative attributes, it is only with trinitarian theology in and after Barth that this question receives forceful statement, with keen awareness of its importance for theological reasoning. To consider the relationship between God's trinitarian being and the events of the gospel is to consider a topic of stimulating significance for dogmatic theology, as I hope to have demonstrated in small measure.

Barth's question is important and not to be ignored. My conclusion though is that Protestant theology since the Enlightenment has in large part failed to provide us with hermeneutical and theological concepts adequate to addressing our question.[4] The catego-

---

[3]Thomas Aquinas, *Summa theologiae* 3.23.1.2.
[4]Compare this dogmatic conclusion with the historical conclusion of Stephen Holmes, *Quest for the Trinity*, 198-200.

ries of historicism in particular, such as "self-determination," "subjectivity," "event," and so forth, are in my judgment unable to account adequately for the identity of the one who is the author and end of history, the eternally and intrinsically replete Trinity, who graciously communicates the riches of his triune fellowship to us through the Son and the Spirit. To find words and concepts adequate for stammering about this glorious reality, we must pursue the path of *ressourcement*, mining the resources available in the storehouse of the church's exegetical and theological tradition. Contemporary theological renewal, at least at this point in the history of modern Protestant theology and on this particular doctrinal topic, is to be found through the retrieval of theological concepts until recently forsaken or ignored by much contemporary trinitarian thought.

As I hope also to have demonstrated, reappropriating concepts such as the analogy of being or the doctrine of God's simple perfection does not require banishing notions such as self-determination or narrative identity. I have tried to indicate how such notions may find a home within a program of retrieval, helping us more clearly to explicate what it means for God graciously to extend relations which are internal to his perfect being to those for whom history is their native habitat. *Ressourcement,* properly understood, is not a reductive but an inclusive and enlarging venture. It is never a matter of simple repetition or repristination but rather of tapping into a vital root, of relearning a lost grammar, of being enculturated in the theological communion of saints, all in service of thinking and speaking faithfully about God in the present.

This, at least, has been the aim of the present book: to serve evangelical theology in its vocation to think and speak responsibly about God according to the gospel. Whatever the shortcomings of the various positions surveyed in the present volume may be, including my own, this remains an inspiring and invigorating vocation.

BIBLIOGRAPHY

Allen, Michael. *The Christ's Faith: A Dogmatic Account*. London: T & T Clark, 2009.

Allen, Michael, and Scott Swain. "The Obedience of the Eternal Son." *International Journal of Systematic Theology* (forthcoming).

Anselm. *Proslogion*. Translated by M. J. Charlesworth. Oxford: Claredon, 1965.

Aquinas, Thomas. *Commentary on the Gospel of John, Chapters 1–5*. Translated by Fabian Larcher and James A. Weisheipl. Washington, DC: Catholic University of America Press, 2010.

———. *Summa Theologiae*. Translated by Fathers of the English Dominican Province. New York: Benzinger Bros., 1948.

Asselt, Willem J. van. *The Federal Theology of Johannes Cocceius (1603–1669)*. Leiden: Brill, 2001.

———. "The Fundamental Meaning of Theology: Archetypal and Ectypal Theology in Seventeenth-Century Reformed Thought." *Westminster Theological Journal* 64 (2002): 319–35.

Athanasius. *Orations Against the Arians*. In *The Trinitarian Controversy*, edited by William G. Rusch. Philadelphia: Fortress, 1980.

Augustine. *City of God*. Nicene and Post-Nicene Fathers 2. Repr. Grand Rapids: Eerdmans, 1993.

———. *Confessions*. Translated by Henry Chadwick. Oxford: Oxford University Press, 1991.

———. *The Trinity*. Translated by Edmund Hill. Brooklyn: New York City Press, 1991.

Ayres, Lewis. *Augustine and the Trinity*. Cambridge: Cambridge University Press, 2010.

———. *Nicaea and Its Legacy: An Approach to Fourth-Century Trinitarian Theology*. Oxford: Oxford University Press, 2004.

Babcock, William. "A Changing of the Christian God: The Doctrine of the Trinity in the Seventeenth Century." *Interpretation* 45 (1991): 133–46.

Bac, J. Martin. *Perfect Will Theology: Divine Agency in Reformed Scholasticism as Against Suárez, Episcopius, Descartes, and Spinoza*. Leiden: Brill, 2010.

Badcock, Gary. *Light of Truth and Fire of Love: A Theology of the Holy Spirit*. Grand Rapids: Eerdmans, 1997.

Balás, David L. "Eternity and Time in Gregory of Nyssa's Contra Eunomium."
In *Gregory Von Nyssa und Philosophie*, edited by Heinrich Dörrie, Margarete
Altenburger and Uta Schramm, 128–53. Leiden: Brill, 1976.

Barth, Karl. *Church Dogmatics*. 14 vols. Edited by Geoffrey W. Bromily and
T. F. Torrance. Edinburgh: T & T Clark, 1936–1969.

———. *Die Christliche Dogmatik in Entwurf*. Edited by Gerhard Sauter.
Zürich: Theologischer Verlag Zürich, 1982.

———. *Die Kirchliche Dogmatik*. Vol. 2. Zürich: Theologischer Verlag Zürich, 1980.

———. *Dogmatics in Outline*. New York: Harper and Row, 1959.

———. *Letters 1961–1968*. Translated by Geoffrey W. Bromiley. Grand Rapids: Eerdmans, 1981.

———. *Protestant Theology in the Nineteenth Century*. Translated by Brian Cozens and John Bowden. Grand Rapids: Eerdmans, 2002.

———. *The Göttingen Dogmatics: Instruction in the Christian Religion*. Translated by Geoffrey W. Bromiley. Grand Rapids: Eerdmans, 1991.

Bauckham, Richard. "The Throne of God and the Worship of Jesus." In *The Jewish Roots of Christological Monotheism*, edited by Carey C. Newman, James R. Davila and Gladys S. Lewis, 43–69. Leiden: Brill, 1999.

Bauckham, Richard, et al., eds. *The Epistle to the Hebrews and Christian Theology*. Grand Rapids: Eerdmans, 2009.

Bavinck, Herman. *Reformed Dogmatics*. 4 vols. Translated by John Vriend. Grand Rapids: Baker, 2004.

Becker, Matthew L. *The Self-Giving God and Salvation History: The Trinitarian Theology of Johannes Von Hofmann*. London: T & T Clark, 2004.

Behr, John. *Asceticism and Anthropology in Irenaeus and Clement*. Oxford: Oxford University Press, 2000.

———. "The Paschal Foundation of Christian Theology." *St. Vladimir's Theological Quarterly* 45 (2001): 115–36.

Bingham, D. Jeffrey. "Christianizing Divine Aseity: Irenaeus Reads John." In *The Gospel of John and Christian Theology*, edited by Richard Bauckham and Carl Mosser, 53–67. Grand Rapids: Eerdmans, 2008.

Bobrinskoy, Boris. *The Mystery of the Trinity: Trinitarian Experience and Vision in the Biblical and Patristic Tradition*. Translated by Anthony P. Gythiel. Crestwood, NY: St. Vladimir's Seminary Press, 1999.

Bockmuehl, Markus. "*Creatio Ex Nihilo* in Palestinian Judaism and Early Christianity." *Scottish Journal of Theology* 65 (2012): 253–70.

Boethius. *De Trinitate*. In *The Theological Tractates and The Consolation of Phi-*

losophy, translated by H. F. Stewart, E. K. Rand and S. J. Tester. Cambridge, MA: Harvard University Press, 1978.

Bonaventure. *Breviloquium*. Edited by Dominic Monti. Works of Saint Bonaventure. Vol. 9. St. Bonaventure, NY: Franciscan Institute Publications, 2005.

———. *Disputed Questions on the Mystery of the Trinity: An Introduction and Translation*. Edited by Geroge Marcil. Translated by Zachary Hayes. Works of Saint Bonaventure. Vol. 3. St. Bonaventure, NY: Franciscan Institute Publications, 1979.

———. *The Tree of Life*. In *Bonaventure—The Soul's Journey to God, The Tree of Life, The Life of Saint Francis*, translated by Ewert Cousins. Mahwah, NJ: Paulist, 1978.

Braaten, Carl E., and Robert W. Jenson, eds. *Christian Dogmatics*. Philadelphia: Fortress, 1984.

Brakel, Wilhelmus à. *The Christian's Reasonable Service*. 4 vols. Translated by Bartel Elshout. Grand Rapids: Reformation Heritage Books, 1992–1995.

Brueggemann, Walter. *Theology of the Old Testament: Testimony, Dispute, Advocacy*. Minneapolis: Fortress, 1997.

Buckley, Michael J. *At the Origins of Modern Atheism*. New Haven and London: Yale University Press, 1987.

Bullinger, Heinrich. *The Decades of Heinrich Bullinger: The First and Second Decades*. Cambridge: Cambridge University Press, 1859.

Bultmann, Rudolf. "New Testament and Mythology." In *Kerygma and Myth*, edited by Hans Werner Bartsch and translated by Reginald H. Fuller, 1–44. London: SPCK, 1964.

———. *Theology of the New Testament*. Vol. 1. Translated by Kendrick Grobel. New York: Charles Scribner's Sons, 1954.

Burkert, Walter. *Greek Religion*. Translated by John Raffan. Cambridge, MA: Harvard University Press, 1985.

Burrell, David. "Creation, Metaphysics, and Ethics." *Faith and Philosophy* 18 (2001): 204–21.

———. "Creator/Creatures Relation: 'The Distinction' vs. 'Onto-Theology.'" *Faith and Philosophy* 25 (2008): 177–89.

———. "Distinguishing God from the World." In *Language, Meaning, and God*, edited by Brian Davies, 75–91. London: Geoffrey Chapman, 1987.

Calvin, John. *Institutes of the Christian Religion*. Translated by Ford Lewis Battles. Philadelphia: Westminster John Knox, 1960.

Charlesworth, James H. *Old Testament Pseudepigrapha*. 2 vols. New York: Doubleday, 1983, 1985.

Coakley, Sarah. "Persons in the 'Social' Doctrine of the Trinity: A Critique of the Current Analytical Discussion." In *The Trinity: An Interdisciplinary Symposium*, edited by Stephen T. Davis, Daniel Kendall and Gerald O'Collins, 123–144. Oxford: Oxford University Press, 2004.

Coakley, Sarah, ed. *Re-Thinking Gregory of Nyssa*. Oxford: Blackwell, 2003.

Collins, John J. *Between Athens and Jerusalem: Jewish Identity in the Hellenistic Diaspora*. 2nd ed. Grand Rapids: Eerdmans, 2000.

Cornelius, Emmitt. "St. Irenaeus and Robert W. Jenson on Jesus in the Trinity." *Journal of the Evangelical Theological Society* 55 (2012): 111–24.

Craig, William Lane. *Time and Eternity: Exploring God's Relationship to Time*. Wheaton: Crossway, 2001.

Crisp, Oliver. *Divinity and Humanity*. Cambridge: Cambridge University Press, 2007.

———. *Revisioning Christology: Theology in the Reformed Tradition*. Farnham, UK: Ashgate, 2011.

———. "Robert Jenson on the Pre-existence of Christ." *Modern Theology* 23 (2007): 27–45.

Dahl, Nils A. "The Neglected Factor in New Testament Theology." *Reflection* 73 (1975): 5–8.

Davidson, Ivor J. "'Not My Will but Yours Be Done': The Ontological Dynamics of Incarnational Intention." *International Journal of Systematic Theology* 7 (2005): 178–204.

Davidson, Ivor J., and Murray A. Rae, eds. *God of Salvation: Soteriology in Theological Perspective*. Farnham, UK: Ashgate, 2011.

Davies, Brian. *The Thought of Thomas Aquinas*. Oxford: Claredon, 1992.

Dempsey, Michael T., ed. *Trinity and Election in Contemporary Theology*. Grand Rapids: Eerdmans, 2011.

Desmond, William. *Hegel's God: A Counterfeit Double?* Aldershot: Ashgate, 2003.

Dionysius. *Pseudo-Dionysius: The Complete Works*. Translated by Colm Luibheid. New York: Paulist, 1984.

Dixon, Philip. *"Nice and Hot Disputes": The Doctrine of the Trinity in the Seventeenth Century*. London: Continuum, 2003.

Dorner, Isaak August. *A System of Christian Doctrine*. Vol. 1. Translated by Alfred Cave. Edinburgh: T & T Clark, 1888.

Downing, Gerald F. "Common Ground with Paganism in Luke and in Josephus." *New Testament Studies* 28 (1982): 546–59.

Driel, Edwin Christian van. *Incarnation Anyway: Arguments for Supralapsarian Christology*. Oxford: Oxford University Press, 2008.

———. "Karl Barth on the Eternal Existence of Jesus Christ." *Scottish Journal of Theology* 60 (2007): 45–61.

Durand, Emmanuel. "A Theology of God the Father." In *The Oxford Handbook of the Trinity*. Edited by Gilles Emery and Matthew Levering, 371–86. Oxford: Oxford University Press, 2011.

Edwards, Jonathan. *Charity and Its Fruits*. Edinburgh: Banner of Truth, 1969.

Eitel, Adam. "The Resurrection of Jesus Christ: Karl Barth and the Historicization of God's Being." *International Journal of Systematic Theology* 10 (2008): 36–53.

Emery, Gilles. "The Immutability of the God of Love and the Problem of Language Concerning the 'Suffering of God.'" In *Divine Impassibility and the Mystery of Human Suffering*, edited by James F. Keating and Thomas Joseph White, 27–76. Grand Rapids: Eerdmans, 2009.

———. *The Trinitarian Theology of St. Thomas Aquinas*. Translated by Francesca Aran Murphy. Oxford: Oxford University Press, 2007.

Emery, Gilles, and Matthew Levering, eds. *The Oxford Handbook of the Trinity*. Oxford: Oxford University Press, 2011.

Fee, Gordon. *God's Empowering Presence: The Holy Spirit in the Letters of Paul*. Peabody, MA: Hendrickson, 1994.

Frede, Michael. "Monotheism and Pagan Philosophy in Later Antiquity." In *Pagan Monotheism in Late Antiquity*, edited by Ploymnia Athanassiadi and Michael Frede, 41–67. Oxford: Clarendon, 1999.

Friedman, Russell L. *Medieval Trinitarian Thought from Aquinas to Ockham*. Cambridge: Cambridge University Press, 2010.

Gabler, Johann P. "An Oration on the Proper Distinction Between Biblical and Dogmatic Theology and the Specific Objectives of Each." In *The Flowering of Old Testament Theology*, edited by Ben C. Ollenburger, Elmer A Martens and Gerhard F. Hasel, 492–502. Winona Lake, IN: Eisenbrauns, 1992.

Gaffin, Richard B. *Resurrection and Redemption: A Study in Paul's Soteriology*. Phillipsburg, NJ: P & R, 1987.

Gatewood, Tee. "A Nicene Christology? Robert Jenson and the Two Natures of Jesus Christ." *Pro Ecclesia* 18 (2009): 28–49.

Gathercole, Simon. "Pre-existence, and the Freedom of the Son in Creation and Redemption: An Exposition in Dialogue with Robert Jenson." *International Journal of Systematic Theology* 7 (2005): 38–51.

Gavrilyuk, Paul L. *The Suffering of the Impassible God: The Dialectics of Patristic Thought*. Oxford: Oxford University Press, 2004.

Gioia, Luigi. *The Theological Epistemology of Augustine's "De Trinitate."* Oxford: Oxford University Press, 2008.

Glomsrud, Ryan. "Karl Barth and Modern Protestantism: The Radical Impulse." In *Always Reformed: Essays in Honor of W. Robert Godfrey*, edited by R. Scott Clark and Joel E. Kim, 92–114. Escondido, CA: Westminster Seminary California, 2012.

Gockel, Matthias. *Barth and Schleiermacher on the Doctrine of Election: A Systematic-Theological Comparison*. Oxford: Oxford University Press, 2007.

———. "Mediating Theology in Germany." In *The Blackwell Companion to Nineteenth-Century Theology*, edited by David A. Fergusson, 301–18. Oxford: Blackwell, 2010.

Goodwin, Mark J. *Paul, Apostle of the Living God: Kerygma and Conversion in 2 Corinthians*. Harrisburg, PA: Trinity Press International, 2001.

Grant, Robert. *Gods and the One God*. Philadelphia: Westminster, 1986.

Grenz, Stanley J. *Rediscovering the Triune God: The Trinity in Contemporary Theology*. Minneapolis: Fortress, 2004.

Gundry, Robert H. *Soma in Biblical Theology: With Emphasis on Pauline Anthropology*. Cambridge: Cambridge University Press, 1976.

Gunton, Colin E. *Act and Being: Towards a Theology of the Divine Attributes*. Grand Rapids: Eerdmans, 2003.

———. "Augustine, the Trinity and the Theological Crisis of the West." *Scottish Journal of Theology* 43 (1990): 33–58.

———. *The Triune Creator: A Historical and Systematic Study*. Grand Rapids: Eerdmans, 1998.

———, ed. *Trinity, Time, and Church: A Response to the Theology of Robert W. Jenson*. Grand Rapids: Eerdmans, 2000.

Habets, Myk, and Phillip Tolliday, eds. *Trinitarian Theology After Barth*. Eugene, OR: Pickwick, 2011.

Hardy, Edward R., ed. *Christology of the Later Fathers*. Louisville: Westminster John Knox, 1954.

Harnack, Adolf von. *Lehrbuch der Dogmengeschichte*. 5th ed. Tübingen: J. C. B. Mohr [Paul Siebeck], 1931.

Hart, David Bentley. *The Beauty of the Infinite: The Aesthetics of Christian Truth*. Grand Rapids: Eerdmans, 2003.

———. "The Lively God of Robert Jenson." *First Things* 156 (October 2005): 28–34.

Hays, Richard B., and Beverly Roberts Gaventa, eds. *Seeking the Identity of Jesus: A Pilgrimage*. Grand Rapids: Eerdmans, 2008.

Hector, Kevin. "God's Triunity and Self-Determination: A Conversation with Karl Barth, Bruce McCormack, and Paul Molnar." *International Journal of Systematic Theology* 7 (2005): 246–61.

———. "Immutability, Necessity, and Triunity: Towards a Resolution of the Trinity and Election Controversy." *Scottish Journal of Theology* 65 (2012): 64–81.

Hengel, Martin. *Judaism and Hellenism: Studies in Their Encounter in Palestine During the Early Hellenistic Period*. Translated by John Bowden. Philadelphia: Fortress, 1981.

Hesselink, I. John. *Calvin's First Catechism: A Commentary, Featuring Ford Lewis Battles's Translation of the 1538 Catechism*. Louisville: Westminster John Knox, 1997.

Hill, Edmund. *The Mystery of the Trinity*. London: Geoffrey Chapman, 1985.

Hodgson, Peter C. *God in History: Shapes of Freedom*. Nashville: Abingdon, 1989.

Holmes, Stephen R. "Divine Attributes." In *Mapping Modern Theology: A Thematic and Historical Introduction*, edited by Kelly M. Kapic and Bruce L. McCormack, 47–66. Grand Rapids: Baker Academic, 2012.

———. *Listening to the Past: The Place of Tradition in Theology*. Grand Rapids: Baker Academic, 2002.

———. "The Attributes of God." In *The Oxford Handbook of Systematic Theology*, edited by John Webster, Kathryn Tanner and Iain Torrance, 54–71. New York: Oxford University Press, 2009.

———. *The Quest for the Trinity: The Doctrine of God in Scripture, History and Modernity*. Downers Grove, IL: IVP Academic, 2012.

Horton, Michael. *Lord and Servant: A Covenant Christology*. Louisville: Westminster John Knox, 2005.

Howard, Thomas Albert. *Protestant Theology and the Making of the Modern German University*. New York: Oxford University Press, 2006.

Hugenberger, Gordon. *Marriage as a Covenant: Biblical Law and Ethics as Developed from Malachi*. Grand Rapids: Baker, 1998.

Hunsinger, George. *Disruptive Grace: Studies in the Theology of Karl Barth*. Grand Rapids: Eerdmans, 2000.

———. "Election and the Trinity: Twenty-Five Theses on the Theology of Karl Barth." *Modern Theology* 24 (2008): 179–98.

———. "Robert Jenson's Systematic Theology: A Review Essay." *Scottish Journal of Theology* 55 (2002): 161–200.

Hurtado, Larry. *One God, One Lord: Early Christian Devotion and Ancient Jewish Monotheism*. Philadelphia: Fortress, 1988.

Irenaeus. *Against Heresies*. Ante-Nicene Fathers 1. Repr. Grand Rapids: Eerdmans, 1996.

Jaeger, Werner. *The Theology of the Early Greek Philosophers*. Oxford: Claredon, 1947.

Jenson, Robert W. "A Theological Autobiography, to Date." *Dialog* 46 (2007): 46–54.

———. *Alpha and Omega: A Study in the Theology of Karl Barth*. New York: Thomas Nelson & Sons, 1963. Repr. Eugene, OR: Wipf and Stock, 2002.

———. *Canon and Creed*. Louisville: Westminster John Knox, 2010.

———. "Creator and Creature." *International Journal of Systematic Theology* 4 (2002): 216–21.

———. *God After God: The God of the Past and the God of the Future, Seen in the Work of Karl Barth*. New York: Bobs-Merrill, 1969. Repr. Minneapolis: Fortress, 2012.

———. "God's Time, Our Time: An Interview with Robert W. Jenson." *Christian Century* 123 (2006): 31–35.

———. "Jesus in the Trinity." *Pro Ecclesia* 8 (1999): 308–18.

———. "Karl Barth." In *The Modern Theologians*. 2nd ed. Edited by David F. Ford, 21–36. Cambridge, MA: Blackwell, 1997.

———. "Once More the *Logos Asarkos*." *International Journal of Systematic Theology* 13 (2011): 130–33.

———. "Parting Ways?" *First Things* 53 (1995): 60–62.

———. "Response to Watson and Hunsinger." *Scottish Journal of Theology* 55 (2002): 225–32.

———. "Second Thoughts About Theologies of Hope." *Evangelical Quarterly* 72 (2000): 335–46.

———. *Systematic Theology*. 2 vols. New York: Oxford University Press, 1997, 1999.

———. "Thanks to Yeago." *Dialog* 31 (1992): 22–23.

———. "The Bible and the Trinity." *Pro Ecclesia* 11 (2002): 329–39.

———. "The Church's Responsibility for the World." In *The Two Cities of God: The Church's Responsibility for the Earthly City*, edited by Carl E. Braaten and Robert W. Jenson, 1–10. Grand Rapids: Eerdmans, 1997.

———. *The Knowledge of Things Hoped For.* Oxford: Oxford University Press, 1969.

———. *The Triune Identity: God According to the Gospel.* Philadelpia: Fortress, 1982. Repr. Eugene, OR: Wipf and Stock, 2002.

———. *Unbaptized God: The Basic Flaw in Ecumenical Theology.* Minneapolis: Fortress, 1992.

———. "What Kind of God Can Make a Covenant?" In *Covenant and Hope: Christian and Jewish Reflections,* edited by Robert W. Jenson and Eugene B. Korn, 3–18. Grand Rapids: Eerdmans, 2012.

———. "You Wonder Where the Spirit Went." *Pro Ecclesia* 2 (1993): 296–304.

John of Damascus. *An Exact Exposition of the Orthodox Faith.* New York: Fathers of the Church, 1958.

Jones, Paul Dafydd. *The Humanity of Christ: Christology in Karl Barth's Church Dogmatics.* London: T & T Clark, 2008.

Jüngel, Eberhard. *God as the Mystery of the World: On the Foundation of the Theology of the Crucified One in the Dispute Between Theism and Atheism.* Translated by Darrell Guder. Edinburgh: T & T Clark, 1983.

———. *God's Being Is in Becoming: The Trinitarian Being of God in the Theology of Karl Barth.* Translated by John Webster. Edinburgh: T & T Clark, 2001.

Kant, Immanuel. *The Conflict of the Faculties.* Translated by Mary J. Gregor. New York: Abaris, 1992.

Keating, James F., and Thomas Joseph White, eds. *Divine Impassibility and the Mystery of Human Suffering.* Grand Rapids: Eerdmans, 2009.

Kirk, J. R. Daniel. *Unlocking Romans: Resurrection and the Justification of God.* Grand Rapids: Eerdmans, 2008.

Kooi, Cornelis van der. *As in a Mirror: John Calvin and Karl Barth on Knowing God: A Diptych.* Grand Rapids: Eerdmans, 2005.

Küng, Hans. *The Incarnation of God: Hegel's Thought as Prolegomena to a Future Christology.* Edinburgh: T & T Clark, 1987.

Leftow, Brian. "Eternity and Immutability." In *The Blackwell Guide to the Philosophy of Religion,* edited by William E. Mann, 48–78. Malden, MA: Blackwell, 2005.

Legaspi, Michael C. *The Death of Scripture and the Rise of Biblical Studies.* Oxford: Oxford University Press, 2010.

Levering, Matthew. *Participatory Biblical Exegesis: A Theology of Biblical Interpretation.* Notre Dame: University of Notre Dame Press, 2008.

———. *Scripture and Metaphysics: Aquinas and the Renewal of Trinitarian Theology.* Oxford: Blackwell, 2004.

Lightfoot, J. L. *The Sibylline Oracles: With Introduction, Translation, and Commentary on the First and Second Books*. Oxford: Oxford University Press, 2007.

Lombard, Peter. *The Sentences, Book 1: The Mystery of the Trinity*. Translated by Giulio Silano. Mediaeval Sources in Translation. Vol. 42. Toronto: Pontifical Institute of Mediaeval Studies, 2007.

Long, Steven A. Analogia Entis: *On the Analogy of Being, Metaphysics, and the Act of Faith*. Notre Dame, IN: University of Notre Dame Press, 2011.

Lotz, David W. "Albrecht Ritschl and the Unfinished Reformation." *Harvard Theological Review* 73 (1980): 337–72.

Louth, Andrew. *Maximus the Confessor*. London and New York: Routledge, 1996.

Ludlow, Morwenna. *Gregory of Nyssa: Ancient and [Post]modern*. Oxford: Oxford University Press, 2007.

Luther, Martin. *The Bondage of the Will*. Translated by J. I. Packer and O. R. Johnston. Grand Rapids: Revell, 1957.

———. "The Three Symbols or Creeds of the Christian Faith." In *Luther's Works*, vol. 34, edited by L. W. Spitz, 197–229. Philadelphia: Muhlenburg, 1960.

MacDonald, Neil B. *Metaphysics and the God of Israel: Systematic Theology of the Old and New Testaments*. Grand Rapids: Baker, 2006.

Marcus, Ralph. "Divine Names and Attributes in Hellenistic Jewish Literature." *Proceedings of the American Academy for Jewish Research* 3 (1931–32): 43–120.

Marshall, Bruce D. "*Ex Occidente Lux?* Aquinas and Eastern Orthodox Theology." *Modern Theology* 20 (2004): 23–50.

———. "Trinity." In *The Blackwell Companion to Modern Theology*, edited by Gareth Jones, 183–203. Malden, MA: Blackwell, 2004.

———. *Trinity and Truth*. Cambridge: Cambridge University Press, 2000.

McCabe, Herbert. "Aquinas on the Trinity." In *Silence and the Word: Negative Theology and Incarnation*, edited by Oliver Davies and Denys Turner, 76–93. Cambridge: Cambridge University Press, 2002.

———. *God Matters*. Springfield, IL: Templegate, 1991.

McCarthy, Dennis J. "Notes on the Love of God in Deuteronomy and the Father-Son Relationship Between Yahweh and Israel." *Catholic Biblical Quarterly* 27 (1965): 144–147.

McConville, J. Gordon. "Exodus." In *New International Dictionary of Old Testament Theology and Exegesis*, vol. 4, edited by Willem A. VanGemeren, 601–605. Grand Rapids: Zondervan, 1997.

McCormack, Bruce L. "Election and the Trinity: Theses in Response to George Hunsinger." *Scottish Journal of Theology* 63 (2010): 203–24.

———. *For Us and Our Salvation: Incarnation and Atonement in the Reformed Tradition.* Studies in Reformed Theology and History 1. Princeton: Princeton Theological Seminary, 1993.

———. "God Is His Decision: The Jüngel-Gollwitzer 'Debate' Revisited." In *Theology as Conversation: The Significance of Dialogue in Historical and Contemporary Theology: A Festschrift for Daniel L. Migliore,* edited by Bruce L. McCormack and Kimlyn J. Bender, 48–66. Grand Rapids: Eerdmans, 2009.

———. "Grace and Being: The Role of God's Gracious Election in Karl Barth's Theological Ontology." In *The Cambridge Companion to Karl Barth,* edited by John Webster, 92–110. Cambridge: Cambridge University Press, 2000.

———. "Karl Barth's Christology as a Resource for a Reformed Version of Kenoticism." *International Journal of Systematic Theology* 8 (2006): 243–51.

———. *Karl Barth's Critically Realistic Dialectical Theology: Its Genesis and Development 1909–1936.* Oxford: Claredon, 1997.

———. "Karl Barth's Version of an 'Analogy of Being': A Dialectical No and Yes to Roman Catholicism." In *The Analogy of Being: Invention of the Antichrist or the Wisdom of God?* edited by Thomas Joseph White, 88–146. Grand Rapids: Eerdmans, 2011.

———. "Let's Speak Plainly: A Response to Paul Molnar." *Theology Today* 67 (2010): 57–65.

———. *Orthodox and Modern: Studies in the Theology of Karl Barth.* Grand Rapids: Baker, 2008.

———. "The Actuality of God: Karl Barth in Conversation with Open Theism." In *Engaging the Doctrine of God: Contemporary Protestant Perspectives,* edited by Bruce L. McCormack, 185–242. Grand Rapids: Baker, 2008.

———. "The Ontological Presuppositions of Barth's Doctrine of the Atonement." In *The Glory of the Atonement: Biblical, Historical, and Practical Perspectives: Essays in Honor of Roger Nicole,* edited by Charles E. Hill and Frank A. James III, 346–66. Downers Grove, IL: IVP Academic, 2004.

———. "Why Should Theology Be Christocentric? Christology and Metaphysics in Paul Tillich and Karl Barth." *Wesleyan Theological Journal* 45 (2010): 42–80.

McCormack, Bruce, and Gerrit Neven, eds. *The Reality of Faith in Theology: Studies on Karl Barth Princeton-Kampen Consultation 2005.* Bern: Peter Lang, 2007.

McDonough, Sean M. *YHWH at Patmos*. Tübingen: Mohr Siebeck, 1999.

McFague, Sallie. *Models of God: Theology for an Ecological, Nuclear Age*. Minneapolis: Fortress, 1987.

McFarland, Ian A. "The Body of Christ: Rethinking a Classic Ecclesiological Model." *International Journal of Systematic Theology* 7 (2005): 225–45.

McGuckin, John. *Saint Cyril of Alexandria and the Christological Controversy*. Crestwood, NY: St. Vladimir's Seminary Press, 2004.

Meyendorff, John. *Christ in Eastern Christian Thought*. Crestwood, NY: St. Vladimir's Seminary Press, 1987.

Molnar, Paul. *Divine Freedom and the Doctrine of the Immanent Trinity: In Dialogue with Karl Barth and Contemporary Theology*. London: T & T Clark, 2002.

———. "*Orthodox and Modern*: Just How Modern Was Barth's Later Theology?" *Theology Today* 67 (2010): 51–56.

———. *Thomas F. Torrance: Theologian of the Trinity*. Farnham, UK: Ashgate, 2009.

Moltmann, Jürgen. *The Crucified God: The Cross of Christ as the Foundation and Criticism of Christian Theology*. Translated by R. A. Wilson and John Bowden. Minneapolis: Fortress, 1993.

———. *The Trinity and the Kingdom: The Doctrine of God*. Translated by Margaret Kohl. Minneapolis: Fortress, 1993.

———. *The Way of Jesus Christ: Christology in Messianic Dimensions*. Translated by Margaret Kohl. Minneapolis: Fortress, 1993.

Mühlenberg, Ekkehard. *Die Unendlichkeit Gottes bei Gregor von Nyssa: Gregors Kritik am Gottesbegriff der Klassichen Metaphysik*. Göttingen: Vandenhoeck and Ruprecht, 1966.

Muller, Richard A. "Jonathan Edwards and the Absence of Free Choice: A Parting of Ways in the Reformed Tradition." *Jonathan Edwards Studies* 1 (2011): 3–22.

———. *Post-Reformation Reformed Dogmatics*. 4 vols. Grand Rapids: Baker, 2003.

———. "Toward the *Pactum Salutis*: Locating the Origins of a Concept." *Mid-American Journal of Theology* 18 (2007): 11–65.

Murphy, Francesca Aran. *God Is Not a Story: Realism Revisited*. Oxford: Oxford University Press, 2007.

Neyrey, Jerome H. "'Without Beginning of Days or End of Life' (Hebrews 7:3): Topos for a True Deity." *Catholic Biblical Quarterly* 53 (1991): 439–55.

Nimmo, Paul. *Being in Action: The Theological Shape of Barth's Ethical Vision*. London: T & T Clark, 2007.

———. "Election and Evangelical Thinking: Challenges to Our Way of Conceiving the Doctrine of God." In *New Perspectives for Evangelical Theology: Engaging with God, Scripture, and the World*, edited by Tom Greggs, 29–43. New York: Routledge, 2010.

Norden, Eduard. *Agnostos Theos: Untersuchungen zur Formgeschichte Religiöser Rede*. Stuttgart: B. G. Teubner, 1956.

Norgate, Jonathan. *The Triune God and the Gospel of Salvation*. London: T & T Clark, 2009.

Norris, R. A. *God and World in Early Christian Theology*. New York: Seabury, 1965.

Nussbaum, Martha. *Love's Knowledge: Essays on Philosophy and Literature*. Oxford: Oxford University Press, 1990.

O'Brien, T. C. "The Holy Spirit: Love." In Thomas Aquinas, *Summa Theologiae*, Vol. 7, 252–258. New York and London: McGraw-Hill, 1976.

O'Regan, Cyril. *The Heterodox Hegel*. Albany, NY: SUNY Press, 1994.

———. "The Trinity in Kant, Hegel, and Schelling." In *The Oxford Handbook of the Trinity*, edited by Gilles Emery and Matthew Levering, 254–66. Oxford: Oxford University Press, 2011.

Origen. *Contra Celsum*. Translated by Henry Chadwick. Cambridge: Cambridge University Press, 1980.

Osborn, Eric. *Irenaeus of Lyon*. Cambridge: Cambridge University Press, 2001.

———. *The Emergence of Christian Theology*. Cambridge: Cambridge University Press, 1993.

Owen, John. *Communion with the Triune God*. Edited by Kelly M. Kapic and Justin Taylor. Wheaton: Crossway, 2007.

Pannenberg, Wolfhart. *Basic Questions in Theology: Collected Essays*. Vol. 2. Translated by George H. Kehm. Philadelphia: Westminster, 1971.

———. *Jesus—God and Man*. 2nd ed. Translated by Lewis L. Wilkins and Duane A. Priebe. Philadelphia: Westminster, 1968.

———. *Systematic Theology*. Vol. 1. Translated by Geoffrey W. Bromiley. Grand Rapids: Eerdmans, 1991.

Peters, Ted. *God as Trinity: Relationality and Temporality in Divine Life*. Louisville: Westminster John Knox, 1993.

Plumer, Eric. *Augustine's Commentary on Galatians*. Oxford: Oxford University Press, 2003.

Polyander, Johannes, et al. *Synopsis purioris theologiae*. Edited by Herman Bavinck. 6th ed. Leiden: Donner, 1881.

Powell, Samuel M. *The Trinity in German Thought*. Cambridge: Cambridge University Press, 2001.

Pratt, Richard. *He Gave Us Stories: The Bible Student's Guide to Interpreting Old Testament Narratives*. Phillipsburg, NJ: P & R, 1993.

Price, Robert B. *Letters of the Divine Word: The Perfections of God in Karl Barth's Church Dogmatics*. London: T & T Clark, 2011.

Radde-Gallwitz, Andrew. *Basil of Caesarea, Gregory of Nyssa, and the Transformation of Divine Simplicity*. Oxford: Oxford University Press, 2009.

Rahner, Karl. *The Trinity*. London: Burns and Oates, 2001.

Rainbow, Paul. *Monotheism and Christology in 1 Corinthians 8:4–6*. D.Phil. Thesis: Oxford University, 1987.

Rendtorff, Rolf. *The Covenant Formula: An Exegetical and Theological Investigation*. Edinburgh: T & T Clark, 1998.

Ricoeur, Paul. *Oneself as Another*. Translated by Kathleen Blamey. Chicago: University of Chicago Press, 1994.

Ritschl, Albrecht. *The Christian Doctrine of Justification and Reconciliation*. 2nd ed. Translated by H. R. Mackintosh and A. B. Macaulay. Edinburgh: T & T Clark, 1902.

———. *Three Essays*. Translated by Philip Hefner. Minneapolis: Fortress, 1972.

Robinson, John A. T. *The Body*. London: SCM, 1952.

Rogers, Eugene. *After the Spirit: A Constructive Pneumatology from Resources Outside the Modern West*. Grand Rapids: Eerdmans, 2005.

Root, Michael. "The Narrative Structure of Soteriology." *Modern Theology* 2 (1986): 145–58.

Rowe, C. Kavin. "Luke and the Trinity: An Essay in Ecclesial Biblical Theology." *Scottish Journal of Theology* 56 (2003): 1–26.

Rowe, William L. *Can God Be Free?* Oxford: Oxford University Press, 2004.

Runia, David T. *Philo in Early Christian Literature: A Survey*. Minneapolis: Fortress, 1993.

Russell, Norman. *Cyril of Alexandria*. London: Routledge, 2000.

Sanders, E. P. *Paul and Palestinian Judaism*. Philadelphia: Fortress, 1977.

Sanders, Fred. "Trinity Talk, Again." *Dialog* 44 (2005): 264–72.

Sarisky, Darren. "What Is Theological Interpretation? The Example of Robert W. Jenson." *International Journal of Systematic Theology* 12 (2010): 201–16.

Schaff, Philip, ed. *The Creeds of Christendom*. 3 vols. Repr. Grand Rapids: Baker, 1996.

Schleiermacher, Friedrich. *The Christian Faith*. Edinburgh: T & T Clark, 1989.

Schwöbel, Christoph. *God: Action and Revelation*. Kampen: Kok Pharos, 1992.

Seitz, Christopher R. *Figured Out: Typology and Providence in Christian Scripture*. Louisville: Westminster John Knox, 2001.

———, ed. *Nicene Christianity: The Future for a New Ecumenism*. Grand Rapids: Brazos, 2001.

Sholl, Brian K. "On Robert Jenson's Trinitarian Thought." *Modern Theology* 18 (2002): 27–36.

Shults, LeRon. "The Futurity of God in Lutheran Theology." *Dialog* 42 (2003): 39–49.

Sibbes, Richard. *A Description of Christ*. In *Works of Richard Sibbes*, edited by Alexander B. Grosart. Edinburgh: Banner of Truth, 1979.

Smith, Aaron T. "God's Self-Specification: His Being Is His Electing." *Scottish Journal of Theology* 62 (2009): 1–25.

Sokolowski, Robert. *The God of Faith and Reason*. Notre Dame: University of Notre Dame Press, 1982.

Soskice, Janet Martin. "Athens and Jerusalem, Alexandria and Edessa: Is There a Metaphysics of Scripture?" *International Journal of Systematic Theology* 8 (2006): 149–62.

———. "Naming God: A Study in Faith and Reason." In *Reason and the Reasons of Faith*, edited by Paul J. Griffiths and Reinhard Hütter, 241–54. London: T & T Clark, 2005.

Spence, Alan. *Inspiration and Incarnation: John Owen and the Coherence of Christology*. London: T & T Clark, 2007.

Stead, Christopher. *Philosophy in Christian Antiquity*. Cambridge: Cambridge University Press, 1994.

Stratis, Justin. "Speculating About Divinity? God's Immanent Life and Actualistic Ontology." *International Journal of Systematic Theology* 12 (2010): 20–32.

Studer, Basil. *Trinity and Incarnation: The Faith of the Early Church*. Translated by Matthias Westerhoff. Collegeville, MN: Liturgical Press, 1993.

Stump, Eleonore, and Norman Kretzmann. "Eternity." In *The Concept of God*, edited by Thomas V. Morris, 219–52. New York: Oxford University Press, 1987.

Swain, Scott R. "The Trinity in the Reformers." In *The Oxford Handbook of the Trinity*, edited by Gilles Emery and Matthew Levering, 227–39. Oxford: Oxford University Press, 2011.

Tanner, Kathryn. *Christ the Key*. Cambridge: Cambridge University Press, 2010.

———. *God and Creation in Christian Theology: Tyranny or Empowerment?* Oxford: Blackwell, 1988.

———. *Jesus, Humanity, and the Trinity: A Brief Systematic Theology*. Minneapolis: Fortress, 2001.

———. "Kingdom Come: The Trinity and Politics." *Princeton Seminary Bulletin* 28 (2007): 129–145.

Tappert, T. G., ed. *The Book of Concord: The Confessions of the Evangelical Lutheran Church*. Philadelphia: Muhlenburg, 1959.

Teske, Roland J. *To Know God and the Soul: Essays on the Thought of Saint Augustine*. Washington, DC: Catholic University of America Press, 2008.

Thompson, John. *Modern Trinitarian Perspectives*. New York: Oxford University Press, 1994.

Tipton, Lane G. "Christology in Colossians 1:15–20 and Hebrews 1:1–4: An Exercise in Biblico-Systematic Theology." In *Resurrection and Eschatology: Theology in Service of the Church, Essays in Honor of Richard B. Gaffin, Jr.*, edited by Lane G. Tipton and Jeffery C. Waddington, 177–202. Phillipsburg, NJ: P & R, 2008.

Torrance, Alan J. *Persons in Communion: An Essay on Trinitarian Description and Human Participation, With Special Reference to Volume One of Karl Barth's "Church Dogmatics."* Edinburgh: T & T Clark, 1996.

Torrance, Thomas F. *The Trinitarian Faith: The Evangelical Theology of the Ancient Catholic Church*. London: T & T Clark, 1995.

Turner, Denys. "On Denying the Right God: Aquinas on Atheism and Idolatry." *Modern Theology* 20 (2004): 141–61.

Turretin, Francis. *Institutes of Elenctic Theology*. Edited by James T. Dennison Jr. Translated by George Musgrave Giger. 3 vols. Phillipsburg, NJ: P & R, 1992.

Velde, Dolf te. *Paths Beyond Tracing Out: The Connection of Method and Content in the Doctrine of God, Examined in Reformed Orthodoxy, Karl Barth, and the Utrecht School*. Delft, The Netherlands: Eburon, 2010.

Velde, Rudi te. *Aquinas on God: The "Divine Science" of the* Summa Theologiae. Burlington, VT: Ashgate, 2006.

Vos, Antonie. "Scholasticism and Reformation." In *Reformation and Scholasticism*, edited by Willem J. van Asselt and Eef Dekker, 99–119. Grand Rapids: Baker, 2001.

Vos, Geerhardus. *The Eschatology of the Old Testament*. Edited by James T. Dennison Jr. Phillipsburg, NJ: P & R, 2001.

Watts, R. E. "Exodus." In *New Dictionary of Biblical Theology*, edited by T. Desmond Alexander and Brian S. Rosner, 478–87. Downers Grove, IL: IVP Academic, 2000.

Webster, John. *Barth's Ethics of Reconciliation*. Cambridge: Cambridge University Press, 1995.

———. *Confessing God: Essays in Dogmatics II*. London: T & T Clark, 2005.

———. *God Without Measure: Essays in Christian Doctrine*. London: T & T Clark, forthcoming.

———. "Life in and of Himself: Reflections on God's Aseity." In *Engaging the Doctrine of God: Contemporary Protestant Perspectives*, edited by Bruce L. McCormack, 107–24. Grand Rapids: Baker Academic, 2008.

———. *The Domain of the Word: Scripture and Theological Reason*. London: T & T Clark, 2012.

———. *Word and Church: Essays in Church Dogmatics*. Edinburgh: T & T Clark, 2001.

Weinandy, Thomas. *Does God Suffer?* South Bend, IN: University of Notre Dame Press, 2000.

Westphal, Merold. "Temporality and Finitism in Hartshorne's Theism." *Review of Metaphysics* 19 (1966): 550–64.

White, Thomas Joseph. "Dyothelitism and the Instrumental Human Consciousness of Jesus." *Pro Ecclesia* 17 (2008): 396–422.

Wicks, Henry J. *The Doctrine of God in the Jewish Apocryphal and Apocalyptic Literature*. New York: KTAV Publishing House, 1971.

Wittgenstein, Ludwig. *Philosophical Investigations*. 3rd ed. Translated by G. E. M. Anscombe. New York: Macmillan, 1958.

Wollebius, Johannes. *Compendium of Christian Theology*. In *Reformed Dogmatics*, edited and translated by John W. Beardslee. Eugene, OR: Wipf & Stock, 2009.

Wright, N. T. *The Climax of the Covenant: Christ and the Law in Pauline Theology*. Minneapolis: Fortress, 1993.

———. *The New Testament and the People of God*. Minneapolis: Fortress, 1992.

———. *The Resurrection of the Son of God*. Minneapolis: Fortress, 2003.

Yeago, David S. "Catholicity, Nihilism, and the God of the Gospel: Reflections on the Theology of Robert W. Jenson." *Dialog* 31 (1992): 18–22.

Young, Frances. *Biblical Exegesis and the Formation of Christian Culture*. Cambridge: Cambridge University Press, 1997.

Author Index

Allen, Michael, 64n155

Anderson, Gary A., 199n30

Aquinas, Thomas, 134–37, 150, 165n1, 191

Aristotle, 101, 134, 139

Athanasius, 123n7, 170

Augustine, 79n9, 101, 130–32, 138n97, 146, 148, 150, 176n48, 189

Ayres, Lewis, 179

Barth, Karl, 5, 14–15, 23–25, 32–66, 98n8, 102, 105, 145, 156–57, 209–10, 214–15, 227, 332–34

Bavinck, Herman, 23, 187

Behr, John, 121

Bonaventure, 160

Brakel, Wilhelmus à, 159, 166n4

Brueggemann, Walter, 82n20

Brunner, Peter, 113–14

Bultmann, Rudolph, 106n39, 116, 119n108

Burkert, Walter, 175–76

Calvin, John, 170

Collins, John, 175–76

Crisp, Oliver, 166n9

Cyril of Alexandria, 70

Dorner, Isaak August, 22–23, 38

Driel, Edwin Christian van, 40n39

Edwards, Jonathan, 30, 140, 206–7, 224–25

Gathercole, Simon, 166–67

Gavrilyuk, Paul, 174, 179

Gregory of Nyssa, 134–37, 158n62, 172, 180–81, 186n98

Gunton, Colin, 15n9, 148n15, 203n42

Hart, David Bentley, 15–16, 90–91, 96n, 155, 184–85

Hector, Kevin, 215n32

Hegel, Georg W. F., 21–23, 36, 38, 56, 62, 136n36, 138n97, 196–99, 224–25

Heidegger, Martin, 124

Horton, Michael, 84–85, 181

Hugenberger, Gordon, 149n18

Hunsinger, George, 50n87, 154

Hurtado, Larry, 177n53

Irenaeus, 80, 151–57

John of Damascus, 13

Jones, Paul Dafydd, 54n111

Jüngel, Eberhard, 42n50, 62–63, 104n37

Kant, Immanuel, 20, 22

Küng, Hans, 62

Luther, Martin, 13, 17, 192

Marshall, Bruce, 146–47

McConville, Gordon, 80–81

McCormack, Bruce L., 30–31, 46n63, 49n85, 54n111, 105, 208–27, 231–34

McGuckin, John, 170n24

Melanchthon, Philipp, 17, 39–40

Molnar, Paul, 161

Moltmann, Jürgen, 37n23, 62n150, 64n156, 211n12

Mühlenberg, Ekkehard, 134–35, 186n98

Murphy, Francesca Aran, 15n9, 68n177

Nussbaum, Martha, 69n181

Origen, 179

Osborn, Eric, 177

Owen, John, 204n45

Pannenberg,

Wolfhart, 36, 68, 97–99

Plato, 101

Polanus, Amandus, 40n35

Pratt, Richard, 126n27

Rahner, Karl, 132n63

Ricoeur, Paul, 140

Ritschl, Albrecht, 21

Rogers, Eugene, 201

Schelling, Friedrich, 22

Schleiermacher, Friedrich, 20–21

Schweizer, Alexander, 24n40

Schwöbel,

Christoph, 122n2

Turretin, Francis, 150n21, 157n59

Velde, Dolf te, 43n53

von Hofmann, Johannes, 23

Webster, John, 28, 34, 119–20, 153n32

White, Thomas

Joseph, 192n131

Wicks, Henry, 178

Wollebius, Johannes, 145n1

Wyschogrod, Michael, 124

Yeago, David S., 71n193

Young, Frances, 123n7

Subject Index

adoption, 160–61, 165, 168, 202

Arianism, 100, 123n7

baptism, 71, 115, 190

biblical exegesis, 18–19

Christian piety, 132n63

conditional election, 48

Council of Chalcedon, 128, 202n40

covenant of grace, 42–43, 46–57, 145–57, 162, 210–11, 216, 226

covenants, 14, 28, 148–50, 171–72. *See also* covenant of grace

creation, 83–84, 127, 151–55, 162

Creator-creature distinction, 83–84, 94, 182–83

death, 91–92, 95

divine freedom, 42–44, 210, 220–27

divine love, 30, 40–41, 160–61, 197–202, 212

divine simplicity, 29, 157–72

divine temporality, 66–74, 88, 125–33

double predestination, 47

dramatic coherence, 80, 88–94, 98, 111, 127, 137, 196

Ecumenical Creeds, 69

election, 14, 24n40, 32, 38, 41, 44–55, 211, 215–23

Enlightenment, 18–19, 39, 233

eternity, 135–36, 185–93

evangelical historicism, 63–66, 82–83, 214–15

exodus, 26, 80–88, 105–6

faith, 23, 38, 48, 69, 113–15

free choice, 42–44

Gemeinschaft, 118–19

Gesellschaft, 118–19

glorification, 126, 206

God
  being and perfection of, 39–44, 54, 139, 155–56
  divine properties of, 148–51. *See also* divine freedom; divine love; divine simplicity
  fellowship with, 43, 56, 144
  identity of
    as covenantal, 149–51
    as Father of elect, 29
    as Father of the Son, 29
    as intrinsically trinitarian, 26, 100–106
    as narrative in evangelical events, 68–75, 126–27, 146
    in the New Testament, 96–120
    in the Old Testament, 77–95
  infinite perfection of, 30, 181–85
  knowledge of, 22, 52–54, 175, 213
  names of, 77–95
  nature of, 34, 156
  as personal, 138–39
  presence of, 20–21, 30, 53, 103, 168, 191, 194–95
  self-determination of, 14, 23, 25, 28, 48, 52–55, 65–66, 143–46, 158–62, 192, 203–4, 213
  self-revelation of, 34–38, 40, 82–84, 214
  self-sufficiency of, 29, 152–53
  temporal infinity of, 124–27,

135–37,
186–87. *See
also* divine
temporality
timeless
eternality of,
185–93
union with,
172–73
will of, 42–44,
161–62
Yₕwₕ-Israel
relationship of,
85–103,
176–82
See also Creator-
creature
distinction;
dramatic
coherence;
immutability;
impassibility
gospel, 48–49, 58,
74–75, 106
grace, 23, 25, 29,
38, 156–57. *See
also* covenant of
grace
Greek thought,
124–27, 171–83
Heidelberg
Catechism,
162–63
Holy Spirit
eternal proces-
sion of, 30, 38,
191–92, 213
eternal will of,
47
fellowship with,

28, 195–207
identity of, 74,
110–12
temporal
mission of, 30,
191, 205n49
as unity in the
Godhead,
110–12, 115
homoousios, 69–70,
187n103
human reason, 33
hypostasis, 17,
130–31, 135,
138, 211
immutability, 78,
126–27, 173–77
impassibility, 78,
173–78
incarnation, 23,
28–30, 32,
57–66, 164–93,
204–5, 212
Jesus
atonement of,
26, 56–57,
107–12, 198
church as the
body of,
116–20
and communica-
tion of
attributes,
63–65, 73
as the electing
God, 46–55,
215–16
eternal filiation
and temporal
mission of,

168–93
as fulfillment of
Old Testament
prophecy, 81,
92–95, 98–100
humiliation and
exaltation of,
25, 55–63,
170–71, 211
as mediator,
165–66,
211–12
natures of,
211–12
preexistence of,
26, 97,
100–106, 160
relation to the
Father in the
Spirit, 64–66,
131–33,
195–207
resurrection of,
26, 106–20,
196
as Word of God,
30, 63, 70, 83,
101–3, 164–72,
182–93, 203
See also adoption;
incarnation
law, 60
liberalism, 19n20,
33n3
Lutheran
theology, 64–65,
73, 211–12
Marcionism, 80,
98
metaphysics,

18–22, 64,
122–27, 134–37,
173–83
modalism, 60–61,
129, 216–20
new creation, 133
Nicene Creed,
69–71, 125–26,
179–80, 216,
225
ousia, 17, 130–31,
135, 138
pactum salutis, 29,
47–48, 165–68,
199, 204
persona dramatis,
17, 110, 136
process theology,
136n36
Protestant
orthodoxy,
17–18, 34, 40,
118–19
Protestant
universities,
18–20
reconciliation,
56–66, 108–10,
136, 199–200
Reformation,
17–18, 34
Reformed
scholasticism,
43n53
religious experi-
ence, 33
reprobation, 47
Roman Catholi-
cism, 17–18,
118–19

salvation, 47,
  80–81, 125–27,
  133, 199
Scripture
  and dogmatics,
    17–18
  and narrative
    preexistence of
    Jesus, 102–6
  and preincarnate
    existence of
    Jesus, 101
  reading with the
    rule of faith, 69
  and revelation,
    35–36, 82–84
sin, 91–92, 95,
  107–8
Socinians, 157n59

spiritual purifica-
  tion, 14n3
subordinationism,
  60–61, 128,
  216–20
systematic
  theology, 84n27
temporal infinity,
  129, 135–36,
  139–40
Thomism, 68n177
transcendence, 30,
  136, 188
trinitarian
  ontology, 41–42
Trinity
  and the
    atonement,
    108–12

and the being
  and perfection
  of God, 39–44,
  75
consubstantiality
  of, 187n103,
  220–23
as divine
  relatedness and
  divine
  temporality,
  66, 125–26,
  129–33,
  139–40
"Franciscan" and
  "Dominican"
  logic of,
  213–20
as God's

self-revelation,
  34–38, 183–84
historicized
  account of,
  66–71, 85–95
identity of, 55,
  135–37
modern
  doctrinal
  history of,
  14–24
processions of,
  131–33, 160,
  191–92, 204,
  213, 219,
  225–27
Western and
  Eastern models
  of, 37n20, 131

Scripture Index

OLD TESTAMENT

Genesis
1:1, *83*
18:14, *172*
22:1-19, *168*

Exodus
3–15, *182*
3:8, *105*
3:14, *123, 158*
4:22, *85, 145*
5:2, *81*
8:10, *183*
15:11, *81*
20:2, *81*
20:4, *182*
29:45, *194*
29:46, *81, 127*
33:19, *81*
34:6, *81*
34:9, *81*

Leviticus
26:12, *28, 127,
194*

Numbers
23:19, *181*

Deuteronomy
4:15-19, *182*

1 Samuel
15:29, *181*

2 Samuel
7:14, *145*

1 Kings
8:27, *181*
8:56, *82*

Job
9:32, *181*
36:26, *181*

Psalms
2:7, *104*
16:5-6, *149*
36:8-9, *153*
40:5, *183*
50:7-12, *153*
90:1, *150*
90:1-2, *181*
90:2, *186*
94:8-10, *183*
102:25-27, *152*
102:26-27, *181*
102:27, *179, 181,
186*
113, *105, 181*
113:6, *169*
139, *181*
145:3, *78, 153, 181*

Proverbs
8:30, *160*

Isaiah
40:6, *189*
40:8, *189*
40:9, *28*
40:13-14, *201*
40:16-17, *153*
40:17, *170*
40:18, *183*

40:28, *181*
42:1, *200*
42:8, *158*
45:5-6, *158*
45:14, *158*
53:10, *199*
57:15, *181*
63:16, *147*

Jeremiah
1:10, *70*
3:19, *93*
10:10, *175*
23:23, *181*

Jonah
4:1-2, *85*

Malachi
3:6, *179*

APOCRYPHA

Wisdom of
Solomon
13:1, *175*
13:3-5, *183*

NEW TESTAMENT

Matthew
3:15, *200*
3:16-17, *200*
28:19, *158*

Mark
1:8, *195*
1:11, *190*

1:12, *205*
8:31, *107*
9:7, *190*
12:1-12, *28, 168*
12:11, *199*
12:32, *158*
14:36, *202*
14:61, *107*
15:34, *198*

Luke
1:34-35, *204*
1:35, *190*
1:37, *172, 185*
1:49, *185*
2:52, *205*
4:1-21, *205*
10:21, *200*

John
1, *102*
1:1, *83, 102, 165,
168, 188, 193*
1:3, *188*
1:4, *153, 158*
1:5, *191*
1:8, *168*
1:11, *165, 185, 188*
1:12, *150, 165, 193*
1:14, *165, 170,
172, 189, 193*
1:16, *170, 189*
1:18, *13, 168, 175*
5:19-30, *190*
5:21-25, *153*
5:26, *153, 158*
6:38, *166*
8:58, *102*

10:36, *165*
14:6, *158*
14:16-17, *195*
14:31, *199*
15:26, *201*
16:28, *165*
17:3, *13, 123, 175*
17:5, *152, 161,
  168, 169, 205*
17:24, *160, 169, 171*
17:24-26, *161,
  168, 190, 202*
19:30, *193*
20:17, *28, 145, 193*

Acts
15:8, *201*
17:25, *153*

Romans
1:1-4, *28*
1:3-4, *103*
1:4, *200, 205*
1:20, *176, 181*
1:23, *176, 181*
5:5, *202*
8:3, *189*
8:11, *196*
8:15, *202*
8:16, *201*
8:29, *161*
8:32, *168*
11:33-35, *153*
11:33-36, *153*
11:35, *153*
11:36, *188*

1 Corinthians
2:7, *186*

2:7-8, *200*
2:10, *200*
8:4-6, *176*
8:6, *158, 188*
12:12-27, *93*
14:33, *59*
15, *113, 205*
15:1-4, *28*
15:20, *205*
15:42-49, *205*
15:44, *205*
15:48-49, *206*

2 Corinthians
1:20, *28*
4:4, *206*
6:16, *195*
6:16-18, *28*
6:18, *145, 162*
8:9, *105, 170*

Galatians
3:13, *199*
3:26-28, *205*
4:4, *172, 199*
4:4-5, *168*
4:6, *202*
4:8, *176*

Ephesians
1:4, *65*
1:4-5, *165*
1:6, *161*
1:13-14, *206*
3:14-19, *192*
3:15, *183*
3:19, *170,
  187*
4:4-6, *158*

5:22-32, *195*
5:23, *93*

Philippians
2:6-8, *199*
2:6-11, *105*
2:7, *166*
2:8, *199*
3:21, *206*

Colossians
1, *102*
1:15-16, *161*
1:15-20, *159*
1:16, *188*
1:17, *188*
1:18, *93, 190, 205*
2:9, *189*
2:19, *93*

1 Thessalonians
1:9, *175*

1 Timothy
1:11, *152, 176, 179*
1:17, *176, 179, 181*
3:16, *171, 200, 205*
6:15, *176, 179*

Titus
1:2-3, *186*

Hebrews
1:1-4, *159*
1:2, *161*
1:3, *159, 171, 175,
  188*
1:10-12, *186*
1:10-13, *188*

2:4, *201*
2:5-4:13, *205*
2:10, *171*
2:11, *171*
2:17, *171*
5:8, *205*
5:9, *205*
7:3, *176*
9:14, *200, 205*
10:7, *199*
10:15, *201*
11:6, *123*
11:27, *176*
13:8, *186*

James
1:17, *78, 153, 158,
  159, 161, 181*

1 Peter
1:20, *165*

1 John
1:5, *158*

Jude
25, *186*

Revelation
1:4, *123, 175, 176*
1:8, *123, 175*
4:8, *175*
11:17, *175*
16:5, *175*
21:2, *195*
21:3, *127, 195*
21:7, *145*
22:13, *188*
22:17, *206*

Strategic Initiatives in Evangelical Theology

IVP Academic presents a series of seminal works of scholarship with significan relevance for both evangelical scholarship and the church. Strategic Initiatives in Evangelical Theology (SIET) aims to foster interaction within the broader evangelical community and advance discussion in the wider academy around emerging, current, groundbreaking or controversial topics. The series provides a unique publishing venue for both more senior and younger promising scholars.

While SIET volumes demonstrate a depth of appreciation for evangelical theology and the current challenges and issues facing it, the series will welcome books that engage the full range of academic disciplines from theology and biblical studies, to history, literature, philosophy, the natural and social sciences, and the arts.

Editorial Advisory Board

Hans Boersma, *Regent College*
C. Stephen Evans, *Baylor University.*
Joel B. Green, *Fuller Theological Seminary*
Veli-Matti Kärkkäinen, *Fuller Theological Seminary*
Roger Lundin, *Wheaton College*
Mark A. Noll, *University of Notre Dame*
Margaret Kim Peterson, *Eastern University*
Kevin Vanhoozer, *Trinity Evangelical Divinity School*

Published Volumes

Addiction and Virtue, Kent Dunnington
The God of the Gospel, Scott R. Swain
Incarnational Humanism, Jens Zimmerman
Rethinking the Trinity & Religious Pluralism, Keith E. Johnson
The Triumph of God Over Evil, William Hasker

IVP Academic
An imprint of InterVarsity Press
Downers Grove, Illinois